Nation, Culture, Text

Nation, Culture, Text: Australian Cultural and Media Studies is the first collection of cultural studies essays from Australia, selected and introduced for an international readership. Participating in the 'de-centring' of cultural studies – considering what perspectives other than the European or American have to offer – the contributors raise important issues about the role of a national tradition of critical theory, and about the cultural specificity of theory itself.

As Graeme Turner's introduction outlines, a key theme of the collection is the place of the postcolonial nation within contemporary cultural theory – particularly those aspects of contemporary theory which see the category of the nation as either outdated or suspect. The collection also deals with the role cultural policy plays in constructing the nation, and in the range of interests which combine under the umbrella of cultural studies. The writers tackle subjects ranging from the televising of the Bicentennial to the role of policy in film, television and the heritage industry, from the use of video technologies within remote Aboriginal communities to the role of ethnography in cultural studies.

The contributors: Meaghan Morris, Eric Michaels, Tony Bennett, Elizabeth Jacka, Tom O'Regan, Stuart Cunningham, Virginia Nightingale, Ian Hunter, Noel Sanders, Helen Grace, John and Marian Tulloch, Pam Gilbert and Sandra Taylor.

The editor: Graeme Turner teaches cultural studies at the University of Queensland and is among the founders of Australian cultural studies, a former editor of the *Australian Journal of Cultural Studies* and its international successor, *Cultural Studies*. He is the author of *National Fictions: Literature, Film and the Construction of Australian Narrative*, *British Cultural Studies: An Introduction* and *Film as Social Practice*.

Communication and Society
General Editor: James Curran

What News?
The Market, Politics and the Local Press
Bob Franklin and David Murphy

Glasnost, Perestroika and the Soviet Media
Brian McNair

Pluralism, Politics and the Marketplace
The Regulation of German Broadcasting
Vincent Porter and Suzanne Hasselbach

Potboilers
Methods, Concepts and Case Studies in Popular Fiction
Jerry Palmer

Communication and Citizenship
Journalism and the Public Sphere
Edited by Peter Dahlgren and Colin Sparks

Images of the Enemy
Brian McNair

Seeing and Believing
The Influence of Television
Greg Philo

Critical Communication Studies
Communication, History and Theory in America
Hanno Hardt

Media Moguls
Jeremy Tunstall and Michael Palmer

Media Cultures
Reappraising Transnational Media
Edited by Michael Skovmand and Kim Christian Schroder

Fields in Vision
Television Sport and Cultural Transformation
Garry Whannel

Getting the Message
News, Truth and Power
The Glasgow Media Group

Advertising, The Uneasy Persuasion
Its Dubious Impact on American Society
Michael Schudson

News and Journalism in the UK
A Textbook
Brian McNair

Nation, Culture, Text

Australian cultural and media studies

Edited by Graeme Turner

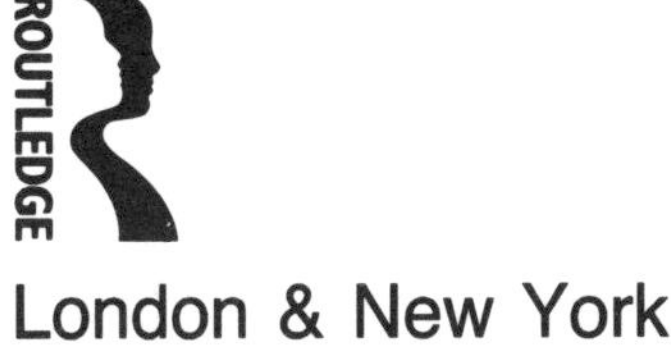

London & New York

First published in 1993
by Routledge
11 New Fetter Lane
London EC4P 4EE

Simultaneously published in the USA and Canada
by Routledge
29 West 35th Street, New York, NY 10001

Editorial matter © 1993 Graeme Turner; individual chapters © the contributors

Set in 10/12 pt Times by Intype, London
Printed and bound in Great Britain by Clays Ltd, St Ives plc

British Library Cataloguing in Publication Data
Nation, Culture, Text: Australian Cultural and Media Studies. –
(Communication & Society Series)
I. Turner, Graeme II. Series 306.0994

Library of Congress Cataloging in Publication Data
Nation, culture, text: Australian cultural and media studies /
edited by Graeme Turner.
p. cm. – (Communication and society)
Includes bibliographical references and index.
1. Australia–Civilization. 2. Australia–Cultural policy. 3. Australia–Popular
culture–History–20th century. 4. Mass media–Australia–History–20th century.
I. Turner, Graeme. II. Series: Communication and society (Routledge (Firm))
DU107.N38 1993
994–dc20
92-21154

ISBN 0–415–088852
0–415–088860 (pbk)

Contents

Contributors

Graeme Turner is Associate Professor in the Department of English at the University of Queensland. His most recent publications include *British Cultural Studies: An Introduction* and (with Stuart Cunningham) *The Media in Australia: Industries, Texts, Audiences*.

Meaghan Morris is a freelance writer. She has published two collections of her essays, *The Pirate's Fiancee: Feminism, Reading, Postmodernism* and *Ecstasy and Economics: American Essays for John Forbes* and is currently working on a book on television and history.

The late **Eric Michaels** was an American anthropologist whose pioneering work on Australian aboriginals and technology has been of profound importance. Among his publications are *For a Cultural Future* and *Unbecoming: An AIDS diary*.

Tony Bennett is Professor in Humanities at Griffith University, Brisbane, Australia. His most recent publications include *Outside Literature* and the forthcoming (co-edited with Larry Grossberg, Simon Frith, John Shepherd and Graeme Turner) *Rock and Popular Music: Policies, Politics, Institutions*.

Tom O'Regan is Senior Lecturer in Humanities at Murdoch University, Perth, Australia. He is an editor of the journal *Continuum*, co-editor (with Albert Moran) of *The Australian Screen*, and is currently writing a book on Australian television for Allen & Unwin.

Elizabeth Jacka is Head of Research at the Australian Film Television and Radio School, and co-author (with Susan Dermody) of the two volume history of the Australian film revival, *The Screening of Australia*. She is currently researching the globalisation of television and its effect on Australian industries.

Stuart Cunningham is Associate Professor in the School of Media and Journalism at the Queensland University of Technology, Brisbane, Australia. He is the author of *Framing Culture: Criticism and Policy in*

Australia and co-editor (with Graeme Turner) of *The Media in Australia: Industries, Texts, Audiences.*

Ian Hunter is Associate Professor in Humanities at Griffith University, Brisbane, Australia. His most recent publications include *Accounting for the Humanities: The Language of Culture and the Logic of Government* (co-edited with Denyse Meredith, Bruce Smith and Geoff Stokes) and *Culture and Government.*

Virginia Nightingale is Senior Lecturer in Media and Cultural Studies at the University of Western Sydney, Australia. She is currently writing a book for Routledge on debates around cultural studies' analysis of television audiences.

Noel Sanders is a musician and academic, who teaches at the University of Technology, Sydney, Australia. He has published widely on Australian popular culture and music and is currently preparing a collection of his essays for Allen & Unwin.

Helen Grace is a photographer and film-maker, best known for the documentary *Serious Undertakings.* She teaches cultural studies and visual art at the University of Western Sydney, Australia and has published a number of essays dealing with the representation of business and the economy in Australian popular culture.

John Tulloch is Professor of Sociology and Head of the School of Social Sciences and Liberal Studies, Charles Sturt University, Bathurst, Australia. He has published widely in the fields of media, literary and cultural studies.

Marian Tulloch is a lecturer in Psychology in the School of Social Science and Liberal Studies at Charles Sturt University, Bathurst, Australia. She has published in the area of child development and children and television.

Pam Gilbert and **Sandra Taylor** teach at, respectively, James Cook University and Queensland University of Technology. They have both published widely on issues around gender and education and are the authors of *Fashioning the Feminine: Girls, Popular Culture and Schooling.*

Acknowledgements

For permission to reprint previously published material, I would like to thank the following: Meaghan Morris, the Institute for Cultural Policy Studies at Griffith University, the editors of *Screen*, Elizabeth Jacka, Jenny Lee, Roslyn Petelin and the Australian Journal of Communication, Noel Sanders, John and Marian Tulloch and Allen & Unwin Australia.

Introduction

Moving the margins: theory, practice and Australian cultural studies

Graeme Turner

In the Australian context I'm working in, the bottom line is really a question mark.

(Meaghan Morris)

TOWARDS A COMPARATIVE TRADITION

Only two or three years ago, it seemed as if cultural studies was heading into its disciplinary phase. Within academic institutions in Britain, North America, Australia and New Zealand, cultural studies was becoming, if not respectable, certainly secure. 'Cultural studies' was increasingly evident in undergraduate course descriptions and graduate degree programmes, even in the 'quality' press, as a term readers were expected to recognise. The installation of cultural studies within undergraduate curricula has created a demand for accounts of its histories, its debates, its central issues and terminologies. The danger of such a demand, and of the strategies publishers and academics employ to satisfy it, is that histories can quickly become history, debates can become debate, and the markers of cultural studies' foundational anti-disciplinarity can look more and more like the emerging protocols of a new discipline.

As cultural studies made its move from Europe to America during the late 1980s, fears about the effect of its popularisation within the American college system grew.[1] The scale of this system and its essentially disciplinary nature suggested a likely future in which cultural studies would either be accommodated within an established discipline such as English, or be forced to articulate its difference by adopting the guise of a discipline itself. Such fears were sharpened by the proposition that the translation of British cultural studies to the American context inevitably meant that it would be emptied of its politics, becoming merely a technical development within various traditions of textual analysis. Anxieties about the political effects of the popularisation of cultural studies have arisen before, of course. Much of the criticism of the so-called theoreticism of British cultural studies of the late 1970s and early 1980s had to do with the advisability of making cultural studies knowledges more accessible by assuming a less informed reader; resistance to this stressed the need for critical theory to disrupt comfortable reading positions and to foreground the demands of theory in the very manner of its writing. The late–1980s export drive to America, then, provoked responses which drew on familiar debates about the politics of cultural studies as an anti-discipline and as a theorised critical practice. America, it seemed, lacked so many of the things held to be central to the foundations of cultural studies in Britain: a long tradition of class analysis, an aesthetic and ethical division over high and popular culture, and most importantly a mature and established, if marginalised, Marxist intellectual culture. It was easy to see how this latest of British cultural exports might go the way of some of the others (Alfred Hitchcock, Cary Grant, Joan Collins!) and wind up being seduced, assimilated and finally claimed by America as its own.

Some of these fears have been realised. The establishment of undergraduate courses in cultural studies has brought new problems in (at least) Britain, North America and Australia. To teach cultural studies in these locations now is to deal with constant pressure from students to frame the field as if it were a unified, uncontested discipline. A further challenge for those teaching what is, after all, genuinely difficult material is that students are often more comfortable dealing with cultural studies as a repertoire of analytical techniques than they are in dealing with the theoretical motivations for these techniques. The move to America has raised different problems which have more to do with the extent of cultural studies' penetration of the American academy and its currently fashionable status. For a critical movement to achieve the degree of acceptance cultural studies has in the US is, probably inherently, worrying for those who value cultural studies' oppositional history. And there is little doubt that cultural studies is being accepted. One only has to conduct a cursory review of the literature of cultural studies to note the extraordinary expansion of American work in the last five years. Significantly, and encouragingly, this has not been a simple matter of appropriation. The American academy's openness to cultural studies is clearly going to produce substantial changes in a number of its disciplines. There has been a revolution in the dominant analytical models used in American studies of television, for instance, in response to cultural studies 'critical' approaches. Finally, and to move beyond the academy, cultural studies has been vigorously – perhaps predictably – taken up by sections of the American media. Whether it is featuring in the demonology of the wave of 'political correctness' and 'French theory' sweeping the humanities when surveyed by an Alan Bloom or a Camille Paglia, or whether it is 'what's hot' for the *Village Voice* book review – Grossberg, Nelson and Treichler's book, *Cultural Studies*,[2] was their cover story in April

1992 – the American media seems to feel that cultural studies is among
the signs of the nineties.

A more worrying trend, in a sense the negative after-image of the
move to America, is the relative slowdown in Britain. I don't pretend to
understand this fully, but among the reasons for what I perceive as the
reduction of energy in British cultural studies would be the deleterious
effects of more than a decade of Thatcherism on the universities and
polytechnics (the Birmingham Centre's preoccupation with its change in
institutional status, for instance, as it takes on undergraduate teaching),
and the perhaps consequent development of a little export industry in
British cultural studies academics moving to America.

I'm not sure that this is the end of the story, however. The conference
from which Grossberg, Nelson and Treichler's *Cultural Studies* emerged
– 'Cultural Studies Now and in the Future', held at the University of
Illinois-Urbana in 1990 – was an event which excited debate about many
of the fears outlined above. The conference was remarkable both for its
sense of a discipline forming around a particularly singular history of the
field, and for the countervailing pressure within cultural studies to remain
faithful to the politics of difference from which it had grown. In the end,
these latter pressures have been the stronger and what may have seemed,
to some at the time, the moment when the new 'universalism' was
installed may well turn out to be the moment when it was displaced.

Since the Illinois conference there have been a number of events which
reinforce a view of cultural studies as a multiplicity of theorised practices
coming from and therefore related to numerous and varied cultural and
national contexts. Those I am aware of include the 'Dismantle Fremantle'
conference in 1991 organised by Ien Ang and John Hartley to 'de-centre'
cultural studies, which formed the basis of a recent issue of *Cultural
Studies* (6 (3), 1992); the 'International Trajectories' conference held in
Taiwan in 1992 aimed at 'internationalising' cultural studies while recognising the 'historical formation of cultural studies within various national
and local contexts'; and the 1993 'Postcolonial Formations' conference
planned for Griffith University in Australia where cultural studies scholars
from Canada, Australia and New Zealand are to gather and share their
views on 'nation, culture and policy'. It would seem, even from these
few indications, that cultural studies may have paused at the brink and
pulled back, ready to re-embrace its own multiplicity and mutability, or
what John Clarke refers to as its own 'undiscipline'.[3]

Even while I believe this to be true, cultural studies has more before
it today than the recovery of its originary critical edge and its refusal to
operate as a discipline. British paradigms may still hold their place within
cultural studies' myths of origin but they no longer operate as the exnominated standards of practice against which all variants are to be measured.
It is widely acknowledged that cultural studies is a critical practice which

takes its place and gains its point within specific historical conditions –
among them the national or geographic location:

> As cultural studies confronts a changing historical world, new intellec-
> tual positions and knowledge, emergent political struggles, and its
> own institutional conditons, it must always contest its own sedimented
> practices by finding new ways to articulate its role. It must continue
> to spell out the relations between the theoretical and the empirical,
> and to rearticulate history in terms of specific material contexts. Even
> notions of context must be constructed contextually: as Meaghan
> Morris points out . . . even history must be defined within the speci-
> ficity of the place from which one speaks.[4]

There are, it needs to be stated, not only varying contexts within which
theory must be tested in practice but also, and as a consequence of this,
there are varying theoretical traditions which make their own use of
cultural studies thought. While many are coming to accept this principle,
it is often very difficult to maintain a practical acknowledgement of it in
one's own work; British and American cultural studies traditions in particular are marked by the ease with they speak from a context that
effortlessly rather than deliberately universalises itself. Such a practice is
especially likely if one does not regularly encounter work from elsewhere
which takes its cultural lcoation too for granted as normative. Without a
comparative tradition which explicitly and routinely admits the contingency of its local analyses and arguments, cultural studies is going to find
it very difficult to avoid the kind of slippage which allows one to write
an article on, for instance, American television but refer to it throughout
as 'television'.

There are hints of a comparative tradition ahead, I believe: Tony
Bennett's recent work on museums strikes me as a particularly rich
example,[5] and John Clarke's recent *New Times and Old Enemies* reveals
both the benefits and difficulties of reading changes across cultures with
full regard for the contextual differences. But there are a number of
preparatory steps we need to take. One is to gain more knowledge about
these other theoretical traditions, and how positions developed elsewhere
require modification and adaptation to be useful in their new conditions.
This is my objective in this selection of essays from Australia: to introduce
examples of some of the contributing streams within Australian cultural
studies.

'POSITIVE UNORIGINALITY' – OR, CENTRAL IDEAS IN MARGINAL PLACES

So far, there are no myths of origins for Australian cultural studies and
I certainly don't intend to start any here. In contrast to cultural studies

in Britain, there are no key institutions around which Australian cultural studies can be said to have formed. Cultural studies is still multiply fragmented in Australia: it takes place on the edge of more established fields such as film and media studies; within the debates over theory and practice in such disciplines as literary studies, fine arts and sociology or, and beyond the academy, within feminism; and as a means of framing arguments within the development and critique of cultural policy. There have been periods when Australian cultural studies attached itself to the developing field of Australian studies – a loosely multidisciplinary association, primarily, between Australian literary studies and Australian history – but this relationship is now breaking down under the pressure of arguments abut 'theory' (we seem doomed to relive the seventies!).[6] It was only in 1990 that the first attempt to form an academic association for cultural studies in Australia occured, and already it is clear that very few of its members would define their interests exclusively as those of cultural studies; rather than a growing discipline, it is a transdisciplinary theoretical tradition widely and variously deployed in the service of different, even contradictory, objectives.

That said, there are key starting points: the journals *Arena* and *Interventions*, the *Australian Journal of Screen Theory* and the *Australian Journal of Cultural Studies* were important early on in providing publishing outlets for Australian material; the major investment in the culture industries by successive federal governments during the seventies and eighties licensed new kinds of critics to speak about Australian culture; new institutions within an expanded higher education sector established in the seventies defined themselves in opposition to the established universities through their interdisciplinary programmes – much in the way of the polytechnics in Britain – and this opened up territory for cultural studies theory to colonise; British cultural studies expatriates – especially Tony Bennett, John Fiske, John Hartley and John Tulloch – played crucial personal roles while establishing journals and research centres, and winning credibility for Australian material with transnational publishers. And cultural studies clearly had much to contribute to the debates about the national identity and contemporary Australian society that have dominated Australian cultural criticism for most of this century.

There are also key attributes which might distinguish Australian cultural studies practice. In general, one would have to say that what has emerged is a body of theory and analysis which is marked by its hybridity. Of course, there is much within it that is seamlessly woven into international debates and issues within cultural studies; Ian Hunter's essay in this collection is such a piece. However, the majority of cultural studies in Australia speaks explicitly from a local position while drawing on a wide range of theoretical influences. Sources which feed into Australian work include American anthropology, 'area' studies methodologies used

in Australian studies courses, British sociological research into deviance
and the press, *Screen* theory, British cultural studies (particularly the
encoding/decoding television research), an indigenous breed of media
studies interested in policy and the construction of national identity, post-
Hallidayan social semiotics, and feminist rewritings of Australian history
– to name a few. As in America, European theory has been immensely
influential; Australian conservatives, too, harrumph about the dangers of
'French theory' – the licentiousness of the signified 'Frenchness' spilling
over to infect 'theory' as if it were some kind of imported contagious
disease. There has been little homogeneity, however, about *which bits* of
European theory are used; while the fine arts group around the Power
Institute in Sydney are applying Lyotard and Baudrillard to a theory of
graphic design, the cultural policy people at Griffith University in Brisbane are reworking Foucault in relation to Australian museums and
heritage policy. In Australian cultural studies, European theory has not
been simply a fashionable avenue for intellectual windowshopping. It is
less respectful than that, as those who raid the European shelves have
little compunction in making major modifications to, or entirely discard-
ing, whatever they find, if it fails to suit local conditions. Indeed, the
relation between Australian cultural studies and European cultural studies
is dominated by the regular practice of appropriation and then modification to local conditions.

Meaghan Morris has had some interesting things to say about appropriation in relation to *Crocodile Dundee*. *Crocodile Dundee* has become a
key text within discussions of Australian film, not only because of its
commercial success but also because once again it raises questions about
the extent to which a national cinema should speak with an exclusively
local accent. Rather than seeing the film, as did so many Australian
critics, as an example of the powerless imitating the powerful – focusing
on the Hollywood genre influences, the lack of formal 'originality' in this
first major box-office success for the Australian film industry – Meaghan
Morris argues that *Crocodile Dundee* demonstrates the positive value of
'unoriginality'. Situating her argument within the rhetorics around the
relationship between the Australian film industry and international
cinema, Morris distinguishes three 'theories of unoriginality and national
cinema'. The first assumes that unoriginality (that is, in this case, the
production of 'international' films, devoid of any cultural specificity) is 'a
Bad Thing, a byproduct of "cultural imperialsm" ', and opposes it by
calling for an 'authentic' local product. The second theory accepts that
unoriginality is a 'necessary and natural thing in modern times', and that
no national cinema is likely to survive without accepting this: 'Film is an
industry in a Western mega-culture, and Australia is simply part of it;
ideals of originality, independence and authenticity are sentimental anach-
ronisms, inappropriate to the *combinatoire* of industrial cinema.'[7] Within

such a view there are no textual signs of a national cinema, only an industrial structure. The third possibility, however, combines the 'cultural assertiveness' of the first theory with the 'economic pragmatism' of the second: 'This is a theory of fully *positive* unoriginality, a context in which, for critics, the privileged metaphors of postmodernism can come in to play – image scavenging, borrowing, stealing, plundering and (for the more sedate) recoding, rewriting, reworking.'[8] *Crocodile Dundee* both steals from and parodies its American models, admires and disdains American power, asserts and undermines Australian nationalisms. Its Hollywood models are, Morris argues, 'comically altered, and disadvantaged, by the narrative', the American public acting as sheep to Mick Dundee's sheepdog in the final scene. The result is a '*takeover* fantasy of breaking into the circuit of media power, to invade the place of control'.[9]

This is not to make an argument for *Crocodile Dundee* as the classic postmodern text – indeed, Morris sees in its 'dead cleverness' an antidote to the postmodern; rather, what attracts me to the inspired perversity of Morris's argument is its endowment of appropriation with the attributes of a measured resistance, a postcolonial politics. I am applying her argument to Australian cultural studies in order to make the simple point that it is not a merely revisionist tradition. As David Morley points out in his discussion of the interaction between 'local definitions and larger communication systems' (drawing on Daniel Miller's analysis of the consumption of American soap operas in Trinidad), the 'local' 'is not to be considered as an indigenous source of cultural identity, which remains "authentic" only in so far as it is unsullied by contact with the global'. Rather, he continues, 'the "local" is itself often produced by means of the "indigenization" of global resources and inputs'.[10] Furthermore, it is important to remember that the ways in which external theoretical influences are 'indigenised' and put to work are themselves overwhelmingly subject to the specific historical conditons in which Australian cultural studies finds itself.

Within these conditons, cultural policy has been a more constant problem than, say, the relation between texts and audiences. From the beginning of the revival of the film industry, Australian cultural studies has been involved in providing a critique of the structure of the national industry as well as of the texts themselves. Within media analysis, issues of ownership and the relation between the press and government has been a permanent issue. The field has been skewed towards the film and television industries, so there is very little analysis of radio, but neither is there a literature on many individual television productions other than soap operas or mini-series. Generally, the fact that one is writing about cultural power from within a relatively powerless nation-state affects the narratives one constructs, the outcomes one expects and the degree to which the arguments made are inherently, explicitly, political. So, while there are many footnotes shared between the Australian and European or American traditions, there are substantial differences in subject matter. Further, it is not only that the contexts within which the arguments take place are different; there is also a degree of cultural specificity in theory itself.

NOMINATING THE NATION

In British television talk shows, from Parkinson through to Aspel and Clive James, there is a subgenre of questions routinely directed to the guest who has just returned from a visit 'abroad' – usually America or Australia. Asked leading questions about their experiences overseas, the guest is licensed to tell stories of fantasy and excess (the postmodern on fast-forward) if their subject is America; and of unsophisticated hedonism and antipodean naivety (modernity on reverse picture-search) if their subject is Australia. The host sits ready to shake his (and it is, always, his) head in amazed appreciation at the 'it could only happen in America' tales, while leaning back in amused superiority (even, interestingly, Clive James does this) at the 'My God, those Australians' stories. From an Australian viewpoint, it is tempting to pause and deal with this xenophobic subgenre and its meanings, but my interest at this moment is elsewhere.

Recently a British comedian was interviewed by Clive James about his trip to Australia. Within a series of routine jokes about Australian males' obsession with masculinity, the comedian observed how different Australian television advertising was to the British variety. Australian television ads, he said, were incredibly nationalistic; he had never heard the word 'Australian' mentioned so many times in connection with so many things as he did during an evening's television. British ads, conversely, were relatively modest in their invocation of nationality and usually only mentioned it when it had some specific point. From this comparison, he presumed an Australian condition of national arrogance, a self-important assertion of the nation as a characteristic and aggressive patriotic tic.

It is possible to read this anecdote another way. The continual naming of Australia within these advertisements could present precisely the opposite of assurance and self-importance; the act of naming becomes incantatory, calling the nation into being. Within a wide range of British representational fields – not only advertising but also much writing within British cultural studies – 'Britain' is exnominated; it is the unquestioned category which needs never to be spoken. In these British representations, nationality seems utterly naturalised, always already in place; in Australian representational genres, Australia is explicitly figured (and interrogated) as image, myth – nation. Similarly, while American representational genres might appear to share this need to nominate the nation, it often seems as if the American nation is ritually spoken of in order to universalise itself – to, as it were, normatively Americanise the world. The British comedian has, I would suggest, failed completely to understand the significance of what he has seen; similarly, it is necessary to realise that in Australian cultural studies the function of the nation cannot be read in terms of the kinds of function it might serve within British or American contexts. So much Australian theory and practice deals with the nation as its primary problematic; while geopolitically and historically a 'given' condition, the nation is anything but surrendered territory for Australian cultural criticism. Simon During argues that 'to reject nationalism absolutely or to refuse to discriminate between nationalisms is to accede to a way of thought by which intellectuals – especially postcolonial intellectuals – cut themselves off from effective political action'. Consequently, During goes on to assert that 'today, writing in a First World colony like Australia, one ought to be nationalistic'.[11] Even with the qualifications During makes to complicate this statement, its nationalism goes far beyond what one might expect ever to encounter within the mainstream of British or American cultural studies.

Of course, all this is not to suggest that Australian TV advertisements for beer or margarine must necessarily be understood, in comparison to their British counterparts, as points of postcolonial resistance. But living in a new country does involve constant encounters with, and definite possibilities for intervening in, an especially explicit, mutable but insistent, process of nation formation. This fact provides so much of the grounding for cultural studies work within the Australian context that one finds it hard to avoid dealing with it at some level or other.

The selection of essays in this book demonstrate this. None of them are 'nationalist' in any sense at all (including During's), yet in the majority of them the category of the nation is fundamental. Meaghan Morris develops a symptomatic history of a particular representational form, examining its enclosure within rhetorics of nationality. Tony Bennett, Tom O'Regan, Elizabeth Jacka and Stuart Cunningham explore from varying perspectives the policy frameworks around the culture industries: through the realtionship between the local and the national, the national and the global, the commercial and the cultural and the ways in which cultural difference might be produced and maintained so that, ultimately, Australia remains 'its own place'. In none of these instances is there a comfortable, unitary definition of what that 'place' might be. Rather, these essays are motivated by an explicit critique of the dominant formations of Australian identity to explore strategies for fracturing or multiplying them. In the remaining essays, where the category of the nation is not explicitly invoked, the postcolonial relation is nevertheless implicit in the localising mode of critique: the scrutiny of globalising perspectives for their specific usefulness within Australian conditons. One can detect such a mode to varying degrees in the essays by Noel Sanders, Pam Gilbert and Sandra Taylor, John and Marian Tulloch and Virginia Nightingale.

I have written at greater length elsewhere on the importance of the category of the nation as a key difference between the cultural studies taking place within postcolonial nations and that accomplished within First World traditions.[12] Without denying its constructedness or its deployment in the establishment of consensus over which social divisions and inequities are to be smoothed over, and without invoking an essentialist notion of authenticity, the category of the nation still has the potential within postcolonial societies to operate as a point where cultural difference can be defended and affirmed. As we shall see in Elizabeth Jacka's chapter, many prefer to keep the idea of 'the national' at arm's length by talking about 'the local' and thus seeing the national only as a necessary instrument for maintaining the integrity of the local.[13] In cultural policy, this preference is often implicated in the habit of legislating at the national level for the regulation of activities which occur at the local level. Overall, however, the problematics of a national culture maintaining its difference against, in spite of, or even in collaboration with, the contemporary pressure towards globalisation has become the ground for Australian cultural studies of all descriptions.

Maintaining the critique of the construction of national identity, resisting nostalgia for a less globalised culture than we now inhabit, and differentiating 'the national' from 'the nationalist' is a necessary but difficult balancing act within Australian cultural studies. So many of the previous, competing, traditions of Australian cultural analysis and criticism – particularly those within social history and literary studies – have been concerned with the unveiling of a 'national character' that the water has been badly muddied. To engage in some deconstructive project on Australian national identity is to risk becoming (or being seen to become) part of the thing one is analysing. There is occasionally, that is to suggest, an unavoidable contradiction in practice between cultural theory and cultural strategy. Of course, this is not an unfamiliar contradiction for the postcolonial, who has to speak the language of the coloniser before he or she can intervene in shaping what it is being used to say. Often, too, this is an internationalising or, more correctly, a universalising language in which the voice of the national and of the local is progressively muted. To speak it is to collaborate in its project; not to speak it is ultimately to accept silence. As will be apparent in the contributions from O'Regan, Jacka and Cunningham, addressing and attempting to act in response to such contradictions has been the primary concern within debates about media policy within Australia, but it is also implicit in Meaghan Morris's very different interest in reorienting our understanding of media histories.

UNDISCIPLINES

The historical conditions which are most easily dealt with through the dominant traditions of cultural studies theory are those of the First World, the northern hemisphere, the West. From 'South of the West',[14] the Eurocentricity (in particular) of the tradition can seem blindingly obvious. For example, much recent debate about globalisation and the role of the citizen assumes as its ground the new 'united' Europe – not Canada, or New Zealand or Australia, where the arguments would be very different. Again, debates about nationalism are dominated by positions articulated within contexts where the idea of the nation is (seemingly permanently) in the capture of a conservative Establishment. Over the last few years other possibilities for nationalism have surfaced even within Europe; now the standard placement of nationalism as categorically reactionary seems far too simple to explain contemporary political events. And in a further example, the often assumed relation between Thatcherism's New Times in the UK, the revival of the New Right in the US, and diagnoses of postmodernism makes little sense within Australia where we have had a majority of Labour governments in the states and a Labour government federally (admittedly none of them in any sense radical) since 1983, but where we can also detect the representational symptoms of the postmodern. In general, within an internationalising cultural studies, theoretical positions that once seemed licensed as global explanations have to accept their provisionality or contingency as they move from the centre to the margins. As Ian Hunter's essay in this collection suggests, it may well be that the very conception of culture with which cultural studies largely works today, its totalised and abstract character, actually inhibits strategic modification when it is deployed onto the analysis of particular instances, specific historical conjunctures.

Hence the epigraph at the head of this introduction; it comes from Meaghan Morris's response to questions about her attitude to the Eurocentricity of cultural studies practice after her paper at the Illinois conference mentioned earlier. In it she underlines the degree of theoretical or analytical 'uncertainty' seen to mark work in Australia (and presumably seen *not* to mark European work), which is a product of the Australian practice of testing theory against the conditions. It is also a product of thinking of Eurocentricity as, Morris suggests, an 'error' which needs to be contested by resisting pressures towards totalisation, asserting the importance of ambiguity and emphasising the need for 'de-centring' cultural studies. As Homi Bhabha says in the same exchange:

> I think the interrogation of Eurocentric practices and concepts is clearly the problematic of what we do. And I think that the important issue is to take the Eurocentric focus and by decentering it, actually open up a whole number of issues which start from a number of other

traditions which have defined themselves both in opposition to Euro-centric positions and in tension and contention with them. So I think it is important to elaborate other starting points and other destinations which would set up very different concepts of historicity, community, temporality, and cultural value generally.[15]

The crucial note here is that the concepts themselves change – not just the way in which they might be operationalised. It is a note that cannot be struck often enough. The virtue of being an 'undiscipline' rather than an established discipline lies in cultural studies' provisionality and its emphasis on praxis. This collection is intended to reaffirm such attributes and to further fuel readers' sense of their importance by offering fresh contributions to the tradition that will be both familiar *and* strange in their theoretical perspectives, local concerns and national origins.

A final task for this introduction is to suggest this book's relation to the large and varied field of Australian cultural studies. The book is divided into four sections, and the introductions to each part will frame and locate the individual contributions. Here, I am concerned to stress that the contributions have been selected from an enormous pool of possibilities. There can be no claims to comprehensiveness as it would be impossible to present a genuinely inclusive overview of Australian cultural studies within one volume; what I have tried to do in this one is to concentrate on issues around the media and popular culture, and on work which speaks from a relatively explicit Australian position. Even within this restricted field there are a wealth of possibilities. Inevitably, a number of distinguished writers have been omitted: among those I particularly regret not being able to include are John Frow, Stephen Muecke, Tim Rowse, Lesley Johnson, Sylvia Lawson, Colin Mercer, Ross Gibson, Robert Hodge and Noel King. Two British expatriates who have contributed immeasurably to the development of cultural studies in Australia, John Fiske and John Hartley, have not been included simply because much of their work is already so widely disseminated.

My opportunity here was to collect work which was unlikely to be known outside Australia in order to bring some new voices and perspectives to an international readership. Most of the selections are drawn from small journals or from monographs published only in Australia. In some cases, such as in Ian Hunter's essay, an international readership is addressed directly; in most instances, however, there is a local specificity about the concerns and the address. While I will attempt to interpret this specificity for a non-Australian readership in the section introductions, I should also stress that it is this very unfamiliarity that I see as the most exciting and productive aspect of this collection. If cultural studies is to remain an undisciplined, contestatory, fluid field of theory and practice, there should be more of it.

NOTES

1 See Cary Nelson, 'Always already cultural studies: two conferences and a manifesto', *Journal of the Midwest Modern Language Association*, 24(1), 24–38.
2 Larry Grossberg, Cary Nelson and Paula Treichler, *Cultural Studies*, Routledge, New York, 1991.
3 *New Times and Old Enemies*, Routledge, London, 1991, p. 1.
4 Larry Grossberg *et al.*, *Cultural Studies*, p. 15.
5 See, in addition to the excerpt in Section 2 from *Out of Which Past? Reflections on Australian Museum and Heritage Policy* (Institute of Cultural Policy Studies, Griffith University, 1988), 'The political rationality of the museum', *Continuum*, 3(1) (1990), 35–55.
6 A more detailed account of this relationship, and the development of Australian cultural studies positions, can be found in my 'It works for me?: British cultural studies, Australian cultural studies, Australian film' in Grossberg *et al.*, *Cultural Studies*. A further discussion occurs in my 'Of rocks and hard places: the colonised, the national, and Australian cultural studies', in the journal *Cultural Studies*, 6(3) (1992).
7 *The Pirate's Fiancée: Feminism, Reading, Postmodernism*, Verso, London, 1988, p. 247.
8 ibid.
9 ibid., p. 248.
10 'Where the global meets the local: notes from the sitting room', *Screen*, 32(1) (1991), 9–10.
11 'Literature – nationalism's other? The case for revision', in Homi Bhabha (ed.), *Nation and Narration*, Routledge, London, 1990, p. 139.
12 See Turner, 'Of rocks and hard places'.
13 There are already signs that this strategy won't work for long. David Morley refers to Coca Cola's cunning characterisation of itself as a 'multilocal' rather than a 'multinational' company in his 'When the global meets the local', p. 15.
14 The title of Ross Gibson's recent collection of essays, published by the University of Indiana Press in 1992.
15 Grossberg *et al.*, *Cultural Studies*, p. 475.

Part I

Nation, Culture, Text

The two essays in this section consider their texts contextually, as the products of specific historical conditions and of particularly defining discursive formations. Meaghan Morris constructs a history of a mass-mediated tradition of 'Australiana' that takes us from the media spectacles of the 1988 Bicentennial to the travel writings of Ernestine Hill; and Eric Michaels examines the ways in which an isolated Aboriginal community makes use of, and how their culture might expect to survive, the technologies of the mass media. Within both essays, and while the idea is never assumed to be unproblematic, the category of the nation is crucially active – powerfully overdetermining but also available for intervention and strategic mobilisation. In the Morris essay, it is a category always in the process of semiosis and thus open for discursive interrogation, but Michaels is interested in a different kind of imagined community: his concern is with the ways in which white Australian definition of the nation delimits and denies the racially defined, but no less imagined, Aboriginal community. His concern with the texts produced by this tribal culture is ultimately an explicitly political concern for the maintenance of racial and cultural difference within the nation-state.

It is hard to imagine a richer site for such a breed of cultural studies than the Australian Bicentennial in 1988. Despite its explicit framing within the increasingly shrill consensus produced by politicians and the entrepreneurial authority charged with running the festivities, the Bicentennial was inevitably and relentlessly fragmented. The signs were there when protesters dogged the path of the prefatory US warships visiting Sydney Harbour in December 1987, and in the long-running scandal about the financial accounts and presumed agenda (first, divisive and later, homogenising) of the Bicentennial Authority. The most powerful and sustained challenge, however, was presented by Australian Aboriginals who renamed Australia Day, 'Invasion Day', and staged their own alternative and non-celebratory events.

Meaghan Morris's essay begins with the panoramic spectacle that was the Australian Bicentennial – initially, with the televisual display of difference in unity, *Australia Live*, a four-hour programme aired on Australia Day (26 January 1988). Morris examines, over what is itself a panorama of textual sites, the media production of a nation making its most exorbitant claims for consensus. Her aim is partly to raise some issues about the relations between live television and the 'live' itself; partly to reframe histories of the mass media in Australia through a history of the work of the Australian writer, Ernestine Hill; and partly to challenge some of the implications of 'the gloomy theory of the media' she identifies with postmodernism. Morris's piece is both a powerful reminder of the need to place theories of the media within specific historical contexts and a partial answer to postmodernist orthodoxies on the media. In her determined reinscription of what she calls 'histories of change', she offers a less apocalyptic vision than Baudrillard or Jameson which acknowledges the mutability (rather than the collapse) of cultural and political relations.

Meaghan Morris's method takes her away, in the centre of her essay, from the Bicentennial to a discussion of the literary career of Ernestine Hill. She uses this example as a means of historicising the 'imaginary spacings of the media', by seeing Hill's career as 'part of the history of the media, mass culture, and popular fiction in the present' – a history which is also that of a tradition of Australian panorama and, ultimately, that of *Australia Live*.

The work of the late Eric Michaels was unique in Australian cultural studies. An American, trained in the anthropological tradition of ethnography, he is one of very few to research the effect of the mass media within rural/tribal Australian Aboriginal communities. In the monograph from which this excerpt is taken, *For a Cultural Future: Frances Jupurrurla Makes TV at Yuendumu*, Eric Michaels examines how Aborigines have made use of the technologies of television, what he calls 'the Aboriginal invention of television', and considers what use might be made of the medium in the future.

The subjects of his analysis are Aboriginal video-makers from the Warlpiri Media Association, a public TV service established in 1985 within the Yuendumu community on the edge of Central Australia's Tanami desert. At the beginning of *For a Cultural Future*, Michaels describes the service in the following way:

> All content the Warlpiri Media Association transmits is locally produced. Almost all of it is in the Warlpiri Aboriginal language. Some is live: schoolchildren reading their assignments, community announcements, old men telling stories, young blokes acting cheeky. The station also draws on a videotape library of several hundred hours of material that had been produced in the community since 1982 [the time of writing is 1985] . . . Yuendumu's four hour schedule was, by percent-

age, and perhaps absolute hours, in excess of the Australian content of any other Australian television station. The transmissions were unauthorised, unfunded, uncommercial and illegal. There were no provisions with the Australian Broadcasting Laws for this kind of service.[1]

He prefaces his account of the ways in which these video-makers produce their work with an outline of the categoric cultural differences necessarily implicated in this appropriation of mass-media technology. Not only is there a 'fundamental mismatch' between culture and medium – 'the bias of mass broadcasting is concentration and unification; the bias of Aboriginal culture is diversity and autonomy' – but the nature of Aboriginal Law, with its restrictions, regulations and conventions (among them a prohibition against fiction) dramatically complicates, for instance, the relation between Aboriginals' fundamental cultural institutions and the transmission of information through representation. The idea of a mass-mediated culture cuts across notions of location and an identification with the land, as well as any hope of regulating the access to information enjoyed by specific groups within the community. Consequently, Michaels's accounts of Aboriginal videos reveal cultural difference vividly in action and palpably under threat. In this excerpt, it is television's threat to Aboriginal culture that is of most concern as Michaels forsakes the objectivity of the ethnographer to frame what is ultimately a policy argument for a particular kind of cultural future.

NOTE

1 Eric Michaels, *For a Cultural Future: Francis Jupurrurla Makes TV at Yuendumu*, Artspace, Sydney, 1987, p. 7.

Chapter 1

Panorama
The live, the dead and the living

Meaghan Morris

In memory of Cecil B. De Mille

MEDIA LANDSCAPE

> 'Live was the operative word, and I couldn't help wondering why.'
> (Peter Robinson, *The Sun-Herald*, 3 January 1988)

The first major media event of the Australian Bicentenary was the satellised, multi-network television broadcast, on 1 January, of a four-hour landscape-special called *Australia Live: Celebration of a Nation*.

There had been many other inaugural events that day. Prime Minister Hawke led the countdown to New Year fireworks at a rain-soaked Melbourne concert; Aboriginal people cast wreaths into the waters of Botany Bay to launch their Year of Mourning; Prime Minister Hawke quoted Abraham Lincoln (while Aboriginal protesters were 'restrained' from approaching the dais) at a pavilion commemorating postmodernism in Sydney's rain-soaked Centennial Park. The reports of these events casually jostled each other, in the usual way, across the newspaper page. They prompted little explicit commentary. It was left to the interested reader to trace ironies running between them.

Australia Live, in contrast, was made an object of serious criticism. As a state-of-the-art communications panorama of 'Australia' past and present, it was a media gift to the Bicentenary, not mere reportage of events. So it acquired the professional status of a self-reflexive text. Almost every 'personality' not seen on the show had something to say about its high-tech aesthetics, its conceptual insufficiencies and its investment of authority in media-celebrity speech. It was described as boring, glib, superficial, embarrassing, myopic and (by Peter Robinson) as a 'shallow, ockerish, noisome bouquet of snippet journalism'. Those critics who praised it seemed unctuous and sycophantic towards their fellow professionals. It was left to a few letter-writers simply to admire the stream of sceneries as 'beautiful' and 'lovely'.

Most writers agreed, in a vexed sort of way, that the programme's content was deliriously formalistic. *Australia Live* had not celebrated a 'nation', in any traditional or substantive sense of that term, but rather its own technical demonstration that four hours of live television could simultaneously be produced and consumed around the globe without too many disasters. The technology itself, some added, wasn't even Australian. We just pushed buttons, twiddled the knobs, and put celebrities on planes to remote locations so we could see, when they were there, that they were there.

Australia Live was not rivetting television. Nor, perhaps, was it meant to be in a dramatically *pointed* sense. Orchestrated by Peter Faiman (director of *Crocodile Dundee*), it placed three talk-show stars in a studio, and tested their skills at burbling into coherence a stream of (1) spectacular landscapes: desert, mine, snow, jungle, sea, ice, mountain, bush, woolshed, beach, town; (2) historicised landscapes: old footage of fire and flood, live presentations of places (Gallipoli, Portsmouth) significant in white Australia's past; (3) celebrity discourse-locations: snatches of speech and song appropriately framed in space – Phillip Adams at Uluru, Olivia in her living room, Ernie Dingo at Botany Bay. In this way was protest and dissent also made panoramic (not pointed): set-piece speeches about the heritage of Aboriginal Australia were smoothed into easy continuity with the spectacle of black English media-import Trisha Goddard gushing, from a hot air balloon, that 'everything in this country has been made by immigrants'.

The panorama is a tolerant form, infinitely indulgent of lapses of attention, momentary or lengthy distraction, shifts of mood and variations of intensity in involvement. A classical panorama (whether produced by painting, cinema, literary description or formal look-out construction) may project this indulgence into the object constructed. So much space to see, so much time for seeing: duration as well as extension become ennobling mythic properties of a ('timeless') spatial *scene*. They signify a there-ness impervious, because supposedly indifferent, to the frailties of the viewer.

The long-lasting but high-speed televisual montage of scenes developed in *Australia Live* is 'panoramic' in another way. It is the performance of keeping it going that matters, the *show* of co-ordinating disparate spaces in time, through time, while moving constantly from scene to scene with minimal jerks and bumps. So much space to see, so little time in any one place: duration and extension as properties of objects are displaced by the *staying-power* of monitoring subjects and the *reach* of the technical system.

With this kind of panorama, there is no need for the viewer to try to watch closely or become absorbed in her vision. To participate, she only needs to check from time to time that it's all still going-on-happening. No single place or scene matters very much. Objects are unimportant. Segments count individually only as pre-texts for conversation later, or as hooks for vagrant story-telling ('I missed that bit, I was doing X or

Y, and . . .'). Where the libidinal economy of classical panorama is imperial, or proprietorial, in structure (seeing is possessing), the self-celebratory, high-tech panorama is primarily touristic (seeing is just passing by). The two structures share, however, a passion for *continuity*: the unbroken vista in the first case, the smooth connection in the second.

A certain dullness was thus a generic feature, and not an aesthetic flaw, of *Australia Live*. Relentlessly repetitive aerial shots and domestic close-ups produced a look-alike effect, an echoing sameness linking places and personalities in a consistent indistinction, which was perfectly appropriate to the project of the show. Airline inflight magazines and travel advertisements are 'dull' in precisely this way.

Australia Live was not a failed portrait of a national identity, nor a poor dramatisation of an Australian social text. It was a four-hour tourist brochure for international, including Australian, consumption. It celebrated Australia as a vast reservoir of exotic yet familiar (cross-culturally accessible) resorts and photographic locations. One of the unifying formal motifs of the presentation was a circle flashing a dot on a tiny bit of map so othewise uninformative that it could only proclaim, 'We are now somewhere else'. Another was a temporal conceit: allusions to racing the twilight across the face of Australia combined with references to time-pressure (the satellite agenda) to create a theme of the *schedule*. With map and schedule to fix our itinerary, a climate-controlled team of studio guides confirmed the touristic mode of address: Jana Wendt (cool and hard) and Ray Martin (warm and mushy) marked the national media context, while Clive James (tepid and oozy) was the international message.

Few other formats could more effectively have declared a gap between, on the one hand, a historical, critical conception of the Bicentenary as an opportunity (however artificial the occasion in a 'nation' eighty-seven years old) for analysis, appraisal and reform, and on the other, an entrepreneurial philosophy of its spectacular 'festive' function. *Australia Live* had no commemorative, or even 'nostalgic', aspirations whatsoever. It produced Australia as a space for visiting, investing, cruising, developing. Its basic theme was (capital) mobility. Comprehensive notes on the risks – drought, grasshopper plagues, restless natives – were included.

In that sense, critical disappointment with the programme's lack of historical 'depth' and 'vision' was, while understandable, inattentive to what it *did* achieve. One writer made fun of its uniformly 'joyous' image of a country without 'blemishes', 'pimples and blotches'.[1] But in a regime of representation where a Cromwellian 'warts and all' approach implies just another style of make-up and not a political shift in aesthetics, it might be more precise to say that *Australia Live* produced a landscape without *shadows*: a surveillance-space where nothing secret, mysterious, troubling or malcontent could find a place to lurk or hide. This 'controlling' fantasy of total visibility and access was, in turn, no secret. Commercial breaks were smoothed into the programme by cartoon images of satellite communication beams ping-ponging from dish to dish, and zapping in unerringly at dot after dot on the map. The immediate historical referent of the show was not two centuries (or even eighty-seven years) of 'Australian' experience, but a classic international video game – *Space Invaders*.

At least, that was its model referent in the history of technique (the media, the technology, and the know-how defining the 'game' of space invasion). Another historical referent in the broader sense of 'history' was a person brought on live to be enjoyed with relish by hosts and critics alike – not just as a model of the show, but of an old national myth that the show worked hard to displace.

Mrs Smith of Kingoonya – the 'mover and shaker', Clive James drooled in anticipation, of a dusty little town with six inhabitants – was the figure who at once epitomised the regime of *Australia Live*, and marked its difference from the historic, pre-satellite, bush-based, white-pioneer, isolationist natural mystique of days gone by. She did both by persistently misunderstanding questions, missing her joke cues, overriding her husband and mixing up James with Martin. In this way, she guaranteed that the live was really *live*. However her propensity for error (like her cultural difference) had already been explained. The Smiths of Kingoonya do not have television.

Just as James announced that Mrs Smith was actually capable of changing her mind and refusing to participate, the camera tracked like a brave pioneer through the house – to catch Mr and Mrs Smith in their lair (the kitchen). It was a rare First Contact experience: media modernity met two of the last surviving pre-televisuals, and the result, all agreed, was spectacular.

In this moment, Mrs Smith of Kingoonya became both a temporary national relic, and a living stereotype.

Scenes of the death of history

I almost think we're all of us Ghosts, Pastor Manders. It's not only what we have inherited from our father and mother that 'walks' in us. It's all sorts of dead ideas, and lifeless old beliefs, and so forth. They have no vitality, but they cling to us all the same, and we can't get rid of them. Whenever I take up a newspaper, I seem to see Ghosts gliding between the lines. There must be Ghosts all the country over, as thick as the sand of the sea.

(Henrik Ibsen, *Ghosts*, 1881)

In the gloomy theory of media developed by Jean Baudrillard, a programme like *Australia Live* could be considered a symptom-text of 'our'
terminal living-condition. It wouldn't be enough to claim that certain
media practices now package a commodified set of differences (national,
in this case, sexual, ethnic, or 'cultural' in others) for an increasingly
undifferentiated, international, consuming class. For Baudrillard, the
media actually do generate as (hyper) *reality* the spectacles they present.
Not only is all television like *Australia Live* – shadowless, depthless,
invasive – but 'reality', or rather what's left of it, is really like *Australia
Live* (even, though not especially, in Australia).

According to this scenario, there is no point in calling for historical
analysis or for critical 'perspective'. After television, imagining the past
in any other relation to the present than that of a period-piece becomes
ontologically impossible for mediatised human beings. Costume dramas
like the mini-series *Captain James Cook*, or the associated theatrics of
historical 're-enactments', function so strongly as simulacra – creating a
past which never before existed – that we become incapable of thinking
either past or future except as genres in the present. Baudrillard's argument is not that these practices distort the 'truth' of history, or naturalise
it as myth, nor even that they displace alternative and dissident versions
of the histories to be narrated. His claim is much more drastic: television
destroys the imagination. In its regime of the all-seeing eye, the fully-
visible space, the inescapable network, there are no obscure places left
to shelter the enigma, and so prompt speculation.[2]

It follows that criticism – at least in its traditional projects of highlighting 'hidden' principles of organisation, revealing faults and clarifying
virtues, looking between the lines and behind the scenes of a text – has
become a futile business. When everything is all out in the open, there's
nothing much to say. That Paul Hogan could introduce *Australia Live*
with a joke about giving the place 'back to the abos' [sic] may (and did)
give rise to indignant commentary about offensiveness and racism. But
the problem is that such a response is programmed by the joke. Because
the joke openly exists to provoke the criticism (shock-horror publicity
value), it is not vulnerable in any way to 'exposure'. As the representative
national viewer, Hogan also supplied *Australia Live* with its own critical
backchat. Asked what it had said about Australians today, he admitted
for us – 'Not much'.

A more sober version of the idea that historical sense is weakening
and critical distance diminishing in contemporary culture is given by
Fredric Jameson in his analysis of postmodernism as a 'cultural dominant'
of late capitalism. Jameson attempts to be argumentatively plausible in
a way that Baudrillard (who takes the postcritical logic of his own theory
seriously) does not. In Jameson's scenario, an electronics-based and glo-
bally integrated capitalist system is increasingly invading the enclaves of

resistant or merely (in Ernst Bloch's phrase) 'non-synchronic' life forms tolerated by previous modes of capitalist organisation. These enclaves are not only localised cultures and residual non-capitalist social systems – once economically exploited, perhaps, but symbolically left alone, in semi-autonomy, to get by – but also what Jameson calls the two 'big targets' of contemporary expansion – Nature, and the Unconscious.[3]

This expansive, invasive, integrationist world-capitalist cultural system bears little relation to the culture once said by Marxists to 'reflect', in various intricate ways, the determinant structures of economic organisation. Since the base-superstructure distinction has collapsed, so, therefore, has the possibility of reflection, and of 'representation' – which always assumes a gap of some sort between at least two orders of reality. In electro-capitalism, culture *becomes* a determinant. The tourist 'industry' provides an excellent example of the systemic integration of economic activity and exploitation, political struggles for power, a technical streamlining of 'nature', the production of dreams and desires and popular cultural practices of having (and making) fun. Tourism, in turn, is laterally connected to a vast range of other enterprises and activities.

To stress 'integration' in this context does not imply that there are no differences or inequalities remaining. On the contrary: as the 'purest form' of capitalism to date, the order that Jameson sees emerging would imply an even greater extension of inequity and exploitation. What it does imply is that there is less and less tolerance of the possibility of critical *exteriority* to the system. Its invasiveness precludes the establishment of positions 'outside' its field of operations.

So the 'critical distance' that separated criticism from its political, social and aesthetic objects has also been abolished. Once again, this does not mean that there are no differences left – although as difference itself becomes commodified, it may mean that the differences at stake in particular conflicts will need to be reconceptualised. What Jameson does claim is that the spatial relations between 'criticism' and its objects have changed: they can no longer effectively be considered as 'external' or 'foreign' to each other; for 'distance in general (including "critical distance" in particular) has very precisely been abolished in the new space of postmodernism'.[4]

One sign of the collapse of critical distance is an increasing inability to distinguish past from present in ways which would allow us to analyse their 'real' relationship. At this point, Jameson's version of the death of history rejoins Baudrillard's. Our access to the past's reality is choked off by a proliferation of historical simulacra (period 'styles', pastiche): 'the historical novel', for example, 'can no longer set out to represent the historical past; it can only "represent" our ideas and sterotypes about that past (which thereby at once becomes "pop history")'.[5]

Although Jameson's unease with these developments is manifest, his point is not to denounce or decry 'pop history', but to argue that a notion of 'oppositional' cultural politics becomes increasingly inappropriate to this new regime of space. With the erosion of distance, the collapse of distinction and the disappearance of positioning 'outside' this new capitalist hyperspace, the old techniques of 'moral denunciation of the Other' have become, for Jameson, 'completely ineffective'. He proposes instead that new forms of political action must develop in response to our *spatial*, as well as social, confusion. Pop history, logically, and despite Jameson's own distaste, should provide one such space for action.

Baudrillard provides no comparable remedial scenario for articulating discontent. In his post-critical fables, the death of history is absolute. Jameson, rather than the more overtly experimental Baudrillard, is the one to point out the limits of his own scenario. Writing about 'contemporary entertainment literature', Jameson comments on the depressing determinism at work in the genre of *high-tech paranoia* – stories featuring 'labyrinthine conspiracies of autonomous but deadly interlocking and competing agencies in a complexity often beyond the capacity of the normal reading mind'.[6] However he adds that conspiracy theory is at least an attempt to think the 'impossible totality' of the 'contemporary world system' – and so, of course, and in a similar way, is his theory of postmodernism.

Ephemera

> Ephemera: Pl. ephemerae, -as . . . *Zool.* An insect that (in its imago) lives only for a day.
>
> (OED)

A conspiracy theorist might see *Australia Live* as evidence for these theories. History was certainly treated as an archival display (old footage) or as a tourist commemorative experience (recitation of 'For the Fallen' at Gallipoli). Moreover, one of its themes was precisely a cliché of Australian pop historiography – the *end* of the 'tyranny of distance'. Thanks to satellites, aeroplanes and computers (three enabling conditions of the show), one version of history, at least, was repeatedly declared dead: Australia as a space of isolation, slow development and eccentricity. Ray Martin called distance 'freedom' (the wide open spaces): and to demonstrate the overthrow of the old tyranny, two residual 'distanced' types were tracked down in the outback and flown to Sydney to be filmed discovering big city life and total contemporaneity. With a thesis so clear to present, it's perhaps hardly fair to say that *Australia Live* had no historical implications.

However there is no need to accept either the exorbitant literalness with which Baudrillard presents particular spectacles as coextensive with all reality, or the literary nostalgia that animates Jameson's paranoia. An event like *Australia Live* is no more representative of a mythic 'television-in-general' than it was reflective of life in Australia. So its uncanny resonance with the *terms* of these theories makes its fiction of Australia as a totally accessible televisual space a useful pre-text for questioning 'paranoia' as a critique of high-tech culture.

As Alice Jardine has pointed out, paranoia involved both a 'fear of the loss of *borders*' and an experience of such a loss.[7] For many critics and historians of culture, to dispute and redraw borders is the same as creating knowledge: despite their differences, both Baudrillard's and Jameson's theories are based on a pained discovery that in the presumed new 'world space' of media, the practice of *discrimination* (dividing mountains from mole-hills, the wood from being the trees) seems to have become more difficult.

This is a temporal, as well as a spatial, problem. Because they are ephemeral (though not necessarily inconsequential) events in people's lives as well as 'texts' that can be recorded, stored in archives and analysed, media products are not easily assimilated to the problematic of the 'durable' which has animated so much classical Marxist criticism as well as the liberalism it opposes. The ephemeral, by definition, lives for one day only: it is transitory, short-lived, poorly differentiated (the *ephemeromorph* is the lowest form of life, 'not definitely either animal or vegetable'). Modern institutionalised criticism, however, has for over a century relaunched and revised its project not only by 'bordering', or differentiating, its objects, but by progressively taking a 'distance' from previous readings of texts that somehow survive through *time*.

Much of the hostility provoked by media criticism in recent years derives, implicitly or explicitly, from assumptions about ephemera. It seems indecent for critics to perpetuate objects that should 'naturally' die in silence after their single day of glory. One response to this assumption is to write histories of 'durability', and how it has been invested in canonical texts by literary critics. Another response is to say that mass-media history, far from being 'dead', has barely begun to be written; that the 'ephemerality' of any television show is in part a product of ignoring the problem of how to think about its relationship to a *media*, and mass-cultural, 'past' and present; and that we can write a critical history of this ignoring, as well as of 'ephemeral' objects, their circulation and their modes of enduring through culture. It is possible, after all, that the disappearing sensation experienced by Jameson is as much a product of the rush of his analysis from early nineteenth-century novels to late twentieth-century media events – without pause to consider the history of mediating structures.

However it is not simply a matter of looking at how media technology develops, and how it changes our experience of culture and our relationships to the past. A history of 'mediation' also involves questioning the conceptual and rhetorical frameworks that have been used in the past to analyse the media and popular culture. The terms of discussion – and how the debates of the past may relate to those of today – are as much a part of the 'history' of media as the technologies on which they depend.

As Andreas Huyssen points out in *After the Great Divide*, early twentieth-century debates about 'high art' and 'mass culture' were already cast in paranoia-producing, borderline terms, which we haven't quite stopped using today. Huyssen argues that modernism constituted itself *as* high art by relegating mass culture to the deathly realm of the Other: modernism's aesthetic and political programme depended on maintaining an 'anxiety of contamination' by an impure force invading from mass culture.[8] 'The Great Divide' is thus for Huyssen not merely a historical moment, but a discourse which can be analysed, and criticised, historically.

However in an Australian context, the rhetoric of 'death', 'divide' (and 'distance') – on which so many accounts of media culture still depend – poses a difficult problem for the writing of cultural history. On the one hand, these are terms historically fundamental to the European invasion of Australia, and the dispossession of Aboriginal people. On the other, they circulate back around as *puns* in Eurocentric media theory: Jameson's scenario in particular would be unimaginable without its conflation of intellectual and political activity (criticism) with spatial representation (landscape) in the metaphor of 'mapping'.

It's easy to explain this convergence as an effect of modern imperialism. But rather than use this sort of generalisation as an all-purpose conclusion, it might be more useful to take it as a point of departure for asking questions. If contemporary critics represent media culture in general as a kind of funereal landscape, for example, how have media critics and practitioners in Australia in the past represented the 'space' – political, geographic, conceptual – of their own activities? To consider this is a way of beginning to historicise the imaginary spacings of media, rather than simply to take them as given.

So it is also a way of seeing shadows on the landscape of *Australia Live*.

SHADOWS

Wending her way for 1,500 miles north, white sails threading through seas and islands lovely as a dream, with her ghastly human cargo unable to stand upright in the hold where they carry the pearl-shell, the leper ship was a nightmare – and a streamer special for the southern Press. Such is a journalist's philosophy. The worse it is, the better it is, transcribing life in printer's ink. For your true journalist . . . prefers a murder to a suicide, and both to a wedding. He skims the cream of science, and the practical experience of years in a few comprehensive phrases, and gives it a snappy title. He is all things to all men, and to him all men, living and dying, are copy.

(Ernestine Hill, *The Great Australian Loneliness*, 1937)

One of the most interesting commentators on early media 'effects' in Australia was Ernestine Hill (1900–72). Her description of the leper ship transporting Aborigines from an island near Roebourne to another near Darwin combines three of the recurring themes of her writing: a descriptive 'dream' of an idyllic land, the 'nightmare' history it contained and concealed, and disturbing new relations created between classically opposed terms (dream/nightmare, description/narrative, landscape/history) by the 'streamer special' of a media sensationalism, and reductive 'snippet journalism'.

A journalist herself, Hill specialised in a kind of writing that was once easily recognisable and very popular in Australia, but which has become quite hard to classify. In the major study of the social and aesthetic context in which Hill was working, *A Study of Australian Descriptive and Travel Writing, 1929–1945*, Margriet Bonnin calls it 'the genre which has been described at various times as landscape writing, travel writing, descriptive writing, frontier writing, and several combinations of these labels'.[9]

Each of Hill's books was as mixed as their general status was uncertain. Today, we might call most of them 'factions'. *The Great Australian Loneliness* (1937) was a volume of highlights from the 'location' journalism she published during several years of travel through Western, Northern and Central Australia in the 1930s. *My Love Must Wait* (1941) was a historical romance, and a biography of Matthew Flinders. *Water Into Gold* (1937) and *Flying Doctor Calling* (1947) were what Hill liked to call 'living history' – idealising portraits of personalities (the Chaffey brothers, Dr John Flyn) projected across a 'landscaped' historical account of their nation-building exploits. *The Territory* (1951) was a remarkable experiment mixing epic, romantic, Western and descriptive conventions to write regional and local history. Her last book *Kabbarli* (published posthumously in 1973) was a 'personal memoir' of Daisy Bates – a character sketch, a biography and, in part, an autobiography. In it Hill claimed that she had ghost-written Bates's own volume of reminiscences, *The Passing of The Aborigines* (1938).

During much of her lifetime, Hill was one of Australia's best-known and widely-read authors.[10] Her popular reputation was not confined to the considerable circulation achieved by her books. Beginning with *Smith's Weekly* (after working as J. F. Archibald's last secretary), she published for over thirty years in almost every newspaper and magazine in Australia. She contributed for decades to *Walkabout*; she was a special correspondent and then editor of the women's pages for the influential wartime *ABC Weekly*; she was an ABC Commissioner from 1942 to 1944; she wrote radio plays, a short centennial history of South Australia ('Story of the state: from wilderness to wealth in a hundred years'), and a Ure Smith proto-coffee-table book called *Australia: Land of Contrasts* (1943).[11]

Today, Ernestine Hill is a barely discernible figure in the field of Australian literature. She no longer really counts as an 'Author', but as one of the innumerable, poorly differentiated ephemera whose writings form the context from which literary authors emerge. Her work has actually 'died' for most of the broad interpretive histories of Australian literature appearing since the 1960s, ranging from the conservative, tradition-constructing project of Leonie Kramer's *Oxford History of Australian Literature*, to the feminist rewriting of tradition in Drusilla Modjeska's *Exiles At Home*.[12]

There are many ways of discussing Hill's non-existence for today's literary past. She does not seem to have counted unambiguously as a 'literary' figure even during the height of her popularity. This is partly a matter of 'landscape' – the political geography of fame. Although she was in contact with many other writers,[13] Hill did not frequent literary circles, or spend substantial periods of time in Sydney and Melbourne when such circles were defining a national literature in the 1930s. While her books were read in Sydney and Melbourne, she favoured Adelaide, Perth and Darwin, and her privileged location was the outback. Those critics who praised her work (like the West Australian J. K. Ewers) were often precisely those who were to be marginalised in the Eastern historical tradition not only as old-fashioned, but as 'regionalist'.

During her lifetime, Hill's work was most admired as 'Australian literature' in precisly those media where much of the material of her books first appeared in 'story' form – newspapers and magazines. The most serious criticism of her books – trenchant to the point of being scathing – usually came from *The Bulletin*, where her writing was pilloried for the sentimentality, purple rhetoric and rosy optimism that made it appeal to a mass, not literary (and feminine, not robust), sensibility.[14] Her work began to go out of fashion generally towards the end of the 1950s, when the style of local 'realism' in which she specialised – folksy anecdotes, stereotypical character sketches, romantic landscape descriptions and melodramatic rhetoric – was confronted by an emergent literary modernism with internationalist aspirations. John Docker's *In A Critical Condition*[15] and Modjeska's *Exiles At Home* have studied the selective historical amnesia entailed by this shift in notions of literary value during the Cold War period, and their analyses would certainly apply in general to the disappearance of Ernestine Hill.

However, Hill did not share the commitment of many literary figures of her generation to organised social change, and she did not belong to the kind of identifiable political *milieu* which interested socialist and feminist historians in the 1970s. While her texts are preoccupied with problems of race, environment and, to a lesser extent, gender, she despised and avoided 'politics' as she understood the term (parties, petitions and unions),[16] preferring to trust to nature, poetry and 'humanity' for improving people's lives. In the framework used by Docker to analyse the literary debates of the 1950s, Hill could not be located either as a radical nationalist or a metaphysical internationalist. She would be a 'metaphysical' nationalist – and so beside the point of that debate, now as well as then.

To speculate on the reasons for Ernestine Hill's exclusion from literary history is not necessarily to argue for a 'revaluation' of Hill as a neglected artist, or to plead for a more expansive conception of literature. Both would be feasible projects, questioning the politics of prevailing criteria for 'durability' (as feminists have done) and/or by redeeming for literature the general field of what is now called 'popular culture'. Another possibility is to accept, rather than contest, the historical tension between these terms, and to look at Hill's disappearance as part of the modern history of the constitution of popular culture. This would assume that the shifts that brought about her exclusion from the literary canon may be studied – along with her work – as part of the history of media, mass culture and popular fiction in the present.

An interesting example of how these shifts could work – creating divisions that set terms for future debate – is provided in a text by a writer who was also long to be ignored by later academic literary criticism. In an article on 'The landscape writers' in 1952 (published just after Hill's major work, *The Territory*), Flora Eldershaw argued that 'three bold stages' make up 'the communal effort called literature': the *folk* stage ('spontaneous, anonymous, and unseparated from the patterns of daily life'), the *co-operative* stage ('in which the sum is more important than the parts'), and the *delegated* stage ('in which power so cumulates in a few individuals that they sum up and are accepted as tokens of the whole').[17] Eldershaw insists that these stages do not succeed each other 'like the rungs of a ladder'. The earlier stages persist, sustained by the 'soil' (a 'blend of earth and social conditions'). This is a model combining natural and political metaphors of literary 'development' to generate great Authors from the anonymous mass – as representative democracy emerges from the people, and the great tree rises from the bushes.

With readings of Fred Blakeley's *Hard Liberty* and Francis Ratcliffe's *Flying Fox and Drifting Sand*, Eldershaw defends landscape writing as a renewal of the old bush-folklore element in Australian literature. In an interesting move, she stresses that it must be understood not only as a *return* to mythic bush origins ('a back to Bool Bool festival'), but as a confrontation with the *difference* made to the bush (and thus to the myth of origins) by new technology and improved communications. Much of the nostalgia of the landscape books was about confronting a loss of old myths, rather than a simple dependence on them. So Eldershaw explicitly places landscape writing in a context of modernisation.

At the end of the article, a tension suddenly appears between her metaphors of development. The text switches from explaining the value of landscape writing to calling it a danger to 'truly creative work'. Her reason for anxiety is economic (and ecological); a scarcity of resources in 'the present depression in Australian publishing'. Landscape writers were then outselling self-consciously literary authors. So the logic of Eldershaw's metaphors suggests that they were like undergrowth choking the trees – or an *uprising* from 'below'. The rebellious possibility (which she does not explicitly consider) is the embarrassing one for the text. Without discussing the comparative failure of 'delegated' artists to mobilise popular support, Eldershaw resolves the tension in her model by switching from earth to water for a natural figure to put landscape writing in its proper political 'place': it should be both *'tributary'* and *'source'* for truly creative work.

The river/empire pun reconciles natural and political hierarchies, but it also allows Eldershaw to eliminate the possibility of rethinking 'truly creative' literature in relation to modernisation. Literature happens in a space not directly affected by the changes in technology or communications – and in the function of old Australian myths – that she had discussed with so much acuity and foresight in her analysis of landscape writing. Her manifesto for creative writing bears no trace of such 'modernist' concerns or their attendant themes of loss, fragmentation, dispersal, new myth-making and experiment. Instead, she looks forward to a literature 'in which man and his environment can be *completely fused and interpenetrated*' (my emphasis). In this moment, Eldershaw nostalgically returns Australian *literature* to a mythic 'source', and confines it to being a 'tributary' creek to that vast imperial river – nineteenth-century English Romanticism. The task of dealing with modernity is left to the popular, now not truly 'creative', field of landscape writing.

Reconsidering this text today, it is tempting to reverse the emphases of Eldershaw's conclusion by making landscape writing a precursor of the creative visual forms of contemporary Australian culture – relegating the 'literature' she admired to the minor field of nostalgia. But the difficulty of playing such border-games – and of definitively placing Ernestine Hill's work now as *either* literature *or* popular culture – is suggested by a commodity, rather than scholarly, category which still easily encompasses both: *'Australiana'*. In general bookshops today, especially those without a specialist literature section, the Australiana shelf can run from undisputed literary classics to coffee-table books to wildlife magazines and politicians' memoirs. The term can be used dismissively ('big tacky picture-books'), but it is more often used commercially as a non-polemical description.

What it describes is not a random collection of books contingently 'about' Australia, but a public space set aside for portable (and competing) mythologies. 'Australiana' openly allows for a *promotional* concept of reified Australian identities: it admits that producing images of Australianness is a commercial acitivity, a mode of entertainment, and a genre of cultural practice. So it subsumes (and still sells) the old categories of 'landscape' and 'descriptive' writing. It embraces cross-media products (novelisations, picture-books about films based on literary texts, the video of the live TV coverage of the Invasion Day festivities . . .), and as a term in general use, 'Australiana' easily extends to media events like *Australia Live*.

Beginning from this context, it is useful to reflect back on the historic confusion noted by Margriet Bonnin about the 'genre' to which Ernestine Hill's work once belonged. In the 1940s and 1950s, 'landscape', 'travel', 'descriptive' and 'frontier' were terms emphasising different aspects of roughly the same vast corpus of texts. They were books by people who went to 'remote' parts of Australia, travelled round and wrote stories for city people about why they went bush, what they saw and how it mattered. The term *'travel* writing' for this activity is perhaps the best today: unlike 'landscape' or 'descriptive', 'travel' allows for the narrative of movement, and the movement of narrative. Unlike 'frontier', it leaves room to consider conflicting, as well as changing, concepts of space, time and motion. It can link *The Great Australian Loneliness* historically not only to *Australia Live*, but to Robyn Davidson's *Tracks*, Bruce Chatwin's *The Songlines*, *Reading the Country* by Krim Benterrak, Stephen Muecke and Paddy Roe, and to Sally Morgan's *My Place*.

It is also a term which faded from the vocabulary of discriminating Australian criticism precisely during the period in which Hill's reputation declined. One of the signs of an advancing 'modernism' in even the most 'traditionalist' Australian criticism after the 1950s was an increasingly reductive concept of literary form. To move from H. M. Green's *A History of Australian Literature: Pure and Applied* (published in 1961, but written over many years) to *Australian Literature 1950–1962* – a 1963 supplement to Green's history published after his death by A. D. Hope – is to pass, in one fell swoop, from the baroque to minimalism. The expansive catholicity of Green's elaborate classification scheme gives way in Hope's booklet to a mere eight categories – one of which is Background, and another Miscellaneous. To pass from Green via Hope to the modernistically spare triad Novel/Poetry/Drama in Leonie Kramer's edition of *The Oxford History of Australian Literature* (1981), is to pass, with a skip and a jump, from the sublime to the ridiculous.

Descriptive and travel writing still had a conceptual place in H. M. Green's 'panoramic' scheme of literary history, as well as in Eldershaw's arborescent one. But a criticism defining literary value through formal minimisation and analytic reduction (the literariness of literature, the qualities of 'quality') could provide few concepts capable of making sense of travel writing as a practice at all. Modernist criticism, with its interest in establishing and demonstrating *purity* of form, was particularly ill-equipped to do so.

With a narrative usually motivated in some way by some notion of the voyage, travel-writing tends to move towards a discovery of, and an encounter with, an experience of *impurity*. Or, to shift the terms away from the historical problematic of modernism (and racism), travel-writing is about difference, incoherence, mixity and trans-formation. It is hard to settle the limits, or fix the borders, of a genre which is usually only recognisable in the first place from a story of crossing borders, defying and redefining limits (geographic, perhaps, but also experiential, cognitive, cultural, political and aesthetic). It is also difficult to 'divide' a travel-writing 'text' from a historical and political 'context' – in the effort to do so, criticism is left struggling with panoramic (and 'metaphysical') concepts like 'movement', or 'voyage', or 'quest'.[18]

Ernestine Hill's work is certainly 'travel writing' in this broader sense. All of her work is organised by narratives of conflict between movement and containment, nomadism and projects for settlement, exotic drive and centralising force. She was fascinated not only by the theme of 'crossing' (by 1951 she claimed to have been 'twice round Australia by land, clockwise and anti-clockwise . . . three times across it from south to north, many times east and west, and once on the diagonal'[19]), but also by the theme of encirclement. Flinders' circumnavigation of the continent was one of her great historical passions, and an experience she 're-enacted' as part of her research for *My Love Must Wait*. An encounter with mythic Others *en route* – most often Aboriginal people, but also Afghans, Chinese, Malays and thrillingly suspect Whites – was not only a major selling-point of her journalism and the theme of most of her stories, but was also allegorically inscribed in her texts as the condition of her activity: she repeatedly represents herself sitting by a lamp 'writing history' as strange 'characters' drift by with a tale to tell.

At the same time, Hill's passion for the primal scenes of travel writing was combined with a commitment to a vision of Australian 'modernity' (if not a stylistic 'modernism'). Like the writers discussed by Eldershaw, Hill was not only fascinated by the bush *mythos* recycled and reappropriated so often in Australia since the 1890s, but by its intersection with the new 'vistas' opened up in Australia by technological change. Her work can now all too easily be dismissed as 'outback' nostalgia by a critical tradition still sufficiently obsessed by the rural component of the 'Australian legend' to keep proving its mythical status. In fact, *Water Into Gold* can equally be described as a case study in the history of industrialisation, *Flying Doctor Calling* as a profile of an experiment in extending public health and medical technology, and both *The Great Australian Loneliness* and *The Territory* as early studies in the politics of tourism. Throughout her career Hill was interested in, and on the whole an ardent exponent of, almost every aspect of what is now casually called 'Development'.

That she placed her fables of modernisation in a largely arcadian bush setting, and wrote them as travel stories drawing on all the conventions of popular romance and the 'streamer special', makes her work very difficult to locate – indeed, invisible – for critics defending (or deconstructing) various versions of 'the city *or* the bush', 'art *or* mass culture', 'modernism *or* the great tradition'.

Ernestine Hill was far from being the only writer of her time with these preoccupations, and she was not the only one to fade from literature. Margriet Bonnin argues that descriptive writing was, especially in the 1920s, a way for a great many writers (Ion Idriess, Dora Birtles, Frank Clune, William Hatfield and Francis Ratcliffe, among those still read today) to foster a broad public debate that was less about 'landscape' in any simple or nostalgic sense, than it was about exploring competing scenarios for a future – and usually 'high-tech' – Australian society. While many cherished arcadian myths (the noble bushman, the 'vanishing' tribes, the fertile desert . . . water into gold),

> in one sense the writers were not romantics. They advocated a new civilisation based on modern technology, which would take advantage of the economic and spiritual benefits that they felt the interior had to offer. They sought to prick the consciences of Australians in the hope that action would be taken on the preservation of the natural environment.[20]

They were also, she notes, popularisers of 'scientific and humanitarian interest in the Aborigines among the general public'.[21] In other words, descriptive and travel writing was a way of creating connections between otherwise disparate elements of Australian life, of reinterpreting past and present in 'constructivist' fictions of the future, and of trying to *mobilise* people to 'enact' those fictions in reality. It is in these respects, rather than in simply sharing a heritage of nostalgic folklore and white male pioneer myths, that Ernestine Hill's travel writing can be read as prefiguring the media landscapes, 'live' panoramas and space-festivals of today.

Ghost writing

For the sixth time in fifty years, a settlement in North Australia was fading down into jungle mould.

'The *Olaf* not having arrived, we are unable to print our serial, *The Skeleton in the Closet*,' announced the *N.T. Times*. A local author was writing a novel, *The Doomed House*, or *The White Ants' Revenge*.

For the rest, they talked snake yarns, gold and the dead.

(Ernestine Hill, *The Territory*, 1951)

Ernestine Hill was in all her ventures an imperialist, a white supremacist and a patriot. *The Great Australian Loneliness* was dedicated 'to the men and women of the Australian outback, and to all who take up the white man's burden in the lonely places'. This emphasis was never substantially modified during the most productive period of her life, which ended with *The Territory*. By the time she wrote *Kabbarli*, she had seen the passing of the genocidal myths of the 'dying race' and the 'half-caste menace', and was able to regret (mostly by way of a critique of Daisy Bates's beliefs) her own part in their re-elaboration for the receptively racist climate of white Australia – and Europe – in the late 1930s.

Her major works were unquestioning of social Darwinist assumptions that Aborigines were naturally doomed to extinction, and that mixed-'race', even mixed-culture, people incarnated an unholy transgression of the border not only between 'black' and 'white', but between nature and culture, the dark past (primitive orgins) and the bright future (civilised destiny) and, ultimately, between 'death' and 'life'. Only when each remained Other to the other could there be a certain love and respect.

She fiercely protested atrocities committed by whites against traditional Aboriginal people. She described massacres, kidnappings, rapes, beatings, forced removal from the land, starvation, slave labour and death camps (in particular, Bates's camp at Ooldea Soak).[22] Most of these stories are presented as local history, complete with names, places and dates. But their significance is usually engulfed in her texts by a meditation on the myth (and the fate) of the Other. They confirm, rather than throw into question, an already established imperial truth. Her books are full of laments for the 'sylvan', 'woodland' people of the 'authentic tribes' (sometimes 'fauns' and 'hamadryads'), scorn and mistrust for 'detribalised' Aborigines (atrocities against whom she occasionally justified), and pity for the 'prison' of the 'dark mind'.

There is nothing exceptional about the phantasmatic structure of the frontier landscape of Hill's travel writing. The most one can say is that it is particularly comprehensive – a compendium of imperial paranoia. If in Stephen Muecke's terms, available discourses for mythifying Aborigines can be classified as Racist, Romantic and Anthropological, then Hill's work displays and deploys them all.[23] Furthermore, she extends the romantic and anthropological treatments to the 'fast-disappearing' *white* society of the outback. Nearly all of Hill's 'characters' are presented as emblematic of a 'type' of life dying out. She saw herself not only as a historian, but as an anthropologist collecting data while there was still time left to do so.

So it is interesting that Hill's texts assume that on the one hand there is something vital about the travel-writer's quest to describe human life ('catch it while you can'), yet on the other, something morbid, even 'doomed', about description. It is an assumption shared by many classic accounts of literary realism, and also by theories of the visual media as a vast descriptive regime for destroying (and for Baudrillard, replacing) 'reality'. Roland Barthes summed up this persistent critical anxiety with a maxim: ' "Capturing life" really means "seeing dead".'[24] 'Capturing life' is not necessarily a good description of description: it is, however, the way that Ernestine Hill (like many media realists today) understood her basic project.

The Great Australian Loneliness, *My Love Must Wait* and *The Territory* can all be read as narratives of a quest to 'capture life' – and as studies in its failure. Hill's narrators and heroes have a classic empirical mission. They are journalists, explorers, scientists, map-makers: they set off to see everything, to observe, record, chart, name and 'characterise' all the peoples and places encountered *en voyage*, and bring it all back home as entertaining and useful knowledge. Yet in each case, the quest is at least partly thwarted. *The Great Australian Loneliness* ends with a lament that the pioneer culture it has idealised is 'swiftly slipping away' – because of 'the aeroplane, the radio and the motor-car' that brought the narrator out West in the beginning (and took her stories back out to the cities). One of the first landscape *tableaux* in the book is a panorama of the country from Perth to Carnavon, 'seen' from an aeroplane: the technical possibility of beginning the text is a portent of doom to come. In this case, the journalistic voyage regretfully participates in the murder of its object.

In *My Love Must Wait*, Flinders' dream of circumnavigating Australia completely – charting every nook and cranny, renaming each beach and crag – is frustrated by contingencies of nature, politics, war and human caprice. Even his home-coming to publish his discoveries is botched. Class disadvantages, poverty and illness conspire to cheat him of his final triumph. In *My Love Must Wait*, the death of the map-maker's referent is taken for granted ('to embrace these natives was to embrace death',[25] the narrator bluntly declares). The real regret this time is that the relentlessly bellicose society from which the voyage for the ultimate map is launched then incessantly interferes with its realisation. Flinders fails to salvage his descriptive dream from the nightmare of history that makes it possible.[26]

In *The Territory*, Hill 'describes' a relationship between the history of space (rather than 'mapping') and death. While the book is full of jocular anecdotes, wry humour and edifying tales of endurance, its tone is overwhelmingly elegiac. Her 'territory' is a landscape of perpetually decaying and disappearing settlements: towns blow away, stations are deserted, boundaries are engulfed by the jungle, washed away by flood or effaced by the sand, while the phases of Darwin's history are variations on a (Darwinian) theme of decay. This space is inhabited by corpses, ghosts, phantoms, skeletons, vanishing tribes, 'riders in mirage' and spectral defenders of a 'freehold in illusion'. Recurring images of death are eerily superimposed: originary scenes of Aboriginal people being murdered and dispossessed by white settlers are overlaid by allegories of a perpetual fading of white colonisation – destroyed by nature, by Aboriginal resistance, by the indifference of the rest of the country. If 'capturing life' may theoretically imply 'seeing dead', the life that Hill sought to capture in *The Territory* was represented as already lived in a gorgeous charnel-house.

So a very strong relation is established in these texts between death and the historical mission of travel writing (narration as well as description). This is partly a matter of their chosen 'landscape': death is a dominant figure in the scenic history of a colonising struggle to conquer the land, the sea and the natives. In their expansionist commitment to Australia's brave white future, Hill's texts are not apparently concerned with any intimations of an absolute 'death of history' – except for Aborigines. They are histories of death: not only because of the colonial scene, but because 'history' is conventionally represented as a narrative of the dead (the past, or the passing). One of Hill's favourite metaphors of narration is 'making history come alive': *My Love Must Wait*, for example, is an allegory of history-writing as an act of necromancy. Flinders himself promised that, 'If the plan of a voyage of discovery were to be read over my grave, I would rise up, awakened from the dead!', and the final chapter – 'The Dead Awakes' – explains that this is what the narrator has hoped to do for his 'graceful shade' by rewriting his voyages.[27]

Perhaps the most lurid allegory of death as a condition of narration in Hill's work occurs not in her own texts, but in the book which she claimed to have ghost-written – *The Passing of the Aborigines*.[28]

In an extraordinary passage at the end of her first chapter ('Meeting with the Aborigines'), Daisy Bates stands by as a group of 'natives' fall upon the body of a dying man, and scuffle to inhale his last breath: 'The man was of course dead when we extricated him, and it was a ghastly sight to see the lucky "breath catcher" scoop in his cheeks as he swallowed the "spirit breath" that gave him double hunting power.'[29] The passage has the intensity of a dream-narrative in which the dreamer figures as a voyeur in the scene of her own dreaming. Placed at the beginning of Bates's chronicle of her own life with Aboriginal people, it works as an uncanny account of the moment in which she receives her own life-vocation as 'last-breath catcher' to the race she believed to be dying – whose culture she would write down and 'preserve' as history.

In the logic of this scene, the field of the Other is not only deathly but *oral*: 'writing' is really the border that finally separates white from black, life from death and 'history' from oblivion.[30] It also defines a vampiric moment that inverts and accompanies necromancy. In *Kabbarli*, Hill would claim in turn to have had this same benevolent vampiric relation with Daisy Bates. Too frail, too ill and too old-fashioned to submit to the constraints of modern journalism, the fading Bates gave her life-story to Hill in the form of an oral narration: 'We decided that she would talk, and I would write.'[31]

However none of Hill's texts are histories of death in any unmediated sense. Her narrators traverse imperial spaces already given and mythologised. They are pioneer sight-seers,rather than battling pioneers, of Empire. Touristic and imperial ways of seeing converge, and sometimes conflict. Even Flinders is a hero of a quest for vision, rather than of a struggle for possession: his disastrous imprisonment by the French is determined by sordid political and personal conflicts over 'territory' that he, pure seer, can barely understand. Hill's narrators claim a certain distance from the deaths they define as history: they are reporters coming after the event, spectators still haunting the scene. Yet they are not irresponsible or innocent: death figures in various ways not only as a condition but as a *consequence* of their mediating – and media – activity.

The least lugubrious of Hill's life-catchers is the gay, slightly giddy journalist of *The Great Australian Loneliness*. As H. M. Green pointed out, she is unusually unobtrusive in her story given that its unity derives only from her experience of the voyage.[32] Unlike many other outback quests, Hill's does not lead to a discovery of personal identity, or a brush with the meaning of life. She often dramatises herself (in a light-hearted way) as silly, or predatory, or both. She is also a repertoire of mass cultural fictions: the book begins with the naive city journalist fantasising, in a Western mode, that she needs a gun to 'brandish in moments of peril' in the outback. When she is rebuked by an experienced traveller ('it would be a ridiculous insult to the finest people in the world, and you would be the joke'), the first utopian myth of the Loneliness as a safety zone in a hostile world is created. So is the narrator's role: she is to be the learner against whose prejudice and limitations the hinterland is defined. The book is in part a *Bildungsroman*, but it is as a flighty urban sensibility, rather than as a questing individual soul, that our tour guide will be (re)educated.

She is sometimes exposed as most brittle and shallow in her perceptions precisely when she poses as securely representative of her urban readers' assumptions. In 'Strange case of Mrs Witchetty', Hill hunts down a white English woman who had married a traditional Aboriginal man and remained in camp, after his death, with his people. Hill's excitement is swiftly exposed as prurience: ' "How did he propose?" I asked, indelicately, but knowing the social limitations of the aborigines, amused and curious.

"He asked me to be his wife," said Mrs Witchetty with dignity . . .'[33]

At the same time, the manipulation here directed at the reader is marked in the text as one of the narrator's more dubious activities as she 'scents' a story with her 'uncanny nose for news'. Hill's newshound is a conscious *stylist*, both of the outback as a represented-world (' "The soft pedal on romance," said my better journalist self'), and of her own persona intervening in it ('I promptly interviewed the captain personally . . . and brought all my innocence and naive earnestness into play').[34] The 'Loneliness' as a reservoir of Australian authenticity is not always clearly distinguished in the text from Hill's presentation of it as a space of special-effects. The tele-visual theme of desert *mirage* (Everything is exaggerated in that unreal light . . . All men are giants, moving in a kind of crystallised slow motion) is one way in which the inventiveness of her landscape description can be both affirmed and denied.

As these throwaway lines accumulate, two issues about journalism emerge as puzzles that persist without being resolved by the text. One is the way that media stories not only style the local realities they claim to report, but have effects at a *distance* that may travel back around in a different form to disturb their original 'location'. The transmission of a story creates an ethical dilemma: as news travels faster and further than the newshound, she no longer covers the *distance* between a story and its significance.

During the writing of this book, Hill was involved in beating up an unfortunate 'streamer special' – the media creation of a gold rush to the Granites in the Northern Territory in 1932.[35] Reading the reports, Depression-ravaged men headed for El Dorado, found nothing, fell ill in appalling conditions and had to be taken home at government expense. *The Great Australian Loneliness* admits to some responsibility ('We translated gold fever into headlines, and some of their copy was much more feverish than mine')[36] but claims that the fiasco served its purpose in focusing the eyes of Australia upon the far-way, unknown Centre. The interest returned in the form of technical improvements. Isolation and hardship were broken down by 'the motor car, the wireless and the telephone': that is, by the enabling conditions of more journalism, and – according to Hill herself – of the decline of the old locales.

Consequently the Granites episode becomes an allegory of the text that contains it: *The Great Australian Loneliness* was effectively a Depression consolation dream of a far-away, unknown Centre where economic problems might be solved by an inrush of population and a bit of modernisation. The text admits, therefore, that reportage is not 'descriptive' (in the realist sense), but polemical and visionary. Description – like the greater good – is an alibi allowing anxiety about the *effects* of media 'vision' to be shunted around in a circle.

The second problem about morbidity and media is related to the problem of destructiveness, but it cannot be dismissed by invoking a greater good. It follows from the idea that writing, and journalism in particular, involves turning human beings into '*copy*'.

Most of Hill's metaphors of writing assume a 'translation', or 'transcription', not only from one order of reality to another, but from the animate to the inanimate – 'life' becomes 'printer's ink', as 'fever' becomes 'headlines'. In the quest to capture life, somehow human life is eliminated and only the medium remains. At one level, Hill's use of these metaphors is merely a reiteration of nineteenth-century aesthetic clichés now so dispersed in everyday culture that they function automatically. But they do function: the aporia of the theory that writing 'captures' life – and so must be in some sense *separate* from, and perhaps inimical to, that life – works in Hill's text not only to disavow the effects that journalism produces in the real that it reports (the descriptive alibi), but also to ensure that writing can be guaranteed a perpetual, impossible quest – for the perfect description, the full story, the 'living' characters of history. 'Copy' remotivates travel.

Casual acceptance of these commonplace assumptions has a complex resonance for the politics of Hill's writing, given the colonial context that she travelled. An example is her portrait of Mrs Witchetty in the Aboriginal camp: 'With no housework to do, she spends all her days in reading hair-raising thrillers, blissfully unconscious *that she is the most hair-raising thriller of the lot*' (my emphasis). Rather than ink or headline, poor Mrs Witchetty has become a living genre-piece. As a result, Hill's use of her 'case' to admit the possibility of a happy crossing of barriers is partly cancelled in the end by the generic recoding of the story as a hair-raising thriller – and of Mrs Witchetty as reader potentially consuming herself as commodity.[37]

This is one of many instances in which the search for the real story, the living history, and the true character in Hill's journalism ends in the (re)production not only of a media sterotype, but one which is formally recognised as such. 'Lubra – A Heroine in Charcoal' is another. A heroic story of a particular Aboriginal woman ('Jane'), is subsumed by a formal race portrait ('Lubra . . . in charcoal'). Colin Johnson has pointed out that when pity inspired some whites ('after the back of Aboriginal resistance was broken') to attempt biographies of Aboriginal people, 'these meatless things often had some point to be proved and the authors were not interested in depicting human beings with all the frailties of human beings'.[38] Johnson's comment applies with particular intensity to Hill's skeletal stories of Aboriginal lives, but it also applies to her general narrative method, her 'portraiture' and its motivating aesthetic. On the one hand, particular stories had ethical or political 'points': Aboriginal people were racially doomed to disappear, Aboriginal people should individually be respected . . . On the other hand, the point of the stories was always the same: *the medium is the message.* In the last line of 'Lubra – A Heroine in Charcoal', the ethical, racial and formal messages converge: 'For such as Jane are history.'

The anxiety about journalism in *The Great Australian Loneliness*, is about *after-effects*. People and places can be harmed by spreading the word about them, and a journalist's 'philosophy' ('the worse it is, the better it is') tends not only towards morbidity but towards reducing all living beings to by-products of media, or 'copy'.[39] It's a mild anxiety: Hill is very far, both in space and in time, from imagining the apocalyptic modes of high-tech paranoia today. However her formulation of the question of media responsibility, small-scale and *insouciant* as it may be, makes explicit one assumption of the paranoid scenario that later versions often suppress. In all her scenes of vampirism, necromancy and 'copying', it is taken for granted that the objects of the deadly arts cannot speak, or write, for themselves. There is only one place, one scene, of media action: the border between the writing and the written-about, the news-hound and her prey, is fixed and absolute.

If Aboriginal people are used as privileged emblems of the Other side of the writing frontier, it is Mrs Witchetty – 'hair-raising' transgression that she is – who can articulate it in the text. Immediately after being called a thriller, Mrs Witchetty says of her life: 'It has been an experience . . . and I am alive to tell the tale.' But then, 'I am afraid my book will never be written. I have become lazy and contented like my husband's people.' The dream of Mrs Witchetty writing a book is both a trace of wishful thinking (the autobiography of a thriller would be lively indeed) and a fable of the inevitability of her destiny as 'copy' (and as commodity). The fact that her Aboriginal 'affinity' (supposedly 'lazy and contented') condemns her to be an object, and not a subject, of the quest to capture life suggests how easily racist and realist theories could meet in Hill's 'doomed house' of travel writing.

In *The Territory*, a spectacular solution is provided to the morbidity of capturing life. Unlike the sharp urban operator of *The Great Australian Loneliness*, and the bookish magician of *My Love Must Wait*, the narrator of *The Territory* has, in some mystical way, crossed over a barrier to the other side. She is 'a pilgrim' among ghosts: an all-seeing, all-knowing, yet still restless phantom – present at every scene, hearing every voice, familiar with every patch of ground and every vanishing character in her 'freehold in illusion'. She isn't an indifferent or transcendent God: she is sometimes an archaic figure returning in her own text ('like Jacob for Rachel I waited seven years for this story'), sometimes an epic poet 'singing' the Territory's people. She includes her past self as a ghost among the ghosts, claiming only the privilege of a greater authority to tell tall tales ('Gold-mine in the sky'), and and a place in legend as the 'Legacy lady' ('Vikings of the Arafura'). Even her prose strives for 'ghostly' effects: phrases recur from passage to passage and chapter to chapter, with increasing insistence until the finale is a chorus of echoes lingering on from the rest of the story.

The image of the ghost in Hill's writing generally invokes ideals of indomitability and persistence, as well as the disturbing possibility of the past returning in the present, or of unhealthy incursions from some 'Other' zone in space. It is in part a Darwinian (and Ibsenesque) anxiety about a deathly interlocking of heredity and 'inheritance': the taint of 'bad blood' and bad deeds reappears in the present to forecast the death of the future. So it is sometimes also a placatory appropriation of the Aboriginal 'white ghost' theory that the invaders were dead Aborigines, returning to their own land. Hill was well aware of this theory, and it could be used not only to explain as 'painless' the displacement of Aborigines from their land, but also mythically to efface the history of conflict. Aboriginal owners and white invaders alike could conveniently be considered, after death, as white ghosts.[40]

However the theme of the ghost in *The Territory* does have a more complex function than simply to admit white Australia's 'skeleton in the closet' and to signify white guilt (both of which it serves to do). The haunting of *The Territory* is also part of Hill's plan to 'capture' the resistant imagination of urban Australians for the North. The book is part western saga (especially chapters like 'Bradshaw's Run' and 'The Diamond Eighty-Eight'), part tropical romance ('Vikings of the Arafura', 'A Lantern in the Scrub'), part horror story ('Chokey'), part traditional bush folklore, as well as a ghost story. It made a calculated appeal to the urban popular culture of Hollywood cinema, comics, pulp paperbacks and magazines. Where *The Great Australian Loneliness* offered Australians in the 1930s a space of splendid isolation, the achievement of *The Territory* was to translate the old outback motifs into the busy pop imaginary of the early 1950s.[41]

The Great Australian Loneliness imitated an actual voyage that could be marked on a map. *My Love Must Wait* observed a chronological model of a human life, from childhood to death. In *The Territory*, there is no longer any attempt at mimetically respecting a realist model of the traversal of space and time. In the history of Port Essington ('Phantoms of Failure'), decades pass in a succession of present tenses so swift that the narrative becomes almost incomprehensible. Other chapters (like

'Dots in the Map') survey vast spaces by spending a few lines in places here and there, then flying on to the next. There is no attempt to narrate the progressive *experience* of travel, and no sense of the voyage as *Bildung*. All places and times are simultaneously and instantaneously available to the ghost narrator, their significance known and moralised. It is a tour of the Empire of the dead: and a tour of a series of genres from 'Winged Victory' at the beginning – a 'war story' of Darwin's history through all the phases of its 'nine lives' – to the quoting of outback-nostalgia in the final chapter, 'The Last Bushman, or *H.M.S. Coolabah Tree*'.

The Territory is an imaginary landscape in which 'normal' laws of human experience are suspended. In this, it is a classical European inter-pretation of the Australian outback. With its 'living history' as a narrative of the dead, it is also a classical justification of White invasion as a natural process with sad, but inevitable, consequences. However in its panoramic myths of movement (without the time of the voyage), survey (without the traversal of space) and Progress (without the *Bildung* of progression), *The Territory* also represents those classical traditions pushing against their limits. If the figure of the ghost involves transgression of frontiers, it is perhaps the confines (rather than the funereal logic) of descriptive travel *writing* that *The Territory* contests. The ghost-narrator's tour does not imitate an actual voyage, but it is nonetheless mimetic of a certain dream of travel: being everywhere, seeing everything, in an instant. A writerly myth of *vision* drives the narrative of *The Territory*: in its vast, 'haunted' landscape, all art, indeed all knowledge, apsires to the triumph over distance that is the (imaginary) condition of television.

Or so a paranoid reading could easily suggest. However Hill's theme in *The Territory* was an epic failure of imperial settlement. The Territory was a land of 'living ghosts', because 'so much worth while in empire-building was thrown away'.[42] The rhetoric of death – and the *threat* of a death of history – is used as a point of departure for a stirring, 'yet another effort' polemic. The tour of the dead aims to inspire shame and regret in the living as well as nostalgia and longing – but above all to solicit commitment to further investment and enterprise. Travel writing becomes an allegory of the need for mobilisation.

In *The Great Australian Loneliness*, a survey of schemes for improving and populating the outback was a casual part of the tour. One of the most 'futuristic' was a programme of genetic engineering by a Dr Cook, who proposed that Aboriginal babies could, unlike 'the Asiatic' and 'the Negro', be bred 'white' in a few generations without any fear of 'throwbacks'.[43] The direct implication was that Aboriginal women could be used systematically to populate the North with the babies they couldn't keep. Hill was sceptical, and the text is in general more concerned to exploit the oneiric attractions for urban readers of an empty space 'far from the rhythm of the "big machine" and the sameness of cities'.

In *The Territory* fifteen years later, there is more urgency and defensiveness invested in the project of population. There is not only the recent memory of war with Japan, but a curious new sense of pressure from an emerging and 'Americanising' urban consumer culture. This time, suburban white women are targets of experiment: populating the outback is a 'home duty' for white wives and mothers. In one passage, a bushman accuses city women of putting the country at risk because they 'can't see no further than the powder on their noses', and goes so far as to define 'half-castes' sympathetically as children cruelly 'turned down' by the white mothers they should have had.[44]

As powdered emblems of consumerism, suburban women are responsible for the economic, as well as sexual, exploitation of Aboriginal women by white men. Another bushman tells 'the story of the "Lochinvar" ': how white men would round up Aboriginal women, kidnap them, teach them to ride, and sell them to drovers and station-owners at £10 a head as 'the world's best stock-boys'. For Hill, the moral is not only the injustice of the black women who colonised the country, but the imperviousness of urban consumers: 'While the cities of Australia were spreading over smug suburbs, universities, parks, picture shows and chain stores, such were the little dramas of progress enacted in the wild and wide.'[45]

Given the tour of pop genres performed by the text, the tele-visual narration, and the proliferation of references to 'picture show' and 'chain store' culture – to the point of using Walt Disney as a source for outback landscape descriptions[46] – there is a circuitous but unmistakable appeal in *The Territory* to suburban women to forsake their smugness and come to the *real* pop territory to be found in the 'wild and wide'.

BIG PICTURES

> With its sands and seas teeming with wealth, and hills and deserts that hold the secret of every known mineral and metal, some day soon, perhaps, this country will begin to realise its destiny. What is needed in the initial stages is the faith and work of the Australians who have forgotten it, with men who know its vagaries at the head of affairs, but, above all, people, people, people.
>
> (Ernestine Hill, *The Great Australian Loneliness*, 1940)

> Here they come wading in over the sodden golf-course in their Dryza-bones and Wellingtons . . . there are now more people here than at Ghandi's funeral. Thank God you've come.
>
> (Clive James at *The Ultimate Event*, Sanctuary Cove, 1988)[47]

The Missouri, *Sydney Cove*

In *Australia: The Last Experiment*, Eric Willmot suggests that 1802 rather than 1788 should mark the beginning of modern Australia. In that year, Aboriginal people on the coast of Arnhem Land saw Matthew Flinders's ship arrive in the bay, as well as the usual Macassan fishing boats – and 'the Europeans, the Asians and the Australians all meet on the shores of the Southland'. It is also the year in which Pemulwuy was beheaded by the British.[48] Only then is the scene set 'for all the actors of modern Australia'.

In a similar way, though in relation to a quite different scale of events, I think that the media Bicentennial scene was set not by any of the nation-wide events on 1 January, or the Syndey-based spectacle of the First Fleet Re-enactment on 26 January, but by the visit of the nuclear warship *USS* ('Dial-A-Sailor') *Missouri* to Sydney Harbour for Christmas, 1987.

The *Missouri*'s significance was not simply to prepare for the Invasion Day arrival of tall ships sporting flags for Coke, and Australia Post/ Intelpost – although it was a warning of just how sentimental a blind to the situation of contemporary Australia the Anglocentric celebrations would be. The main aspect of its visit was expounded by a photo in *The Sydney Morning Herald*, headed 'Making a splash . . . how to arrest a suspect on a surfboard'.[49] A policeman in wetsuit and booties was taking a fabulous dive through the air – soaring, arms outstretched towards the water, like any joyous Sydney person on a fine summer's day – to nab a surfing peace-protestor. The anti-nuclear flotilla was out as usual, and the report said that tugboats helping the US ships to dock were flying anti-nuclear flags. The benevolence of the scene and the sensuality of the policeman's dive predicted exactly the way that the televisual pageant of the Fleet on 26 January would work – State politics, popular protest and partying all making a splash together at the harbourside water-sports carnival.

Wending its way through seas and islands lovely as a dream, the nuclear ship is a banalised nightmare. No streamer specials are provoked by the routine ghastly cargo. The focus of human interest is the life of the ship: its fabulous size, the sailors, American-Australian romances, the familial yearnings of young mariners so far away from home, and the money. The rhetoric of death is part of the landscape: protests, warnings, threats, scenarios and disaster-hypotheticals enhance the event as 'background', or flash briefly into prominence as features of a locale. The *Missouri*'s visit, like Invasion Day, was primarily a spectacle of mass *attendance*, a display of the power to mobilise crowds. There seems to be no room here for 'critical distance'. These are festivals of confluence and critical proximity.

But they are not 'post' or 'anti'-historical, even at the level of a shallow media memory. The policeman's soar was suspended between the family album's summer-holiday snaps, a *Good Living* supplement and a single, spectacular image from the *Missouri*'s previous visit – an anti-nuclear surfer paddling up to the ship, then maniacally riding the prow. As a great moment in the history of proximity, his ride created that intimate, fluid space into which the policeman dives, years later, as a tactical response – his posture heroising, his position (like his booties) absurd. This is a space of *accompaniment* and sensational fellow-travelling, where 'distance' imposed by power is critically defied – and the Law, ephemerally, left floundering.

Those who stayed back on the shoreline in mundane traditional protest were not, however, 'completely ineffective' in their moral denunciation. At the very least, they defined a context in which the surfer's action made political, as well as avant-garde, sense. To become décor, to become ambience, to become setting, to become *stereotype*, is not necessarily to be out of the picture. On the contrary: a living stereotype can always historicise, as well as appear in, the media image of any event. It stubbornly refers to the social conditions of its own appearance in space, and endurance through time – repetition, perpetuation and the possibility of change. As an indomitable trace of a *past* in representation (how many times have I seen that banner, those slogans, before?), a stereotype is the critical accompaniment, and the insistent historical shadow, of simulation as Baudrillard understands it. Like Mrs Smith in *Australia Live* or Mrs Witchetty for Ernestine Hill, the traditional protestor in media today acts a mark of genre – a persisting, negotiable and collective cultural product. As such, we stereotypes can act as a 'historic' reminder – well or ill performed, more or less successful according to contingencies – that unlike God, the media-simulacrum cannot produce and multiply reality in its singular image alone.

'Back to Bool Bool'

It's easy to say that the numerous space-festivals, landscape-displays and national-identity programmes competing to cover 'Australia' for 1988 were producing, even simulating, the places they 'depicted' and the histories they 'portrayed'. It is now a familiar theme for many modes of criticism much less morbid than Baudrillard's that traditions may be invented, communities imagined and spaces generated. The critical problem in any one instance is – so what?

For some critics – like Russell Braddon in his ABC television programmes *Images of Australia* – it is enough to reveal that myths are based in fiction, not historical 'authenticity'. By kindly humanists no less than by apocalyptic postmodernism, some kind of symbolic death is assumed to follow from acts of invention – a death of a 'truth' about the past (Braddon[50]), or a demise of the very possibility of 'real' reality (Baudrillard). Either way, the basic premise remains that if it's fictive, it doesn't exist. Criticism's job is to banish the phantom by demonstrating its lack of reality. Thus Braddon's first programme revealed that most Australians are not and never have been hardy bush pioneers, that we aren't all white or male and that Ned Kelly was a criminal.

Revelation of this kind has a ritual quality. The critique is as venerable as the 'Back to Bool Bool' mythology to which it belongs, and yet it remains silent about its own historic status and offers itself as irreverent. This is perhaps the kind of denunciative activity that Jameson has in mind as 'ineffective'. It doesn't question the varying *use* of similar myths in different places and times, what happens when they are cherished as myths or the rival myths the criticism itself is recommending. Braddon's series was framed by one of the oldest travel stories in the Australian repertoire – the quest for a 'national identity'. Like any quest, it presupposes a gap between the seeker and object sought-for. So it can only operate *as* quest by reassuring us that the gap is still there, the goal never yet reached, and the search necessitated by 'history' – convict origins, colonialism, immigrant amnesia.[51]

An accompanying *critical* quest may then take the form of a voyage through disillusion. We undergo a progressive dismantling of the available myths, all attributed to credulous Others and all found wanting as truth. The logical conclusion of the adventure is not the capturing of an identity but the projection of a big picture – a vision of a *future* Australia in which a true 'identity' may at last be seized. Braddon's picture had familiar features: a pluri-racial, double-gendered, multicultural society with Japanese as a second language, the three R's reimposed in schools, a healthy debate about republicanism, and a high-tech economic outlook. The future produced by unmasking past myths turned out to be (give or take a touch of eccentricity) a widely current policy-guide for a programme of modernisation. The quest for identity is a metaphor of a polemic about the present.

One problem is whether the ritual unmasking of historic national myths in favour of such domestic 'home truths' can effectively address the entrepreneurial logic of a TV Bicentenary. Braddon's demystification of bush myths, for example, barely works now as a critique of *The Great Australian Loneliness*, or *The Territory* – to which it might seem immediately applicable. In Hill's use of pioneer legends, the 'Loneliness', and the 'Territory' are names for dreams of *generating* (rather than 'celebrating') a substantive sense of nation. They are utopian, as well as commemorative, programmes: far from suggesting that we are all white male bush pioneers, they deeply regret that we're *not*. If a plan to restyle a population in the image of a revamped old ideal is certainly open to criticism, criticising the ideal requires a strategy different from proving the plan's premise that it isn't based on 'fact'.

Revamping is an event that changes materials as well as their meanings – and a process that may continue till no trace of 'origins' is left. Ignoring material and formal changes is perhaps more surely to take a nostalgic road than those involved in revamping. Thus Braddon watched people staring at the amateur theatrics of violence and gore at re-enacted convict whippings, and saw a loss of historical reality. In another series, *Aussies*, Jack Pizzey looked at similar footage, and rederived the hardness of 'Australians' from the founding events of the past. Neither considered that in at least one order of reality today, such pantomimes may be enjoyed not only as digests of *The Fatal Shore*, but also as comic reductions of the special effects in any splatter video.

Taxi to Fantasia

In one of the brochure-modernistic passages of *The Territory*, Ernestine Hill assured her readers that 'Walt Disney and his flying crayons never conjured a gayer fantasia in natural history than those vanishing jungles that fade from arsenic green to sulphur yellow and crackle away in fire'.[52]

For Ita Buttrose writing in *The Sun-Herald* ('We can't take tourism for granted'), people can't be lured North now with just a sketch of Disney scenery. Recalling a boat trip along the Katherine Gorge, she criticised the service offered tourists – no water on board, bad English from the guide. Gaiety now is not a sulphur yellow jungle, but a couple of cans of lemon squash.[53]

Ernestine Hill's fantasia was designed for an ethos of settlement, and a 'populate or perish' imperative. Her panorama of the wide-open spaces stresses their vulnerability to invasion and pleads for a kind of strategic closure. The problem is a disparity between rich natural resources and poor supplies of people. *The Great Australian Loneliness* looked to 'transport' as one solution and racial engineering as another. *The Territory* dreamed of luring white women away from the suburbs. Both books aim at *mobilisation*. They are space-*time* fantasias, using 'landscape' to project big pictures of national development to be realised in the future by moving people around.

Media space-festivals today involve notions of 'development' and techinques of mobilisation quite different from those envisaged by the landscape writers. Their demand is for crowds, not population: people are needed to pass through a space (and be filmed or photographed) rather than to inhabit it with communities. Where imperialism wanted settlers for security, tourism needs visitors for endorsement. One regime values permanence and accumulation, the other transience and turnover. One fears invasion, the other metaphorically solicits it. Threatened by the 'foreign', the 'primitive', and by 'ghosts', imperialist discourse tends towards closure: it paranoically defends the borders it creates. A touristic space must be liberal and open: the foreign and the primitive are commodified and promoted, ghosts are special-effects: the only 'barrier' officially admitted is strictly economic.

There is also a difference in rhetoric. Hill's was overtly *sectarian*: suburban white women are targeted as metonymic bearers of the ideal people they should help to create. The appeal of tourist discourse is *universalising*: rather than proposing to create a nation from one of its elements, it aims to bring the world (including Australians) temporarily to particular spots. The touristic 'nation' already accepts that identities are mythic, plural – and obsolescent. But the 'nation' is also addressed by its entrepreneurs as a beneficiary of the flow of people-and-money to be lured through particular spots: nationality is not here the object of a quest, but a field of big-business philanthropy. Certain duties follow for the population, who 'profit' from the flow: this is the space of 'our' national debt, 'our' credit rating, 'our' need to please the consumer.

It is easy now to mock the absurdity – as well as the fictiveness – of a dream of creating an enclosing high-tech paradise by sending people from the coast to the wide open spaces to fence the land, dig holes and have white babies. Yet today, the image of Australia as panoramic spread of tourist resorts has sufficient credibility in media to pass as a plan for 'national' salvation. Australia is a space wide open: people come in, cruise around, photograph spectacles and leave their money behind. 'Nationalism' becomes, not a quest for identity or repertoire of myths, but 'our' willingness to redesign everyday life as a landscape for rigorous tourists.

Pointing out that tourism rivals meat and wheat as an Australian 'revenue earner', Ita Buttrose suggested a plan to 'get our act together'. It included 'questioning' overtime and penalty rates in the hospitality sector, revised work practices in the service industry and special catering for Japanese tourists. The *pièce de resistance*, however, was a campaign to re-educate Sydney taxi drivers. Besides better 'class', better manners and a better sense of direction, many will need re-education in 'personal hygiene'. Much depends on this politics of bodies in proximity: for if the tourist trade goes elsewhere, 'then what will happen to our balance of payments?'

However widely disseminated, discussed and even acted upon, these mediated scenarios are no doubt mere caricatures (or in Peter Robinson's phrase, 'puerile stereotypes') of projections by serious 'big picture' thinkers of natural development – whether in our own time or in Ernestine Hill's. But they are images of 'our' future that circulate now in our lives. Part of their power as popularisations is to act as everyday guides that can at any moment be repudiated (in newspapers, on chat shows) as too

local, too simple, too schematic. For every clear, bold picture offered
the public, there is always a bigger one somewhere, full of details, blanks
and messy patches that only expert professionals can read. (A 'big picture'
in that sense is a paranoid myth of information and of the limits of public
intelligence.)

Some philosophers have claimed that this is an age of decline in 'meta-
narratives' – grand stories of humanity's origins and destiny (Progress,
Emancipation) that justify local incidents.[54] This seems a strange argument
about media (if not the history of philosophy): what is striking on television is the wild *proliferation* of meta-discourses. There are more of them
around, not less: Emancipation may be unpopular, but Development (like
Doom) is thriving. So big pictures should perhaps still sometimes be
questioned in the large terms on which they depend.

How *big* is any big picture, what sort of *time* does it imply? Ita's image
of tourist Fantasia seems eternal: vivid scenery, pleasing service-industry
figures styled in rigorous detail – and for background, a blur of visitors
streaming in from everywhere, nowhere, 'Japan'. How many Fantasias
are possible? How far does Fantasia extend? Why is it the stream of
people, not the Territory, that now seems limitless, inexhaustible? One
writer in a Northern Fantasia, using the same premise as Buttrose ('every
week a new musuem opens somewhere in the UK, and the museum/
tourist business is the 3rd largest moneyspinner in the country') suggests
a big picture different from hers, yet just as 'Australian' a landscape:

> Who is going to do all this touristing? Tourism is supposed to generate
> employment so that people thus employed may go and play tourist
> themselves? . . . Closed circuits. There is something nice about the
> idea that today's museums and tourist resorts are tomorrow's ruins
> and ghost towns.[55]

Crocodile, Sanctuary Cove

Tomorrow isn't a concept vital to Fantasia or for high-tech-paranoid
critique. Both invest in 'futures': speculative projections based on models
of trends today. Tomorrow is more uncertain than the future: it is closer,
and yet more distant, somehow right on the *edge* of today. It's not an
imaginary space in which anything could happen, but a time in which
something *will*. In Baudrillard's Hyperreality, there is no tomorrow, no
politics of temporal proximity. There is a future (the perpetual present),
but in it we will exist, as now, as chronic *after-effects*. We are now, and
now always will be, always already programmed as an effect of what
went before. In Hyperreality, the image, not the Word, is a *fiat*. At best
we can only thwart, overload or parody the programmes that precede us.

Curiously, big live media *events* (if not necessarily 'images') imply a different kind of temporality. They do envisage tomorrow: not as the predictable space of a future continuous with the present, but as a moment towards which calculations tend, but *about* which nothing is sure.

One such event was a Bicentennial side-show: the opening of a residential and tourist resort, Sanctuary Cove (The Ultimate Address), with a concert starring Frank Sinatra (The Ultimate Event). As a private development, Sanctuary Cove formally had nothing to do with the official Bicentenary. But as the product of a legendary deal between its developer, Michael Gore, and a politician (Sir Joh Bjelke-Petersen), it had *status* as a model of how governments can go about doing 'national' business. The January opening, the promise of Sinatra's 'historic' return to shores he had long foresworn, and Gore's own media profile made The Ultimate Event seem a part of the one big party.

Attendance was poor for preliminary festivities. The media criticised Sanctuary Cove for confusing sectarian and universalising modes of address in its promotional publicity. A high-priced, high-security, residential 'vivarium'[56] with public leisure enclaves, Sanctuary Cove is a sectarian establishment with an inbuilt populist appeal. But the advertisement for residents forgot about tourism, and revamped the old frontier code of discriminatory closure: '*The streets these days are full of cockroaches, and most of them are human. . . .*' Critics predicted that crowds might feel already excluded on specious (if not strictly racist) criteria.

When tomorrow came and the vital people materialised, Gore shed tears of relief on television and drew the moral of Sanctuary Cove. At the end of the Event, a young man wanted Sinatra's autograph to take back to his dying father. Sinatra had already gone, so Gore fetched his stool from the stage. Zooming off later down the road, Gore drove past the young man, hitch-hiking – stool clasped proudly in his arms. And Gore beheld, in this poor vestige of his crowd, a great and ennobling truth: he, the rich man in his castle, might have thrown the stool away – not questioning, as at last he had, his own living priorities. This was the real value of the Events at the Address: the poor man's gift of enlightenment to Gore was the ultimate endorsement.

Apart from the flood of gratitude that followed any act of effective people-moving, Sanctuary Cove was hooked into the official space-festival circuit by the anxiety circulating in advance about what people would do on the day – come or not come, give or withhold consent to the Bicentenary, be good or misbehave. It is as though the people who can, if they will, become crowds, have their greatest power in the time *before* an event, when suspense about tomorrow is at its most intense. Thus some of the most extensive and favourable coverage of Aboriginal politics seen for years on Australian television preceded Invasion Day, or came on in the aftermath of gratitude that nothing had marred the show. There was a convergence of speculation about what *might* happen on 26 January, talk about the criticism that *could* be beamed around the world by overseas press in Australia – and preparations *for* the Muirhead inquiry into Aboriginal deaths in custody.

This 'time' of suspense between today and tomorrow is a 'space' for action, organisation and invention that simulation cannot precede. As a period defined by anticipation, it is invisible and unthinkable for the myth of the permanent Aftermath that Baudrillard calls 'hyperreality'. A paranoid imaginary of 'space' alone cannot think the media *event*. Ignoring time, movement and agency, it presumes that nothing critical can happen. Where media activism thinks a little time ahead, simulation forever thinks back.

Convergent space-festivals like The Ultimate Event are planned to pre-empt moments of crisis. For live survey shows, however, the possibility of crisis is built into the format to generate narrative interest. With a dispersive, *longue durée* show like *Australia Live*, to hope for unpredicted events is the *only* narrative interest.

Several critical moments enlivened *Australia Live*. The most trying was the bad timing of the Russian cosmonauts in space. The promise of a meta-satellite hook-up was the ultimate panoramic fantasy – exchange and feedback between two surveillance-control cockpits, one down here (nuclear) and one up there (orbital). Alas: when the moment came, the cosmonauts were out to lunch, and stayed out for most of the show. The nuclear model collapsed, and with it the conceits of Australia's centrality and the primacy of 'our' schedule.

Another was a wildly threshing crocodile caught alive in Darwin Harbour – chomping, munching, lashing out and nearly biting its way to freedom. The studio guides had unusual trouble in streaming into the show. Clive James, in particular, oozed panic. Decision loomed between missing a vital connection (panoramic catastrophe), or leaving the croc still struggling (narrative disaster). But there was a discursive as well as a technical hitch. James had begun the segment by boasting about his recent crocodile hunt. The raging beast at last subdued, the Wildlife Officer in Darwin had just a split second left to produce, from the shadows of his boat, a miniscule baby croc – James's catch and the longed-for punchline to his carefully programmed joke.

What haunts the imaginary space of the live is not the dead (history/ footage), nor a Baudrillardian zombie horde of living-dead ('live' personalities *in situ*, silent masses at home), but the volatile force of the living. The 'live', in this frame of reference, has a rather peculiar meaning. Live television is an operation guaranteed, and yet contested, not by an opposite or a negation (the not-live: the prerecorded, the archival, the simulacrum, the ghostly, the 'dead') but an array of vague possibilities associated with *life*: unprogrammed events, breaks in continuity, accidents, missed connections, random occurrences, unforeseen human and technical recalcitrance. The descriptiveness of live television is not that of a theoretical 'still life', or *nature morte*. It doesn't presume an eternal essence of its object once time and movement has been subtracted. It doesn't generate a chronic hyper-reality in its own perpetual static image. On the contrary: the live pursues the living for its transient and fugitive potential, its veer towards instability.

The live and the living interact in a mode of hostile complicity. Overcoming and subjecting to schedule the vagaries of the living is the aim of live television. It depends on the spectre of failure and breakdown to 'prove' the rule of its success. So it shuttles between drive towards total control, and desire for the test of catastrophe. For this system the living are not ghostly after-effects of media, as Baudrillard's fables would have it. The living animate the media event by ignoring its critical limits.

Broadway, Kingoonya

It was the live appearance of Mrs Smith that reminded me of Ernestine Hill, the kind of 'history' she wrote and the problems her texts raise today about imperialism and racism, media and distance, panorama and historical criticism. Hill's work was already what Jameson calls 'pop' history: it invented a past by revamping and sometimes criticising stereotypes that were already (in the pop sense) 'historic' – last bushmen, sylvan tribes, white women pioneers. To turn casually, as I have in this essay, from a few minutes of live TV creating a current 'version' of one of these, to a few books by a dead woman writer, is to engage, to some extent, in much the same sort of activity.

It is televisual activity, where 'seeing at a distance' translates as images available for reinterpretation in idiosyncratic local settings. It is associative activity, putting quite different elements (TV shows, media memories, political events, academic research notes on Ernestine Hill) into 'cultural', or commodity, proximity. It is also a mediated activity, in which people are confused with their image and never directly addressed.

The reviews of Mrs Smith's live 'performance' (like this essay) ignored her living existence completely. They were not written for her: it is as though, despite the reach of the communications industries, separate linguistic worlds are created not only by an academic essay and 'Kingoonya' (a stereotypical distinction) but by Broadway pop critics as well. In each of these worlds we can talk about others as though they will not hear or respond to what we say – or if they do, will use another language, in a different place. Stress on the gap between 'academic' and 'ordinary' language hides the proliferation of such gaps in everyday culture, which Barthes called the 'division' – or 'war' – of languages: 'on the scale of the nation, we understand each other but we do not communicate: putting things at their best, we have a *liberal* practice of language.'[57]

Putting things at their worst, it is as though the principle of Hill's writing about Mrs Witchetty is applied on an ever expanding scale, turned back invasively on the society that produced it until the cohesive myths of a 'society' become quite difficult to sustain. Yet in the process, as Iain Chambers points out, a 'strong' sense of singular opposition becomes a 'weak' sense of detailed differences. 'The "Other" becomes the "others".'[58] There is no single 'source' making sense of the world in communication with a captive audience. Complaints about collapsing standards (in aesthetic quality, in reality-values or in degrees of critical distance) are side-effects of this process. It is not that aesthetic standards cannot be stated, historical reality asserted or distance maintained (critics do these things all the time) – but that there is no guarantee of 'a' public who will care to validate the outcome or be 'mobilised' by the result.

A paranoid border-rhetoric cannot begin to come to terms with the intimate proximities lived today between people and media. There isn't necessarily a happy or liberating proximity – there is depression, boredom, anger, deception, addiction, oppression, indifference and lies. But only by beginning to think of media as accompanying experience, and as time (not just 'space') for action, can criticism respond to an event like the Aboriginal protest march on Invasion Day, and its reoccurrence in subsequent playbacks.

The Aboriginal demonstrations – the march, the flags, the boats, the tents, the voices shouting and wailing and the confluence of different people from all over the country – in fact did mobilise an effective force of *'singular oppostion'* – without enacting a myth of the Other. That role was prepared for Aboriginal people by the First Fleet Re-enactment context (making any Aborigines present play themselves in the European script), by the panoramic telecast (showing them 'on shore' as the ships came in) and by the history of the *form* of Invasion re-enactments.[59] (The 'simulacrum' immediately preceding this one was the 1938 re-enactment: a group of Aborigines were kidnapped from near Menindee, held captive for a week, and forced to play 'their' part in the Sydney proceedings.)

The 1988 protest showed that precedents, like simulacra and scripts, can be destroyed as well as revised. Aborigines had already changed the re-enactment's significance by proclaiming a Year of Mourning – and by making a Landing impossible. So proceedings began in open admission that the ceremony was not a 'factual' mimicry of the past, but a political event in the present. Once the basic premise had been altered, the ceremonial 'present' became, for the official script on the day, a field of suspense and evasion. Speech after speech from the dais skipped hastily from 'the mistakes of the past' to expressions of faith in 'the future'. The *significant* present was elsewhere: with people lying in the sun, having picnics, watching boats and milling about, but above all with the insistent critical accompaniment of the Aboriginal protest. Audible and visible in most telecasts on the day,[60] extending later into media commentary, news items, current affairs shows and the television archive of future Aboriginal images – that protest effectively historicised, on Aboriginal terms, an entrepreneurial 'national' event.

In 'Paranoid Critical Methods' – a response to Peter Fuller's book *The Australian Scapegoat* – Ross Gibson argues against the nostalgic *return* to nature involved in seeing mediation as alien to a 'naturally' natural world of hands-on landscape painting. He suggests instead 'a *redefinition* of what is nature *nowadays*'. For Gibson, redefining 'nature', 'landscape' and 'environment' to include the mass media – *and* their dangers, and so an 'ecology' of their use – is a way of polemically rejecting the Frontier imaginary (and its spectres of cultural degeneracy menacing from the Other side):

> not only sunshine, clouds, landforms and all things 'green', but also the cinema, television, pop music, books, motor cars, magazines and all available mass-mediated images and sounds are part of my nature. All this nature is part of my culture. Such is the environment I perceive and accept as a natural (though mutable) fact.[61]

'Mutable' is the vital term for this polemical *collapsing* of critical distance between 'spaces' of nature and culture. Mutable media forms can not only be thought of historically, but challenged, and changed, 'historically'. But like Eric Willmot's revision of the beginnings of modern Australia, this change is only made possible by rethinking temporal, as well as spatial, experiences of mediation – and thus our histories of change.

NOTES

This chapter first appeared in Paul Foss (ed.), *Island in the Stream: Myths of Place in Australian Culture*, Pluto Press, Sydney, 1988.

My grateful acknowledgements got to the Humanities Research Centre, Australian National University, Canberra, for their support of a fellowship for my research on Ernestine Hill in 1986. I also thank Margriet Bonnin for permission to quote from her thesis, from which I have learnt far more than my references may suggest.

1 Keith Dunstan, 'But what about the country's pimples?,' *The Sydney Morning Herald*, 5 January 1988.
2 These theses are mainly developed in *De la séduction*, Galilée, Paris, 1979, and *Les stratégies fatales*, Grasset, Paris, 1983. A basic outline of the theory of simulation on which his work on television depends is 'The precession of simulacra', in *Simulations*, Semiotext(e), New York, 1983.
3 Fredric Jameson, 'Postmodernism, or the cultural logic of late capitalism', *New Left Review*, 146 (1984), 77.
4 ibid., p. 86.
5 ibid., p. 71.
6 ibid., p. 79.

7 Alice Jardine, *Gynesis: Configurations of Woman and Modernity*, Cornell University Press, Ithaca and London, 1985, ch. 4 ('Spaces for further research: male paranoia'). For a different argument, see Elizabeth Grosz, 'Every picture tells a story: art and theory re-examined', in Gary Sangster (ed.), *Sighting References*, Artspace, Sydney, 1987.

8 Andreas Huyssen, *After the Great Divide: Modernism, Mass Culture, Postmodernism*, Indiana University Press, Bloomington and Indianapolis, 1986.

9 Margriet Bonnin, 'A study of descriptive and travel writing, 1929–1945', PhD Thesis, University of Queensland, 1980, p. 2.

10 *The Great Australian Loneliness* was one of the most famous descriptive books of the early 1940s. It was reprinted many times for over twenty years, sold well in Britain and (as *Australian Frontier*) in the United States, and it was issued as a 'textbook' on Australia for American troops in the Pacific war. *My Love Must Wait* (1941) – written with the assistance of the Commonwealth Literary Fund – was a bestseller which long remained the most commercially successful of Australian novels published in Australia. It was studied as literature in schools, and it was broadcast as a serial (with Peter Finch as Matthew Flinders) repeatedly by the ABC.

11 'Story of the state' was published in *The Centenary Chronicle, 1836–1936*, Advertiser Newspapers, Adelaide, 1936. One of Hill's radio plays, 'Santa Claus of Christmas Creek', is in Leslie Rees (ed.), *Australian Radio Plays*, Angus & Robertson, Sydney, 1946. She also published a book of verse, *Peter Pan Land*, in Brisbane, 1916.

12 Kramer, *Oxford History of Australian Literature*, Oxford University Press, Melbourne, 1981; Modjeska, *Exiles at Home*, Angus & Robertson, Sydney, 1981.

13 Mary Gilmore, George Mackaness, Mary Durack, Henrietta Drake-Brockman, Katherine Susannah Prichard, Xavier Herbert and Eleanor Dark were among her correspondents. See Hal Porter's portrait of Hill, at a literary gathering in Adelaide just before her death, in *The Extra*, Nelson, Melbourne, 1975, pp. 177–9.

14 On the critical reception of descriptive books in general, cf. Bonnin, *Study*, pp. 45f., and on Hill pp. 72–3. On the feminisation of mass culture, cf. Huyssen, *Great Divide*, ch. 3 ('Mass culture as woman: modernism's Other').

15 Docker, *In a Critical Condition*, Penguin, Melbourne, 1984.

16 Cf. *The Territory*, ch. XIX, 'On with The motley'.

17 Flora Eldershaw, 'The landscape writers', *Meanjin*, 11(3) (1952), 216.

18 A classic metaphysical study which has great trouble differentiating 'travel' from 'narrative' is Percy G. Adams, *Travel Literature and the Evolution of the Novel*, University Press of Kentucky, 1983. Other recent studies of travel writing relate its modern forms to the history of imperialism, studying how particular texts use an encounter with difference to construct a mythic problem of 'Otherness'. Cf. Michael de Certeau, *Heterologies: Discourse on the Other*, Manchester University Press, Manchester, 1986; Mary Louise Pratt, 'Scratches on the face of the country; or, what Mr Barrow saw in the land of the Bushmen', in Henry Louis Gates Jr. (ed.) *'Race', Writing and Difference, Critical Inquiry*, 12(1) (1985), 119–43; and Georges Van den Abbeele (ed.), *The Discourse of Travel, L'Esprit Créateur*, 25(3) (1985).

19 Cited in W. Wilde, J. Hooton and B. Andrews (eds), *The Oxford Companion to Australian Literature*, Oxford University Press, Oxford, 1985, p. 341.

20 Bonnin, *Study*, p. 392.

21 ibid., p. 240.

22 In *The Territory*, Hill also recognised the 'pioneer' economy's dependence on Aboriginal labour – in particular, the role played by women in the cattle industry. Cf. Ann McGrath, *'Born in the Cattle': Aborigines in Cattle Country*, Allen & Unwin, Sydney, 1987; and Bill Rosser (ed.), *Dreamtime Nightmares*, Penguin Books, Melbourne, 1987 (Australian Institute of Aboriginal Studies, 1985).

23 Stephen Muecke, 'Available discourses on Aborigines', *Theoretical Strategies, Local Consumption Series*, 2(3), Sydney, 1982, 98–111.

24 Cited in Michel Beaujour, 'Some paradoxes of description', in Jeffrey Kittay (ed.), *Towards A Theory of Description, Yale French Studies*, 61 (1981), 47.

25 *My Love Must Wait*, Angus & Robertson, Sydney, 1941, p. 180.

26 The relation between them is highly ambiguous. Cf. Christina Thompson, 'Romance Australia: love in Australian literature of exploration', *Australian Literary Studies*, 13(2) (1987), 161–71.

27 *My Love Must Wait*, p. 453.

28 More precisely, she said that she had written the original serial called *My Natives and I* in the Adelaide *Advertiser*, syndicated in newspapers all over the country. She attributed final responsibility for Bates's book to persons unknown: 'To my surprise, when the book appeared as *The Passing of the Aborigines* it was shorn of the earlier chapters, and of her life story very little appeared' (*Kabbarli: A Personal Memoir of Daisy Bates*, Angus & Robertson, Sydney, 1973, p. 154).

29 *The Passing of the Aborigines*, John Murray, London, 1983, p. 8.

30 Cf. Henry Louis Gates Jr., 'Writing "race" and the difference it makes', in *'Race', Writing and Difference*, pp. 9f.

31 *Kabbarli*, p. 142. Bates, however, unlike the Aborigines, had the chance to read over and correct Hill's 'copy' of her life.

32 H. M. Green, *A History of Australian Literature* (ed. and revised by Dorothy Green), vol II, Angus & Robertson, Sydney, 1985, p. 1389.

33 *The Great Australian Loneliness* (hereafter *G.A.L*), Angus & Robertson, Sydney, reprinted 1963, p. 272.

34 Cf. *G.A.L*, pp. 63, 208, 261, 279.

35 Cf. Bonnin, *Study*, pp. 23–6. In *Tragedy Track: The Story of the Granites* (Frederick Ehrenfield, Sydney, 1933). Eric Baume specifically blamed Hill for the incident in his preface, 'She started it all'. During this period Hill was also involved with promoting Daisy Bates's claim that she had saved an Aboriginal baby from being eaten by its mother. She later tried to dissociate herself from the story (cf. *G.A.L.*, p. 254).

36 *G.A.L.*, p. 312.

37 *G.A.L.*, pp. 274–5. The last scene with Mrs Witchetty has her a 'scuttling lubra', shutting her door 'tight against the prowling of the debil-debil'.

38 Colin Johnson, 'White forms, Aboriginal content', in Jack Davis and Bob Hodge (eds), *Aboriginal Writing Today*, Australian Institute of Aboriginal Studies, Canberra, 1985, p. 22.

39 Bonnin points out that 'the power of the popular press in Australia and the ethics of journalists were both subjects of great concern to writers during the 1930s, even . . . to those descriptive writers who were also journalists'. Bonnin, p. 20.

40 *Water into Gold*, Robertson & Mullens, Melbourne, 1937, revised edition *Study*, 1946, p. 19. On the Aboriginal 'white ghost' theory, cf. Henry Reynolds, *The Other Side of the Frontier: Aboriginal Resistance to the European Invasion of Australia*, Penguin Books, Ringwood, Vic. 1982, ch. 2.

41 On the deliberate appeal by Hill and other landscape writers to city audiences, cf. Bonnin, *Study*, pp. 39, 235–6, 302–5.
42 *The Territory*, Angus & Robertson, Sydney, reprinted 1985, p. 227.
43 *G.A.L.*, pp. 225–32.
44 *The Territory*, p. 392. Bonnin points out that this address of discussion about miscegenation to white city women was 'overwhelmingly' common in descriptive books: 'If the empty spaces of Australia were to be populated by whites, it was up to the women to act' (*Study*, p. 234). For an Aboriginal history of the context of this discussion, cf. Rosser, *Dreamtime Nightmares*.
45 *The Territory*, pp. 310–12.
46 *The Territory*, p. 18. Cf. Bonnin, *Study*, pp. 304–5, on Hill's descriptive vocabulary.
47 Cited in 'Today's people', *The Sydney Morning Herald*, 11 January 1988.
48 Eric Willmot, *Australia: The Last Experiment*, 1986 Boyer Lectures, ABC Enterprises, 1987, p. 33.
49 23 December 1987.
50 For a similar approach, see Martin Thomas, 'Centennial dreamings: the tyranny of a discourse', *The Age Monthy Review* (December 1987–January 1988).
51 When national identity is taken to be a condition already achieved, the result is that staple sub-genre of imperial travel-writing, the 'race portrait'. Thus in Jack Pizzey's programmes *Aussies*, 'the Australian' was sketched (from an English immigrant point of view) in a manner formally improving on Hill's portraits of Aborigines only by the 'courtesy' of a second-person form of address.
52 *The Territory*, p. 18.
53 21 February 1988.
54 Cf. Jean-François Lyotard, *The Postmodern Condition: A Report on Knowledge*, Manchester University Press, Manchester, 1984.
55 Paul Willemen, unpublished paper, 1988.
56 Cf. Mike Davis, 'Urban renaissance and the spirit of postmodernism', *New Left Review*, 151 (May–June 1985), and '*Chinatown*, Part Two? The "internationalisation" of Downtown Los Angeles', *New Left Review* 164 (July–August 1987).
57 Roland Barthes, *The Rustle of Languages*, Blackwell, Oxford, 1986, p. 107.
58 Iain Chambers, 'Maps for the Metropolis: A Possible Guide to the Present', *Cultural Studies*, 1(1) (1987), 9.
59 Cf. Thomas, 'Centennial dreamings'.
60 This account conflates different interpretations by different networks. The ABC was least responsive to the Aboriginal protest, and so its telecast was the least critical.
61 Ross Gibson, 'Paranoid critical methods', *Art & Text*, 26 (1987), 63.

Chapter 2

The Fire Ceremony
For a cultural future

Eric Michaels

In 1972, anthropologist Nicolas Peterson and film-maker Roger Sandall arranged with the old men to film a ritual of signal importance for the Warlpiri: Warlukurlangu, the Fire Ceremony. In a subsequent journal article,[1] Peterson described these ceremonies in terms of the functions of Aboriginal social organisation. He identified such Warlpiri ceremonies as a means of resolving conflict, or of negotiating disputes, a kind of pressure valve for the community as a whole. One pair of patrilines (or 'side') of the community acts as Kurdungurlu (stage manager or witness), and arranges a spectacular dancing ground, delineated by great columns of brush and featuring highly decorated poles. The Kirda (performer) side paints up, and dances. Following several days and nights of dancing, they don elaborate costumes festooned with dry brush. At night they dance towards the fire, and are then beaten about with burning torches by the Kurdungurlu. Finally, the huge towers of brush are themselves ignited and the entire dance ground seems engulfed in flame. Following some period (it may be months or even years) the ceremony is repeated, but the personnel reverse their roles. The Kurdungurlu become Kirda, and receive their punishment in turn.

Visually and thematically, this ceremony satisfies the most extreme European appetite for savage theatre, a morality play of the sort Artaud describes for Balinese ritual dance – what could be more literally signalling through the flames than this? Yet I do not think the Peterson/Sandall film does this, partly due to the technical limitations of lighting for their black-and-white film stock, and partly because of the observational distance maintained throughout the filming. The effect is less dramatic, more properly 'ethnographic' (and, perhaps wisely, politically less confrontative). It was approved by the community at the time it was edited in 1972 by Kim McKenzie, and joined other such films in the somewhat obscure archives of the Australian Institute of Aboriginal Studies, used mostly for research and occasional classroom illustration.

Remarkably, the ceremony lapsed shortly after this film was made.

When I arrived at Yuendumu in 1983, the Fire Ceremony seemed little more than a memory. Various reasons were offered:

- one of the owners had died, and a prohibition applied to its performance;
- it had been traded with another community;
- the church had suppressed its performance.

These are not competing explanations, but may have in combination discouraged Warlukurlangu. The interdiction by the church (and the state, in some versions) was difficult to substantiate, though it was widely believed. Some of the more dramatic forms of punishment employed in the ceremony contradict Western manners, if not morals. There seemed to be some recognition among the Warlpiri that the Fire Ceremony was essentially incompatible with the expectations of settlement life, and the impotent fantasies of dependency and development they were required to promote. The Fire Ceremony was an explicit expression of Warlpiri autonomy, and for nearly a generation it was obscured. The question arises, as it does also in accounting for the ceremony's recent revival: what role did introduced media play in this history?

Yet Warlukurlangu persisted in certain covert ways. The very first videotape which the community itself directed in 1983 recorded an apparently casual afternoon of traditional dancing held at the women's museum. Such spontaneous public dance events are comparatively rare at Yuendumu. Dances occur in formal ceremonies, or during visits, in modern competitions and recitals, or in rehearsal for any of these. Yet this event appeared to meet none of these criteria. Equally curious was the insistence on the presence of the video camera. These were early days – Jupurrurla had not yet taken up the camera, and Japanangka and myself were having trouble arranging the shoot. A delegation of old men showed up at each of our camps and announced that we must hurry; the dancing wouldn't start till the video got there. What was taped was not only some quite spectacular dancing, but an emotional experience involving the whole community. When I afterwards asked some of the younger men the reason for all the weeping, they explained that people were so happy to see this dance again. I later discovered I had seen excerpts of the dances associated with the Fire Ceremony.

Some months later, I was invited to a meeting of the old men in the video studio. They had written to Peterson, asking for a copy of the film, and now were there to review it. I set up a camera and we videotaped this session. As it was clear that many of the on-film participants would now be dead, how the community negotiated this fact in terms of their review was very important. The question of the film's possible circulation was raised. Following a spirited discussion, the old men (as mentioned above) came to the decision that all the people who died were 'in the background': the film could be shown in the camps. Outside, a group of women elders had assembled, and were occasionally peeking through the window. Some were crying. They did not agree that the deceased were sufficiently backgrounded, and it made them 'too sorry to look'. These women did not watch the film, but didn't dispute the right of the men to view or show it.

It became clear that the community was gearing up to perform the Fire Ceremony again for the first time in this generation. As preparations proceeded, video influenced the ritual in many ways. For example, the senior men announced that the Peterson film was 'number one Law', and recommended that we shoot the videotape of exactly the same scenes in precisely the same order. (When this did not happen, no one in fact remarked on the difference.) Andrew Japaljarri Spencer, who acted as first cameraman, stood in Kurdungurlu relationship to the ceremony. This meant that he produced an intimate record of the ceremony from his 'on the side' perspective.

We are at close-up range for some of the most dramatic moments, alongside the men actually administering the fiery punishments. Jupurrurla absented himself from this production. Although he was willing to do certain preproduction work, and subsequent editing and technical services, he would not act as cameraman because he would be a Kirda for this event. Quite sensibly, he pointed out that if Kirda were cameramen, the camera might catch on fire. Jupurrurla was not unaware, like many of the younger men, that he too might catch on fire, so at the climax of the ceremony they were nowhere to be found.

The tape of this major ceremony was copied the very next day and presented to a delegation from the nearby Willowra community, who were in fact in the midst of learning and acquiring the ceremony for performances themselves. This is a traditional aspect of certain classes of ceremonies. In oral societies where information is more valued than material resources, ceremonies can be commodities in which ritual information is a medium of exchange. This exchange may take years, and repeated performances, to accomplish. For instance, there was a dramatic (if not unexpected) moment when a more careful review of the tape revealed that one of the painted ceremonial poles had been rather too slowly panned, rendering its sacred design too explicit. This design had not yet been exchanged, and so the Willowra people might learn it – and reproduce it – from the tape. Runners went out to intercept the Willowra mob, and to replace their copy with one that had the offending section blanked out.

These new tapes of the Fire Ceremony circulated around the Yuendumu community, and in their raw state were highly popular. In fact, it became difficult to keep track of the copies. This was one of the motivations to proceed with broadcasting – more to assure the security of the video originals and provide adequate local circulation of tapes than to achieve any explicitly political intent. But perhaps there was a broader public statement to be made with the record of these events. I recommended, and was authorised to propose to the Australian Institute of Aboriginal Studies, that we edit together the tapes to produce an account which would describe both the ceremony and its reproductions. We had the Peterson film, the community dance, the review of the film, and the extraordinary footage of the 1984 performance. This seemed to me an excellent and visually striking way to articulate the ceremony in terms of some of the more fundamental questions concerning the place of such media in Warlpiri life. The Institute did not support the idea, and when one of the central performers died shortly thereafter, the community dropped the matter. The tapes took their place on a shelf in the archive that Jupurrurla labelled 'not to look'. Later, however, the Institute did transfer the Sandall/Peterson film to videotape, and put it into general distribution without, to my knowledge, informing the community that this was being done.

There is no point in isolating any one instance of this failure to address or resolve the problems that the appropriation of Warlpiri images poses. The situation is so general that it proves how fundamental the misunderstandings must be. Alien producers do not know what they take away from the Aborigines whose images, designs, dances, songs and stories they record. Aborigines are learning to be more careful in these matters. But the conventions of copyright are profoundly different from one context to the other. Perhaps these urgent questions will never be solved: 'Who owns that dance now on film?', 'Who has the authority to prevent broadcast of that picture of my father who just died?', 'How can we make sure women will not see these places we showed to the male film crew?', 'Will we see any of the money these people made with our pictures?' . . . Whenever 'appropriate' Australian authorities are confronted with such questions, they go straight to the too-hard basket, not only because they are truly difficult questions, but also because they refer to equivocal political positions.

Underlying the problem is not only a failure to specify the processes of reproduction and their place in oral traditions; there is also a contradiction of values regarding the possibilities for Aboriginal futures, and the preferred paths towards these. Many Aborigines do wish to be identified, recognised and acknowledged in modern media, as well as to become practitioners of their own. They recognise the prestige, the political value, the economic bargaining position that a well-placed story in the national press can provide. They attempt to evaluate the advantages – and what they are told is the necessity – of compromising certain cultural forms to achieve this. But the elements of this exchange, the discrimination between what is fundamental and what is negotiable, resists schematisation. On neither side is there a clear sense of what can be given up and what must be kept if Aborigines are to avoid being reprocessed in the great sausage machine of modern mass media. For them, it is the *practices* of cultural reproduction that are essential. If by the next generation the means of representing and reproducing cultural forms are appropriated and lost, then all is destroyed. What remains will just be a few children's stories, place names for use by tourist or housing developments, some boomerangs that don't come back, a Hollywood-manufactured myth of exotica. These will only serve to mask the economic and social oppression of a people who then come into existence primarily in relation to that oppression.

The criteria for Aboriginal media must concern these consequences of recording for cultural reproduction in traditional oral societies. Warlpiri people put it more simply: 'Can video make our culture strong? Or will it make us lose our Law?'

The problem about answering this sort of question as straightforwardly as it deserves, is that it usually is asked in deceptive cause/effect terms: what will TV do to Aborigines? The Warlpiri experience resists this formulation. Jupurrurla demonstrates that such questions cannot be answered outside the specific kin-based experiences of their local communities. His productions further demonstrate that television and video are not any one, self-evident thing, a singular cause which can then predict effects. Indeed, Yuendumu's video-makers demonstrate that their television is something wholly unanticipated, and unexplained, by dominant and familiar industrial forms.

Here I want to emphasise *the continuity of modes of cultural production across media*, something that might be too easily overlooked by an ethnocentric focus on content. My researches identify how Jupurrurla and other Warlpiri video-makers have learned ways of using the medium which conform to the basic premises of their tradition in its essential oral form. They demonstrate that this is possible, but also that their efforts are yet vulnerable, easily jeopardised by the invasion of alien and professional media producers.

My work has been subject to criticism for this attention to traditional forms and for encouraging their persistence into modern life. The argument is not meant to be romantic: my intent has been to specify the place of the Law in any struggle by indigenous people for cultural and political autonomy. In the case of Warlpiri television, the mechanisms for achieving this were discovered to lie wholly in the domain of cultural reproduction, in the culture's ability to construct itself, to image itself, through its own eyes as well as the world's.

In the confrontation between Dreamtime and Ourtime, what future is possible? The very terms of such an inquiry have histories that tend to delimit any assured, autonomous future. For example, if it were true that my analysis of Warlpiri TV provided no more than a protectionist agenda, then the charge of romantic indulgence in an idealised past might be justified. I would have failed to escape a 'time' that anthropologists call the 'ethnographic present' – a fabricated, synchronic moment that, like the Dreamtime, exists in ideological space, not material history. It is implicated in nearly all anthropology, as well as most ethnographic discourse. Certainly, the questions of time that seem essential here cannot be elucidated by constructs of timelessness.

It seems likely that grounding Aborigines in such false, atemporal histories results in projecting them instead into a particular named future whose characteristics are implied by that remarkable word, 'Lifestyle'. This term now substitutes everywhere for the term culture to indicate the latter's demise in a period of ultra-merchandise. Culture – a learned, inherited tradition – is superseded by a borrowed, or gratuitous model; what your parents and grandparents taught you didn't offer much choice about membership. Lifestyles are, by contrast, assemblages of commodified symbols, operating in concert as packages which can be bought, sold, traded or lost. The word proves unnervingly durable, serving to describe housing, automobiles, restaurants, clothes, things you wear, things that wear you – most strikingly, both 'lifestyle condoms' for men and, for women, sanitary napkins that 'fit your lifestyle'. Warlpiri people, when projected into this Lifestyle Future, cease to be Warlpiri; they are subsumed as 'Aborigines', in an effort to invent them as a sort of special ethnic group able to be inserted into the fragile fantasies of contemporary Australian multiculturalism. Is there no other future for the Warlpiri than as merely another collectivity who have bartered away their history for a 'lifestyle'?

I propose an alternative here, and name it the Cultural Future. By this I mean an agenda for cultural maintenance which not only assumes some privileged authority for traditional modes of cultural production, but argues also that the political survival of indigenous people is dependent upon their capacity to continue reproducing these forms.

What I read as the lesson of the Dreaming is that it has always privileged these processes of reproduction over their products, and that this has been the secret of the persistence of Aboriginal cultural identities as well as the basis for their claims to continuity. This analysis confirms Jupurrurla's and Japanangka's claims that TV is a two-edged sword, both a blessing and a curse, a 'fire' that has to be fought with fire. The same medium can prove to be the instrument of salvation or destruction. This is why a simple prediction of the medium's effects is so difficult to make. Video and television intrude in the processes of social and cultural reproduction in ways that literate (missionary, bureaucratic, educational) interventions never managed to accomplish. Its potential force is greater than guns, or grog or even the insidious paternalisms which seek to claim it.

But in a cultural future, *Coniston Story* operates over time to privilege the Japangardi/Japanangka version of that history, to insert it bit by bit into the Dreaming tracks around Crown Creek until the tape itself crumbles and its memory is distributed selectively along the paths of local kinship. In this future, when the mourning period for that old Japangardi is passed, his relations will take the Fire Ceremony tape from the 'not to look' shelf and review it again, in regard to the presence or absence of recent performances of the ceremony. Audiences at Yuendumu will reinterpret what is on the tape, bring some fellows into the foreground and disattend to others. They might declare this 'a proper law tape', and then go on to perform the ceremony exactly the same, but different. I expect, in the highly active interpretative sessions that these attendances have become, there will be much negotiation necessary to resolve apparent contradictions evoked by the recorded history. I expect that a cultural future allows the space and autonomy for this to happen.

In a lifestyle (ethnic, anti-cultural) future, it's not so certain that anyone will be there at Yuendumu to worry about all this. Why should they? After all, the place has only cultural value, lacking any commercial rationale for the lifestyle economy. But if people are to be situated in this future, we can assume that they will be faced with a very different kind of, and participation in, media. Their relation to the forces and modes of cultural reproduction will be quite passive: they will be constituted as an audience, rendered consumers, even though there's not much money to buy anything (the local store is reduced to selling tinned stew and Kung Fu video tapes). But it would be mistaken to claim that the ethnic cultural policy has ignored Aborigines. In fact, they play a major part in the construction of the national, multicultural image; in this scenario, they become niggers. Then they will be regularly on the airways, appearing as well-adjusted families in situation comedies, as models in cosmetic ads, as people who didn't get a 'fair go' on *60 Minutes*. Nationally prominent, academically certified Aborigines will discuss Aboriginality on the ABC and commercial stations, filling in the legislated requirements for Australian content. In the lifestyle future, Aborigines can be big media business.

The people at Yuendumu will watch all this on their government-provided, receive-only satellite earth stations; but we can only speculate about what identifications and evaluations they will make. Perhaps the matter will not be inconsequential. Imported programs supplant, but may not so directly intrude on, cultural reproduction. Rather, it is when some archivist wandering through the ABC film library chances on an old undocumented copy of the Peterson Fire Ceremony film, one of the competing versions of the Coniston massacre, or even some old and valuable Baldwin Spencer footage, circa 1929, of Central Australian native dances, that something truly momentous happens. In pursuit of a moment of 'primitivism', the tapes go to air, via satellite, to thousands of communities at once, including those of its subjects, their descendants, their relations, their partners in ritual exchange, their children, their women (or men). One more repository guarded by oral secrecy is breached, one more ceremony is rendered worthless, one more possible claim to authenticity is consumed by the voracious appetite of the simulacra for the appearance of reality. At Yuendumu, this already causes fights, verbal and physical, even threatened payback murders, in the hopeless attempt to ascribe blame in the matter, to find within the kin network the one responsible, so that by punishing him or her the tear in the fabric of social reproduction can be repaired. However, the kin links to descendants of Rupert Murdoch or David Hill or Bob Hawke may prove more difficult to trace, and the mechanisms for adjudication impossible to uncover.

A cultural future can only result from political resistance. It will not be founded on any appeal to nostalgia: not nostalgia for a past whose existence will always be obscure and unknown, nor a nostalgia we project into a future conceived only in terms of the convoluted temporalities of our own present. The tenses are difficult to follow here – but in a sense, that is precisely the critical responsibility now before us. Francis Jupurrurla Kelly makes, is making, television at Yuendumu. He intends to continue, and so assure a cultural future for Warlpiri people. His tapes and broadcasts reach forward and backwards through various temporal orders, and attempt somehow to bridge the Dreaming and the historical. This, too, is a struggle which generates Jupurrurla's art.

The only basis for non-Warlpiri interest in their video must recognise these explicitly contemporary contradictions. Channel Four at Yuendumu resists nostalgic sentiment and troubles our desire for a privileged glimpse of otherness. It is we who are rendered other, not its subject. Ultimately, it must be from this compromising position that such work is viewed.

NOTE

This chapter first appeared in Eric Michaels, *For a Cultural Future: or Francis Jupurrurla Makes TV at Yuendumuu*, Artspace, Sydney, 1987.

1 N. Peterson, 'Bulawandi: a Central Australian ceremony for the resolution of conflict', in R. M. Bernt (ed.), *Australian Aboriginal Anthropology*, University of Western Australia Press for the Australian Institute of Aboriginal Studies, Perth, 1970, pp. 200–15.

Cultural Policy and National Culture

The place of cultural policy studies within cultural studies has been the subject of fresh and vigorous debate over the last few years. A concern with cultural policy has been established for many years (indeed, it occupied a central position in Raymond Williams's earliest considerations of communications and the media), but it did take a back seat for much of the 1980s as cultural studies pursued the trajectory which took it from texts to audiences and then back once more to 'everyday life'. Within Australian cultural studies, policy has never been far from the foreground. There are many reasons for this – among them, the prominence of work on Australian film within Australian cultural studies and, within that, the centrality of policy issues. In general, however, the relation between cultural studies and cultural policy in the newer, postcolonial nations seems particularly important. In such societies, as the following three chapters will demonstrate, the process of nation formation is extremely explicit; cultural policy is debated precisely in terms of its 'national' potential. And yet, paradoxically, the products of such policies are usually assessed in terms of how 'naturally' they speak of the nation; so, the Australian film industry is continually judged in terms of how well, accurately or confidently it reproduces an already established image of the nation. There is a defensive imperative, too, where cultural policy is deployed through regulations aimed at protecting the national identity – often the same national identity seen elsewhere to be in the process of explicit and programmatic construction. In Australia, as in Canada, there is a long history of cultural critique which centres itself on cultural policy and which sees the culture industries as a crucial site for nation formation and thus for interrogation and intervention.

The first chapter in this section is an extract from Tony Bennett's *Out of Which Past? Critical Reflections on Australian Museum and Heritage Policy*. This is a relatively new area for Australian cultural studies, but one where there is a strong relationship between the policy-makers and cultural critics. In a model of what a comparative cultural studies could look like, Tony Bennett draws on examples of museums, historical exhibitions and theme parks from the United Kingdom, the United States, and Australia in order to analyse how Australia's museum and heritage policy goes about its task of 'nationing' – of figuring forth a highly specific version of nationhood as their primary semiotic function.

In this excerpt, Bennett pursues two major effects of this process. The first involves the insertion of Aboriginals into a history which constructs an homology between the white invasion of Aboriginal Australia and Aboriginals' transcontinental migration some 40,000 years earlier. Any disruption in this 'never-ending story' is elided by 'enfolding its different phases into a discourse of development which tells the history of the nation as a "continuing story of the transformation of Australia from a country of hunter-gatherers to an industrial nation" '. The nationalised narrative of the museum display, despite its benevolently inclusive intentions, effectively understands Aboriginal histories, indeed Aboriginality itself, as simply a step along the way to white Australia.

The second concern is reached through another narrative strategy – one which tells a story of Australian settlement through the selective and deeply ambiguous motifs of the bush and the prison. As museum policy is increasingly driven by the demands of tourism, so are the effects of what Bennett calls the 'rural gerrymander' – the 'disproportionate concentration on the lives of pioneers, settlers, explorers, goldmining communities and rural industries in the nineteenth century at the expense of twentieth-century urban history'. Bennett notes how this concentration diverts attention from the present and from the more immediate histories out of which it emerges. Further, he warns of the culturally regressive effect of such a policy, the backwardness of its gaze: 'such a policy', he says,

> runs the risk of fashioning a past which meets the demands of foreign visitors for tourist locations which seem to embody the virtues of the exotic, the eccentric and the authentic – in short, which seem to be the antithesis of the metropolitan centres from which they travel.

Within such a scenario, the national past is once again in danger of being produced through the gaze of, rather than in opposition to, the defining Other from elsewhere.

The concern about the Other from elsewhere reappears in Tom O'Regan's chapter, too; there, what is at risk is the Australian television industry. O'Regan outlines the extraordinary political economy of Australian television in the last years of the 1980s, when all three metropolitan networks changed hands at least twice; when two of the three went into receivership while the remaining one (the market leader) went into debt for the first time for decades; when the new owners – in particular the corporate raiders Alan Bond and Christopher Skase – engaged in such questionable business and ethical practices that Bond has spent some time in jail and Skase is only evading a similar fate by hiding in Majorca.

The media shakeup of the 1980s was breathtaking in its comprehensiveness. During the period 1986–90, all the metropolitan television stations, most commercial radio stations, and a significant proportion of the national and metropolitan press changed owners. This after decades of stability in which family dynasties such as the Packers and the Fairfaxes had seemed permanent. As an image of the consequences of a deregulated media market, this period in Australian media history offers a frightening warning to Britain and other European markets of their possible futures.

While the effects of these changes in ownership were dramatic, the causes – as O'Regan points out – were complex and varied. It is clear, however, that government media policy, in particular its deliberate facilitation of the development of national television networks – something hitherto foresworn by governments of all political complexions – played a major role.

Media policy in Australia is tightly articulated to arguments about national sovereignty and the maintenance of national difference within the context of a globalised television and communications market. Unlike most other Western countries, Australia actually has the option of maintaining Australian control of its broadcasting content – at the moment, anyway. The geographic isolation of Australia is, in this respect, an advantage in that it protects local media producers from outside competition. Unlike Canada, for example, we have no large producer just across the border who can address our audiences whether we like it or not. Further, and again given the size of the Australian continent and the distribution of its population around the coastline, broadcasting (first in radio, and then in TV) has been an essential mechanism for addressing a physically dispersed but imaginatively connected Australian nation. Broadcasting has played a central role in the process of 'nationing' Tony Bennett describes in his article, and is thus a prime area of cultural as well as communications policy. With the deregulation of the financial and media markets for those few brief years, however, the Australian media were effectively disarticulated from this cultural function and actually flirted with an 'internationalisation' of Australian TV. By the time this flirtation had run its course, the damage was done.

In O'Regan's essay we encounter a graphic demonstration of the basic contradiction, in principle and in practice, between nationalist cultural policy and a deregulated market. O'Regan describes the effects it achieved on Australian television in this way:

> The Australian commercial TV system managed to successfully erode its comparative advantage of a debt-free TV service . . . It diminished

its production levels and production capacity. It increased production costs with no accompanying increase in standards – and then later stripped down productions with a loss in standards. It lost the possibility of managing internationalisation on its own terms and so had it managed for it. It lost a possible place as a successful medium level international producer. Now it was just another one struggling in a difficult environment.

Not an unfamiliar story in Australian cultural policy, where a small and economically weak nation is torn between adjusting what it does in order to compete internationally (and these adjustments often seem to mean the denial of specificity, the thorough internationalisation of its activities), or alternatively maintaining a close relation between its activities and a sense of national identity – even where this incurs economic penalties. While television is a lively site for such arguments, the primary site over the last two decades has been the Australian film industry and it is here that Elizabeth Jacka's article focuses.

Again the Bicentennial looms, this time as an event which 'has made it virtually impossible to speak about nation or national identity without intense disqualification and discomfort'. As we have already seen, however, within an Australian context it is virtually impossible to discuss cultural policy *without* the idea of the national. The double bind for the Australian cultural critic is admirably encapsulated in the trajectory of Jacka's piece. It begins with a reasoned critique of film policy and its textual consequences which leads her into rejecting the idea of 'the national' altogether in favour of 'the local'. By the end, however, the lack of any institutional structure for 'the local' necessitates considering how the objectives of the local might be served through national policy initiatives.

Even in postcolonial countries, where the 'national' can so often operate as a point of resistance, a policy of supporting culture industries in order to protect, maintain or further contribute to a national culture can produce extremely conservative results. Jacka was among those who worked hard to present the film industry's case for subsidisation, but she is also among those who now question whether all their effort, on the evidence of the films it helped to produce, was worthwhile. While the film industry may have prospered in terms of the number of films it has produced since the revival of the 1970s, the texts themselves have offered little in the way of new perspectives on, or new voices within, Australian culture. The original objectives of leftist support for nationalist cultural policies have been poorly served. The consequent disenchantment leads Jacka to pose a fundamental question: whether it is the case in these days of a globalised information and entertainment industry that 'the ideal of a national cinema' is simply 'naive and anachronistic'.

Certainly, the view from Europe has long suggested this is the case, but Australia has held out longer than most – for the kind of reasons outlined in the introduction to this book.

As Jacka suggests, even the best-intentioned national cinema is going to have to 'internationalise' in order to compete on world markets; depending on how fully this is done, the point of having a national cinema in the first place could disappear entirely. Jacka centres her discussion around contemporary debates dealing with 'Australian content' in film and television. The occasion was an inquiry into Australian content regulations conducted by the chief regulatory body, the Australian Broadcasting Tribunal. Jacka demonstrates how conservative and restrictive these well-intentioned ethics are in practice, and how difficult it is to logically justify a process of cultural protectionism. If we want an 'Australian content' that goes beyond the Crocodile Dundee factor, peppering films with shots of kangaroos, koalas and Bryan Brown's torso, and especially if we want an Australian content that is progressively critical of Australian society, then the current policy process is doing little to assist in this endeavour. Jacka sees nationalism and 'the national' (she usefully distinguishes between the two), the conservatism implicit in their supporting ideologies if not in their actual intentions, as key reasons for this. Nevertheless, and with a degree of reluctance, Jacka concludes that it may be the case that 'only by preserving the Australian nature of the production process' can we also 'create the space for the local'. And so, while 'regulation of Australian content then is not a sufficient condition' for a cinema that can be 'surprising, shocking, uncomfortable' or just simply contemporary and local, 'perhaps it is a necessary one'.

Chapter 3

The shape of the past

Tony Bennett

THE PAST IN THE PRESENT

In elaborating the educational advantages of museums, the Pigott Committee[1] stressed their ability to 'dispense with those layers of interpretation which, in most media, separate an object or evidence from the audience', suggesting that 'a gold nugget found at Ballarat in 1860 or a "Tasmanian Tiger" trapped in 1900 will be lacquered less with layers of interpretation in a museum hall than in a film, history book, television documentary, photographs or song'.[2] Kimberley Webber strikes a similar note when, in criticising the aura of sanctity attached to the exhibits in the Australian War Memorial, she suggests that the cultivation of a serious sense of Australia's past 'must rest upon a clear distinction between the rhetoric of the relic and the reality of the artefact'.[3]

While occasionally challenged, the 'culture of the artefact' which underlies both positions continues to provide the primary terms of reference governing debate within the museum world. Yet the distinction on which it rests is a false one. For the artefact, once placed in a museum, itself becomes, inherently and irretrievably, a rhetorical object. As such, it is just as thickly lacquered with layers of interpretation as any book or film. More to the point, it is often lacquered with the same layers of interpretation. For it is often precisely the presuppositions derived from other media that determine both which artefacts are selected for display in museums and how their arrangement is conceived and organised. No matter how strong the illusion to the contrary, the museum visitor is never in a relation of direct, unmediated contact with the 'reality of the artefact' and, hence, with the 'real stuff' of the past. Indeed, this illusion, this fetishism of the past, is itself an effect of discourse. For the seeming concreteness of the museum artefact derives from its verisimilitude; that is, from the familiarity which results from its being placed in an interpretative context in which it is conformed to a tradition and thus made to resonate with representations of the past which enjoy a broader social circulation.[4] As educative institutions, museums function largely as repositories of the already known. They are places for telling, and telling again, the stories of our time, ones which have become a *doxa* through their endless repetition. If the meaning of the museum artefact seems to go without saying, this is only because it has already been said so many times. A truly double-dealing rascal, the museum artefact seems capable of lending such self-evident truths its own material testimony only because it is already imprinted with the sedimented weight of those truths from the outset.

The authenticity of the artefact, then, does not vouchsafe its meaning. Rather, this derives from its nature and functioning, once placed in a museum, as a sign – or, more accurately, a sign-vehicle or signifier. The consequences of this are far-reaching. All of the developed theories of language available to us are in agreement that, apart from a few special classes, individual signifiers have no intrinsic or inherent meaning. Rather, they derive their meaning from their relations to the other signifiers with which they are combined, in particular circumstances, to form an utterance. This has the obvious consequence that the same signifiers may give rise to different meanings depending on the modes of their combination and the contexts of this use.

That this is true of museum artefacts is amply confirmed by those instances in which changes in the systems of classification governing museum displays have led to a radical transformation in the signifying function of identical artefacts. One of the best known examples concerns Franz Boas's breach with the typological system for the display of ethnographic materials. In this system, developed by Pitt Rivers, tools and weapons were extracted from their specific ethnographic origins and arranged into evolutionary series, leading from the simple to the complex, in order to demonstrate the universal laws of progress. Boas, by contrast, insisted that ethnographic objects should be viewed in the context of the specific cultures of which they formed a part and promoted tribally-based displays with a view to demonstrating 'the fact that civilisation is not something absolute, but that it is relative, and that our ideas and conceptions are true only so far as our civilisation goes'.[5]

Given this, it is clear that the significance of particular history museum displays or heritage sites is not a function of their fidelity or otherwise to the past 'as it really was'. Rather, it depends on their position within and relations to the presently existing field of historical discourses and their associated social and ideological affiliations – on what Patrick Wright has called their past-present alignments.[6] To consider the shape of the Australian past from this perspective requires that the past-present alignments embodied in its new and extended forms be considered in their relations to the political ideologies to which, in the main, they have been articulated. While a detailed study of this type cannot be attempted here, a brief consideration of some of the more distinctive past-present alignments currently characterising the national past will suffice to high-light the ambivalent yield of its recent reformation.

THE NEVER-ENDING STORY

We have noted that, for Anderson, nations seem always to loom out of an immemorial past. He goes on to add, however, that they seem also to 'glide into a limitless future'.[7] In so far as they are 'imagined communities' – ways of conceiving the occupants of a particular territory as essentially unified by an underlying commonality of tradition and purpose – nations exist through, and represent themselves in the form of, long continuous narratives. As ways of imagining, and so organising, bonds of solidarity and community, nations take the form of never-ending stories which mark out the trajectory of the people-nation whose origins, rarely precisely specified, are anchored in deep-time just as its path seems destined endlessly to unfold itself into a boundless future. Eric Hobsbawm makes a similar point when he notes, apropos the development of national traditions in late nineteenth-century Europe, that the continuity such traditions evoked was 'largely fictitious', stretching the imaginary continuity of nations back beyond the period of their establishment as identifiably distinct cultural and political entities.[8]

This process of stretching the national past so as to stitch it into a history rooted in deep-time is particularly evident in the case of new nations where, however, it also gives rise to peculiar difficulties. In the case of settler societies which have achieved a newly autonomised post-colonial status, this process has to find some way of negotiating – of leaping over – their only too clearly identifiable and often multiple beginnings: 1788 and 1901, for example. The formation of the National Estate has been of especial significance in this respect. Its role in ironing out the ruptures of Australia's multiple beginnings to produce a national past which flows uninterruptedly from the present back to 1788 is especially clear. This is accomplished, in the main, by two means. First, the classification of cultural artefacts from the period prior to 1901 as parts of the National Estate serves to wrench those artefacts from the histories to which they were earlier connected – those of Empire, for example – and thus to back-project the national past beyond the point of its effective continuity. Equally important, the very concept of the National Estate entails that all particular histories are deprived of their autonomy as their relics – private homes, disused factories, explorers' tracks, marked trees – are dovetailed into the putative unity of the national past. It would, in this respect, be mistaken to conclude from the demotic structure of the National Estate – that is, its all-embracing inclusiveness, encompassing the histories of subordinate as well as elite groups – that it is democratic also. The very concept of a national heritage is, of necessity, demotic;

its *raison d'être* is to enfold diverse histories into one, often with the consequence that the histories of specific social groups are de-politicised as their relics come to serve as symbols of the essential unity of the nation, or to highlight its recently achieved unity, by standing for a divisiveness which is past.[9] Whether or not the results of these processes can be described as democratic depends less on which is included within a national heritage than on the discourses which organise the relations between those artefacts.

Yet the Australian National Estate consists not merely of artefacts relating to the period of European settlement. Its other main classifications are the natural environment and Aboriginal sites. David Lowenthal, writing shortly after the publication of the first Register of the National Estate, notes the consequences of this precisely:

> The Australian heritage incorporates not only the few decades since the European discovery but the long reaches of unrecorded time comprised in Aboriginal life and, before that, in the history of nature itself, the animals and plants and the very rocks of the Australian continent. Thus the felt past expands, enabling Australia to equal the antiquity of any nation.[10]

He might also have noted the similar function of the increased significance accorded maritime history in recent museum and heritage policy. This has emerged as a major area of interest within each of the States whose various maritime collections will receive a point of national co-ordination when the National Maritime Museum opens toward the end of 1988 – a year that will see the nation's maritime past conspicuously foregrounded through the First Fleet re-enactment, the Tall Ships events and the national tour of the Bicentennial Shipwreck exhibition. More generally, the Commonwealth Historic Shipwrecks Act of 1976 has officially annexed pre-settlement maritime history to the national past in declaring all wrecks found in Australia's coastal waters a part of the National Estate. The temporary return to Australia of Hartog's plate – currently the property of the Rijksmuseum in Amsterdam – for the period of the Shipwreck exhibition's tour is symptomatic of the role maritime history plays in pushing the national past as far back beyond 1788 as possible to include the voyages of the explorers. Yet this particular way of extending the past also meets a broader purpose. To the degree that they are fashioned to represent both the outgoing history of Europe and the incoming history of Australia, the inclusion of the voyages of the explorers within the national past allows at least some of the various European constituencies in a multicultural Australia to anchor the 'shallow' histories of their recent immigration in the structures of a deeper time. At the same time, this rooting of the nation in a broader history of contact also serves to liberate the national past from the British dependency which results from an exclusive focus on the moment of settlement.

Much of this is not surprising. Nor, in itself, is it in any way deplorable. That said, this process of elongating the national past does have some questionable aspects of which, here, I want to focus on two: the use of Aboriginal culture as an instrument of nationing, and the forward trajectories of the nation to which these newly created deep pasts – of the land and of the sea – are connected.

The following excerpts from the 1982 *Plan for the Development of the Museum of Australia* offer a convenient illustration of the first of these concerns:

> The Museum of Australia will be a museum about Australia; a museum with which every Australian can identify. It will tell of the past, present and future of our nation – the only nation which spans a continent. It will tell the history of nature as well as the history of the Australian people . . .
>
> Much of the history of Australia – the driest continent – has been shaped by its climate, its geological antiquity, its vast distances and its island isolation. Because of this, its flora and fauna are unique, and the same timeworn landscape conceals ancient life forms and enormous mineral resources.
>
> Australia's human history is ancient and distinctive. Aboriginal people populated Australia early in the colonising surge of modern peoples across the world. Over a period of at least 40,000 years, the Aboriginal people developed a spiritually complex society with an exceptional emphasis upon ritual life and attachment to place. Through time, Aboriginal societies modified the environment and, in their turn, adapted to it with considerable regional variation.
>
> As the nation approaches the bicentenary of European settlement it has become a complex multicultural society. The continuing story of the transformation of Australia from a country of hunter-gatherers to an industrial nation is one of tragedy, triumph, persistence and innovation. It should be told with vigour and objectivity, using our collective heritage to promote the consciousness and self-knowledge which foster a mature national identity.[11]

In 1975, the Pigott Committee was sharply critical of the tendency, in late nineteenth-century museums, for Aboriginal remains and artefacts to be exhibited as parts of natural history displays.[12] The function of such exhibits was clear. Occupying a twilight zone between nature and culture, Aboriginal materials served both to differentiate the two while also accounting for the transition between them. Placed on the lowest rung of the ladder of human evolution, they represented culture at the stage of its emergence out from nature – a sign whose value was purely negative in demonstrating how far humanity had progressed beyond its 'pre-historic' origins. The above passage clearly intends a decisive breach with such conceptions in the significance it accords Aboriginal culture as well as its inclusion of Aborigines within the national subject ('every Australian') it constructs and addresses. Yet it would be an indulgent reading which remained at this level. Indeed, what is most striking about the passage are the respects in which it retains Aboriginal culture in the same representational space (the relations between nature and culture) albeit transforming the function of that space in using it as a device of nationing. For the role assigned Aboriginal peoples is that of a mediating term connecting the history of European settlement to the deep history of the land (its 'geological antiquity' and 'timeworn landscapes') and of its flora and fauna ('ancient life forms'). In thus overcoming the cliff-edge of 1788 to anchor the nation in the structures of a deeper time, this conception fulfils a number of further risks. First, it overcomes any sense of rupture between the phases of pre- and post-settlement in suggesting that Aborigines be viewed merely as a first wave of settlement (they just came 'early in the colonising surge of modern peoples') who, just as did their successors, adapted the environment to their needs. In this way, an essential unity is constructed for a 40,000 year span of history by enfolding its different phases into a discourse of development which tells the history of the nation as a 'continuing story of the transformation of Australia from a country of hunter-gatherers to an industrial nation', a never-ending story of 'tragedy, triumph, persistence and innovation'. This also enables the discourse of multiculturalism to be back-projected into the mists of time where it finds its support in the regional variation of Aboriginal cultures.

It might be thought that this is making too much of a few paragraphs from a relatively early planning document. Certainly, in many of its details, the Museum of Australia may well turn out differently. Yet, they are key paragraphs – the first definitive statement of the concept of the Museum – and accurately indicative of the nationing rhetoric governing its conception as a co-ordinated arrangement of three galleries; the Gallery of Australia since 1788, the Gallery of Aboriginal Australia and the Gallery of the Australian Environment. There seems little doubt, from more detailed plans, that the Gallery of Aboriginal Australia will be seriously critical in its depiction of the effects of European settlement on Aboriginal peoples. Yet, to some degree, this will be overshadowed by the overall conception of the Museum which, in its very structure, is unavoidably deeply ambiguous in the connecting role it accords Aboriginal history.

At the very least, these remarks should suggest the inappropriateness of displaying Aboriginal materials within the frameworks of nationalised narratives. There is, however, a further problem with such narrativisations of the national past, one deriving from the discursive pressure to which they are subject from the broader cultural environment. This is particularly true of forms of narrativisation which, like that embodied in the plan for the Museum of Australia, are organised in terms of a discourse of development in view of the degree to which this discourse has been annexed to the public imagery of Australia's leading business corporations. Paul James has usefully shown how, in the aftermath of the 'new nationalism', such corporations sought to renovate their public images and, in doing so, to attach the forward impetus of the new nationalism to their corporate interests.[13] Yet, in thus claiming to embody the future trajectory of the nation, the advertising strategies of such corporations have also sought to connect pre-existing nationalised images and traditions – the iconography of the Australian landscape, the frontier spirit, the motif of 'the quiet achiever' – to their public images. The meaning potential of such images and traditions is consequently now significantly overdetermined by the corporate imagery which has become attached to them through extended and highly influential advertising campaigns. In BP Australia's 'Quiet Achiever' advertisements, for example, both the Australian land and its surrounding oceans are represented in terms of a discourse of development which presents the corporation's exploratory activities as the outcome of a long story of exploration and development reaching back into the remote history of the continent.[14] Nor have the thematics of multiculturalism proved any less immune to corporate appropriation. The Bond corporation's Bicentennial advertisement, for example, also represents the story of the nation as a continuous story of 'tragedy, triumph, persistence and innovation' in portraying successive waves of settlers and immigrants, all those 'who thought they'd never make it', whose differences are finally annulled as they make their way through to their ultimate historical reward and destiny: a glass of Swan lager.

In his examination of the British national past, Patrick Wright characterises one of its dominant past-present alignments as 'the complacent bourgeois alignment':

> This alignment makes it possible to think of historical development as complete, a process which finds its accomplishment in the present. Historical development is here conceived as a cumulative process which has delivered the nation into the present as its manifest accomplishment. Both celebratory and complacent, it produces a sense that 'we' are the achievement of history and that while the past is thus present as our right it is also something that our narcissism will encourage us to visit, exhibit, write up and discuss.[15]

The past-present alignment embodied in corporate advertising strategies might appropriately be characterised an an active bourgeois alignment.

For it, too, views the past as a cumulative process which has delivered the nation into the present as its accomplishment. Yet that present, while marking an accomplishment, does not mark a completion; rather, it stands poised as a moment between a past and a future cast in the same mould. The future trajectory for the nation which it marks out is governed by the logic of 'more of the same'; a never-ending story of development in which multinational corporations figure as the primary representatives of a process of uninterrupted development which seems to emerge naturally out of the relations between the very land itself and its inhabitants. The temptation, by no means limited to the Museum of Australia, to work along with such narratives in view of their familiarity and, therefore, ready intelligibility, is understandable. However, given the degree to which those narratives have been hijacked by particular sectional interests, it is a temptation that should be actively resisted.

THE PENAL PAST

When Millbank Penitentiary opened in 1817, a room festooned with chains, whips and instruments of torture was set aside as a museum.[16] Thus did a new philosophy of punishment committed to the rehabilitation of the offender through the detailed inspection and regulation of behaviour distance itself from an earlier regime of punishment which had aimed to make power manifest by enacting the scene of punishment in public. The same period witnessed a new addition to London's array of exhibitionary institutions. In 1835, after decades of showing her waxworks the length and breadth of the country, Madame Tussaud set up permanent shop in London. Her new establishment included, as a major attraction, the Chamber of Horrors where, among other things, the barbarous excesses of past practices of punishment were displayed in gory detail.[17] As the century developed, the dungeons of old castles were opened to public inspection, as they still are and, in many places, as the centre-pieces of museums – as at Lancaster Castle, for example, or at York's Castle Museum, located in two eighteenth-century prisons. And Madame Tussaud's now has a rival in the London Dungeon, one of the city's most popular tourist attractions, where special-effects technologies reproduce the mutilation of the body in scenes of torture and punishment from yesteryear.

These developments are not merely of an anecdotal significance. Although little remarked upon, there is an important symbolic symbiosis between the development of imprisonment as the major modern form of punishment and the simultaneous tendency for museums and related institutions to include past forms of penality within their repertoire of representational concerns.[18] It is the logic of the penitentiary that punishment should remain hidden from public view. To the degree that this is so, the penitentiary's reforming rhetoric – its claim to embody humane forms of punishment orientated toward the rehabilitation of the offender – is deprived of public validation. The exhibition of the excesses of past regimes of punishment thus provides the penitentiary with the visible supports which Whiggish views of its history require. The very openness of past scenes and practices of penality to public inspection helps to ensure that the doors of the penitentiary remain well and truly shut in conjuring up visions of such barbarity that the prison, whatever its defects, could not but seem benevolent in comparison.

These considerations are especially pertinent to Australia in view of the unique importance accorded representations of penality within the structure of the national past. Yet this, too, is a relatively new development. Twenty to thirty years ago, most penal institutions from the convict period were either disused or dedicated to other government functions. Since then, the number of such institutions – as well as late nineteenth-century prisons – which have been converted into museums is truly remarkable. Port Arthur, Hyde Park Barracks, Old Melbourne Gaol and Old Dubbo Gaol are among the most obvious examples, but these are complemented in innumerable local prisons which have been converted to house local history displays with several more destined to make a similar transition in the course of 1988 – the opening of Narrabri Old Jail Heritage Centre, for example. Yet it is not simply the marked increase in the quantitative significance accorded representations of penality that most distinguishes their function. This derives from the fact that such representations usually play in two registers simultaneously: as parts of Whiggish views of penal history, and as components of discourses concerning the nation's origins.

Where the former concern predominates, the emphasis falls on depicting the harshness of the convict system or that of the penal institutions developed to deal with indigenous crime in the course of the nineteenth century. It is thus that Jim Allen urges that Port Arthur should be primarily concerned to demonstrate the failure of the convict system. Similarly, although, in its day – like Port Arthur – embodying the ideals of nineteenth-century penal reformers in their aspiration to use imprisonment as a mode of rehabilitation, Old Melbourne Gaol now functions as a testimony to the harshness of a penal regime that is represented as past. In its display of the instruments of prison discipline (the cat, truncheons, a whipping post), the scaffold (reconstructed for the film *Ned Kelly*), the condemned cell, the white masks prisoners were obliged to wear outside their cells and the death masks of hanged felons, the Gaol fulfils the same function in relation to Australia's modern penal system as did the museum within the Millbank Penitentiary for the mid-nineteenth century: it locates penal severity in the past.

The more distinctive rhetoric, however, is that which retrieves the convict population as one of the cornerstones of the nation. In this respect, the penal past forms a part of a broader process in which attitudes toward the convict period have been significantly transformed – so much so that the discovery of convict ancestry is now one of the most sought-after prizes of genealogical inquiry.[19] A healthy demotic tendency, no doubt. What is more questionable is the accompanying tendency for the convicts to be cast in the role of enlisted immigrants or early pioneers in order to provide an early point of reference to which the subsequent histories of settlers, squatters, miners and so on can be connected in a relationship of uninterrupted continuity. As an official catalogue glosses the lessons of Port Arthur.

> Gradually a tourist traffic developed, until today, visitors from all corners of the globe come in their thousands to Port Arthur to catch a vision of bygone days and relive a history of which we should be very proud, for it is the story of the pioneers, bond and free, who laboured together to build the foundations of the Tasmania we know and enjoy today.[20]

The same rhetoric is evident at The Rocks where, in being combined with a nationalised version of the Whiggish view of penality, it serves the unlikely purpose of establishing a moment of origin for the nation which, in its developmental tendency, is represented as free of conflict. Cadman's Cottage and the First Impressions sculpture in The Rocks Square thus both suggest that the only forms of conflict to mar early Australian history were those imported from the old world in the form of the antagonistic relations between the colonial administration and the marines on the one hand and the convicts on the other. Yet these antagonisms – alien intrusions imposed by a past and foreign regime of punishment – are retrospectively erased once Australian history proper gets under way as the convicts and marines, when granted land, are portrayed as rubbing shoulders with the settlers in laying the foundations for a free, democratic and multicultural society.[21]

While it may seem fairly innocuous, this transformation of the penal past into a device of nationing has the further consequence of pre-empting the uses to which that past can be put. The use of a nationing rhetoric is never an innocent choice; its consequences have to be assessed partly in terms of the alternatives it excludes. Thus, in according the penal past the role of a foundational chapter in the history of the nation, that past is simultaneously detached from other histories to which it might be more intelligibly, and certainly more critically, related – in particular, the broader and subsequent history of Australian penality. This would involve different representational choices at both the synchronic and diachronic levels: synchronically, in relating prisons to other historically contemporary penal institutions – asylums, for example, or institutions for destitute women and their children – and diachronically in relating the penal past to present-day forms of punishment. In their singular failure even to gesture in this direction, all of the institutions mentioned above serve a crucial role in institutionalising amnesia with regard to contemporary practices of punishment.[22] In aligning the penal past to the present within the framework of a rhetoric of national development, and in representing that past as one whose excesses have been overcome, contemporary forms of punishment are bereft of any public history except that which, axiomatically, declares their benevolence.

THE TOURIST PAST

Dean MacCannell has argued that 'the best indication of the final victory of modernity over other sociocultural arrangements is not the disappearance of the nonmodern world, but its artificial preservation and reconstruction in modern society'. Museums and heritage sites 'establish in consciousness the definition and boundary of modernity by rendering concrete and immediate that which modernity is not', rendering the past present 'as revealed objects, as tourist attractions'.[23]

While a useful general comment on the amount of social effort modern societies devote to the social production and preservation of their pasts, MacCannell's observation applies with particular force to living-history or open-air museums. The rapid development of this form – at Sovereign Hill, Timbertown and Old Sydney Town, for example – has constituted the most distinctive addition to Australia's museum complex over the last two decades, and certainly the most popular: Sovereign Hill attracted five million visitors in the twelve years after its opening in 1970. It is also, seemingly, the most democratic of museum forms in its concern to reproduce the timbre of the everyday lives of ordinary people in past forms of community.

Yet such appearances are often deceptive. The history of open-air folk museums is a deeply ambiguous one. Michael Wallace traces the prehistory of the form to

> such eighteenth-century aristocratic productions as Marie Antoinette's play peasant village (complete with marble-walled dairy), French *folies* such as Parc Monceau, and the great landscape parks of the English gentry which excised all signs of daily peasant activity and eradicated any sense of time other than the artificially constructed 'natural'.[24]

The late ninteenth-century Scandinavian open-air museum movement – conventionally regarded as the origins of the form – was strongly influenced by romantic conceptions of folk culture as an imaginative antidote to the degradation of capitalism, and, accordingly, tended toward an idealised depiction of past social relations cast in the mould of a pre-

Edenic organic community. The same was true of the development of the form in the United States in the 1920s and 1930s, except that – as at Henry Ford's Greenfield Village – the lives of the pre-industrial folk to which open-air museums were dedicated were so fashioned as to emblematise 'the "timeless and dateless" pioneer virtues of hard work, discipline, frugality, and self-reliance' – exemplary precursors of capitalism rather than its imaginary antithesis.[25]

In brief, the form has tended to be populist rather than democratic in conception, finding a place for the lives of ordinary people only at the price of submitting them to an idealist and conservatively inclined disfiguration. Of course, this is not an intrinsic attribute of the form as such. There is nothing in principle to prevent open-air museums using the resources of the form – which are, in essence, theatrical – to offer a more critical relation to the pasts they produce.[26] None the less, the form's history does tend, in practice, to exert a pressure on the ways in which its uses are conceived, often with the consequence that serious museum enterprises are side-railed into the heartland of conservative mythologies.[27] An added difficulty is that the form now comes under pressure from another source, one whose development it facilitated: Disneyland, whose evocation of Main Street USA draws substantially on the earlier restoration of Colonial Williamsburg.

This is not to suggest a relationship of equivalence between Disneyland (and its imitators) and open-air museums. But they are institutions which overlap, and in several ways. Their thematics are often similar. If Disneyland mimics Colonial Williamsburg, Dreamworld's goldmining sector calls Sovereign Hill to mind. They are, moreover, connected by virtue of their closely related positions within the tourist's itinerary. A survey of Disneyland visitors reveals that a high proportion of them regard a trip to Disneyland and visiting historic sites as closely related activities.[28] While there is no equivalent information for Australia, it seems likely that associations of meaning are carried over from one type of institution to the other within the tourist's itinerary.

Perhaps most important, however, are the distinct similarities between the ways in which Disneyland and open-air museums organise how their visitors negotiate and experience the relations between their constructed interiors and the outside world. Moreover, these constitute the respects in which Australian open-air museums most strongly resemble one another even though, in other respects, they are quite distinct. Most obviously, they differ with regard to the styles of performance regulating the ways in which costumed museum workers mediate the relations between the visitors and their reconstructed historical milieux. At Timbertown, the stress falls on the use of such staff as living history props, costumed complements to the historical setting. The same is true of Sovereign Hill, except that costumed staff will step out of their roles, rupturing their illusionistic function, if asked for information, while there are also non-costumed site interpreters. By contrast, the staff at Old Sydney Town specialise in what can be best characterised as historical hi-de-hi, mixing the routineness of vaudeville theatre and holiday camp hosts to produce a jocular relation to the past which, at one level, they are meant to embody. When such differences are acknowledged, however, there remain two overriding common features which – precisely because it embodies them to excess – a comparison with Disneyland usefully illuminates.

Perhaps the most important similarity between the two institutions consists in their miniaturisation of past social relations. At Disneyland this is achieved by a reduction in the scale of historical reproduction. The buildings on Main Street USA, for example, are at least an eighth less than their true size. 'This costs more', Walt Disney explained, 'but made the street a toy, and the imagination can play more freely with a toy. Besides, people like to think that their world is somehow more grown up than Papa's was.'[29] While open-air museums rarely go to the same lengths, their effects are similar. In clustering together, in a compressed space, every conceivable building type – workers' cottages, school, hotel, church, saddlery, smithy, stables, store, sawmill, newspaper office – they offer the visitor the illusion of knowable, self-enclosed little worlds which can be taken in at a glance, revealed to the tourist's gaze in their entirety in the course of a morning's stroll. Or, as at Timbertown, laid open to a controlling vision via the railway ride which – like the one at Dreamworld – circles the site and establishes its perimeters, separating it from the bush with which, however, it also merges imperceptibly. As the brochure prepares the visitor for the experience which beckons:

Step back into the past . . . and take a stroll through Australia's history. Timbertown is an entire village, re-created to demonstrate the struggles and achievements of our pioneers. It reflects the way they lived, the way they worked, their hardships and their skills.

It is not a lifeless museum . . . it lives! It's an authentic, vital township where the steam train still runs, timber is still sawn, the bullock team still trudges with its heavy load, the woodturner transforms natural timber into works of art, and the general store sells home-made wares and lollies in glass jars . . .

Hear, too, the noises of yesteryear . . . the whistle of the steam train, the bellowing of the bullocks, the clanging of the blacksmith's iron. And, as you pass the old hotel, you hear the sounds of the pianola or true Australian folk music, the happy sounds that entice the folk of the village into the tavern for a hearty singalong . . .

And in this atmosphere of rural serenity, its [sic] likely that the township fringes will reveal kangaroos, wallabies, kookaburras, bower birds and other species of Australian fauna.

Timbertown . . . a fascinating reflection of how people lived and worked in the simplicity and ruggedness of 19th Century Australian bush life.

A number of difficulties coalesce here. The first consists in the false naturalisation of past social relations which results from their miniaturisation and, more particularly, from their self-enclosure. Timbertown is not merely a compressed and knowable little world, it is also an isolated one; the railway does not lead out of the town, connecting it to a wider set of social and economic relations, but rather encircles it, closing it in on itself. The consequence is that the tale of pioneer hardship which the museum tells – largely in the form of push-button commentaries which relate the conditions of work in the sawmill or in the forest – seems to be one which flows from the harshness of nature itself. If the millworkers' living conditions were spartan and their working days long and arduous, this is because the bush was a stern taskmaster. It has seemingly little to do with the encompassing system of economic relations which governed the structure of the timber industry – the conditions of ownership prevailing within it, the organisation of the world market, the degree to which its profits were retained in Australia or returned to Britain – and thus powerfully influenced the ways and standards of living within timber towns as well as their internal structures of power and authority,

In brief, by excerpting the reconstructed township from any sense of a broader historical context, Timbertown mystifies past social relations, transforming a particular phase in the capitalist exploitation of Australia's natural resources into a rural idyll where the village folk troop off to the tavern every night for a communal singalong. This screening of past economic relations is complemented by the ways in which Timbertown simultaneously masks the economic relations which secure its own existence. As is true of many open-air museums, this venture in living history rests on a dual economy. A part of the function of such museums is to deliver a market for the various retail outlets – selling refreshments, craft products, tourist curios, historical fetishes – which constitute a significant proportion of their interiors. While sometimes run by salaried staff, such enterprises are often run privately by local entrepreneurs who, much like side-stall operators at amusement parks, are leased their premises on a concessionary basis. Although the rent charged such private businesses helps to meet overheads and salary costs – including those associated with the special displays which provide one of the major tourist enticements – these are mostly provided for through admission charges.

Both aspects of this dual economy tend to be shrouded. Transactions with costumed retailers are conducted in an imaginary mode, as if the visitor were buying a genuine historical article from an authentic inhabitant rather than paying for a commodity decked out in the attire of history from an entrepreneur or salaried worker. The masking of the economic relations associated with the demonstration of past crafts and skills has a somewhat more complex structure. At Timbertown, most of the forms of labour displayed are manifestly unproductive on their own terms: a team of bullocks drags the same log round the same circle several times a day, and is yoked and unyoked in a demonstration of traditional skills; an operating sawmill is activated at set times, but it cuts no timber. A significant amount of social labour with no readily discernible end-product, its productivity consists entirely in the revenue which its display generates. It is, in other words, labour as spectacle, labour transformed into a form of tourist consumption whose nature as such, however, is withdrawn from the arena in which it is performed to the degree that the transactions which sustain it take place off-site, outside the boundaries of the fabricated historical milieu in the buffer zone which regulates the visitors' transition between the site's inside and its outside, between past and present.

The markers of such transition zones are many and various. Those at Old Sydney Town are perhaps the most elaborate, beginning in the car park ('Park your car here and leave the twentieth century behind'), continuing through the entry building – a large, modern complex of tourist kiosks which urge the visitors to make sure they have all they need before they pass through the turnstiles, as there were no cameras, batteries or films in 1788 – and then, once the price of admission has been paid, through a barbecue and tea-house area before entering a tunnel which gives access to the zone of history, to 1788. Although not so complex, the buffer zones of Sovereign Hill and Timbertown are essentially similar in nature. Timbertown is fronted by a hyper-modern building within which the boundary between past and present is marked by a turnstile (staffed by costumed museum workers) which divides the foyer (modern and functional) from a period setting which gives way to a passageway displaying equipment associated with the timber industry – adjustment zones leading to the zone of history proper. The effect of these markers is reinforced by their virtual absence within the reconstructed historical milieux of the museums' interiors. These are rigorous in their exclusion of any signs of modernity. Sovereign Hill is bereft of explanatory notices in case these might detract from the authenticity of the illusion. Old Sydney Town provides historical information in the form of notice-boards which contrive – in their appearance of age, their antiquated spelling and modes of address – to be intended for a citizen of 1788 rather than a modern tourist. Rubbish bins are hidden in barrels. Toilets are coyly signposted as privies and contained within period buildings – as at Timbertown where, as if to deny them official existence, they are not indicated on the plan of the site in the museum's brochure.

Yet nowhere is an inside more effectively separated from its outside than at Disneyland. M. R. Real notes that, apart from the physical boundaries of a huge parking lot, a circulating railway and the ticket booths, the visitors are screened to ensure that prescribed dress codes – no political messages are allowed on patches, buttons or T-shirts – are observed, and that potential unruly elements (drinkers or addicts) are excluded. Perhaps more important, however, is the screening out of money through its replacement by different classes of tickets, special tokens which allow free participation in the entertainments of the interior – but free, of course, only because it has already been paid for. Yet this screening out of money is designed only to secure its more liberal passage when the visitor moves from the entertainments covered by the entry ticket to Disneyland's innumerable retail outlets in encouraging the illusion of a world in which consumption is experienced as play. 'The Main Street facades', as Umberto Eco puts it, 'are presented to us as toy houses and invite us to enter them, but their interior is always a disguised supermarket, where you buy obsessively, believing that you are still playing'.[30] The scale, no doubt, is different; none the less, the principle embodied in open-air museums is essentially similar – stimulating commodity circulation by organising consumption under the sign of history – as are the means by which it is accomplished.

There is, however, a more general problem arising from the relationship between the preserved or reconstructed past and the economics of tourism which open-air museums serve merely to highlight. It is, moreover, a problem which is especially acute in the Australian context and threatens to become more so now that, in contrast with the loftier sentiments of the 1970s, the search for the tourist dollar has become the primary driving force of museum and heritage policy. As Dean MacCannell notes, the logic of historical tourism is to drive a wedge between the modern world and the past by fashioning the latter in the image of modernity's imaginary other; a world which we have supposedly lost and which we retreat to from the present in search of a never-to-be found set of roots or identity. Even as noted a historian as Manning Clark is not immune to the allure of this conception:

> On a journey round the inhabited parts of Australia today the eye of the traveler is rarely given respite from the monuments of the age of the motor car and the jet engine. The motel, the used car lot, the petrol bowser, the fast food dispenser and the bottle shop have become the main features of the scenery in which we live out our lives. In the cities high-rise buildings dominate the horizon, in the country wheat silos have replaced the temples of an earlier age.

Yet from time to time, in places such as Windsor in New South Wales, Carlton in Victoria, Burra in South Australia, Kalgoorlie in Western Australia, Roma in Queensland, Evandale in Tasmania, Gungahlin in Australian Capital Territory or Darwin in the Northern Territory, the traveller or the local inhabitant is immediately aware of another Australia, remote from the Australia of the skyscraper and conspicuous waste: there is also an old Australia.[31]

It is clear even to casual observation that the structure of the Australian past is the victim of a rural gerrymander which brings with it a marked temporal imbalance owing to its disproportionate concentration on the lives of pioneers, settlers, explorers, goldmining communities and rural industries in the nineteenth century at the expense of twentieth-century urban history. Nor is this simply a matter of the preponderance of museum and heritage sites devoted to such themes. In tourist literature, with a consistency which belies exception, the past is represented as precisely something to get away to, often in the register of the Dreamworld jingle 'Take a trip away from the everyday'. Michael Bommes and Patrick Wright, noting a similar tendency in the British context, argue that it serves to de-historicise both past and present to the degree that the former becomes a tourist spectacle precisely because it is divorced from the present while the latter – or, more accurately, the recent past – seems devoid of history precisely because it does not fall within the zone of the officially demarcated past.[32] There is a clear dilemma here. The more the structure of the past is subject to the exigencies of tourism, the greater the likelihood that it will focus on the country rather than the city, and the nineteenth rather than the twentieth century. It will, as a consequence, tend to offer the great majority of Australians an imaginative diversion from their present conditions of existence rather than affording a familiarity with the more immediate histories from which those conditions effectively flow. Such a policy, in the Australian context, runs the further risk – and the more so as tourism becomes an increasingly export-orientated industry – of fashioning a past which meets the demand of foreign visitors for tourist locations which seem to embody the virtues of the exotic, the eccentric and the authentic – in short, which seem to be the antithesis of the metropolitan centres from which they travel. The more the Australian past is fashioned to meet this demand, the greater will be its tendency to represent Australians to themselves through the cracked looking-glass of the Anglo-American gaze in its tendency to cast the national character in the form of a heroic and primitive simplicity – the Crocodile Dundee factor.

NOTES

This chapter first appeared in Tony Bennett, *Out of which Past? Critical Reflections on Australian Museum and Heritage Policy*, Institute for Cultural Policy Studies, Brisbane, 1988.

1 The Pigott Committee was established in 1974 to inquire into the museums and national collections of Australia.

2 *Museums in Australia*, Report of the Committee of Inquiry on Museums and National Collections including the Report of the Planning Committee on the Gallery of Aboriginal Australia, Australian Government Publishing Service, Canberra, 1975, para. 4.17.

3 Kimberley Webber, 'Constructing Australia's past: the development of historical collections 1888–1938', *Proceedings of the Council of Australian Museums Association Conference* (1986), Perth, 1987, p. 170.

4 This discussion of verisimilitude is drawn from Roland Barthes, *Criticism and Truth*, University of Minnesota Press, Minneapolis, 1987, pp. 34–6.

5 Cited in Ira Jacknis, 'Franz Boas and exhibits: on the limitations of the museum method of anthropology', in George W. Stocking Jr. (ed.), *Objects and Others: Essays on Museums and Material Culture*, University of Wisconsin Press, Madison, 1985, p. 83.

6 See Patrick Wright, 'A blue plaque for the Labour Movement? Some political meanings of the national past', in *Formations of Nation and People*, Routledge & Kegan Paul, London, 1984, pp. 51–2.

7 Benedict Anderson, *Imagined Communities: Reflections on the Origin and Spread of Nationalism*, Verso, London, 1983, p. 19.

8 See Eric Hobsbawm, 'Mass-producing traditions, Europe 1870–1914', in Eric Hobsbawm and Terence Ranger (eds), *The Invention of Tradition*, Cambridge University Press, Cambridge, 1983.

9 A good example of this is provided by Lord Chartis of Amisfield ('The work of the National Heritage Memorial Fund', *Journal of the Royal Society of Arts*, 132 (1984) who, in listing a number of items 'saved' by the British National Heritage Memorial Fund, manages to place trade-union barriers cheek-by-jowl with an avenue of elms, Coalbrookdale Old Furnace and the *Mary Rose* without any sense of incongruity.

10 David Lowenthal, 'Australian images: the unique present, the mythic past', in Peter Quartermaine (ed.), *Readings in Australian Arts*, University of Essex Press, Colchester, 1978, p. 86.

11 Museum of Australia, *The Plan for the Development of the Museum of Australia*, Report of the Interim Council, Australian Government Publishing Service, Canberra, 1982, p. 2.

12 ibid., paras 4.27 and 4.30.

13 Paul James, 'Australia in the corporate image: a new nationalism', *Arena*, 61 (1983).

14 The specificity of this rhetoric of the land is highlighted by Bommes's and Wright's discussion of the sharply contrasting rhetoric of preservation which has characterised Shell's advertising in Britain. See Michael Bommes and Patrick Wright, 'Charms of residence: the public and the past', in Centre for Contemporary Cultural Studies, *Making Histories: Studies in History-writing and Politics*, Hutchison, London, 1982.

15 Wright, 'Blue plaque', p. 52.

16 See Robin Evans, *The Fabrication of Virtue: English Prison Architecture, 1750–1840*, Cambridge University Press, Cambridge, 1992.

17 For details, see Richard Altick, *The Shows of London*, The Belknap Press of Harvard University Press, Cambridge, Massachusetts and London, 1978.

18 I have, however, touched on this matter elsewhere. See Tony Bennett, 'The exhibitionary complex', *New Formations*, 4 (spring 1988).

19 See M. Cordell, 'Discovering the chic in a convict past', *Sydney Morning Herald*, 31 January 1987.

20 *Port Arthur Historic Site: Museum Catalogue*, trial version, Tasmania National Parks and Wildlife Service and the Education Department, 1984.

21 I have discussed the Rocks in more detail elsewhere. See Tony Bennett 'History of the Rocks', *Local Consumption*, 1988.

22 The 'Out of Sight Out of Mind' Exhibition to be held at the S. H. Evrin Gallery in Sydney later in 1988 (at the time of writing) promises to be an exception to this general tendency.

23 Dean McCannell, *The Tourist: A New Theory of the Leisure Class*, Schocken Books, New York, 1976, pp. 8–9, 84.

24 Mike Wallace, 'Mickey Mouse history: portraying the past at Disneyworld', *Radical History Review*, 32, (1985), 40.

25 Mike Wallace, 'Visiting the past: history museums in the United States', *Radical History Review*, 25 (1981), 72.

26 For a discussion of a critical experiment with the form, see John Fortier, 'Louisburg: managing a monument in time', in R. E. Rider (ed.), *The History of Atlantic Canada: Museum Interpretations*, National Museum of Canada, Ottawa, 1981.

27 For a discussion of this tendency in the British context, see Tony Bennett, 'Museums and "the People" ', in Bob Lumley (ed.), *The Museum Time Machine*, Methuen, London, 1988.

28 For details, see M. Real, 'The Disney universe: morality play', in *Mass-Mediated Culture*, Prentice Hall, Englewood Cliffs, NJ, 1987, pp. 72–3.

29 Cited in Real, 'Disney universe', p. 54.

30 Umberto Eco, *Travels in Hyper-Reality*, Picador, London, 1986, p. 43.

31 Introduction to Australian Council of National Trusts, *Historic Places of Australia*, vol. 1, Cassell Australia, Sydney and Melbourne, 1978.

32 Bommes and Wright, 'Charms of residence', p. 296.

Chapter 4

The rise and fall of entrepreneurial TV
Australian TV, 1986–90

Tom O'Regan

THE PARLOUS STATE OF AUSTRALIAN TV[1]

In the 1988–9 financial year, the Australian commercial TV industry lost money for the first time since 1957. At the time of writing, in September 1990, two of Australia's three commercial networks – Seven and Ten – are in the hands of receivers. Seven has been that way all year. Ten was put into receivership on 14 September 1990 – a little more than one year after former network owner, Frank Lowy, sold the network at a discounted price to its new owner, Steve Cosser. Leading network, the Nine Network, has recently changed hands for a fraction of its original purchase price; sold by Kerry Packer to Alan Bond's Bond Media group for $A1.1 billion (1 billion = 1,000 million; $A1 = $US0.81, UK 43p), it was repurchased by Packer in a deal which put the value of the Network at an estimated $A410–$A485 million.[2] The financial state of the Australian industry is represented by the Seven Network's earning of $A4.83 million *before* its interest and tax bills are taken into account in the 1988/9 financial year. A similar picture emerges for the other networks. The lowest rating Ten Network lost $A114.3 million in 1988/9 and expects to lose $A85–95 million in the 1990 calendar year.[3] This crippled financial state has led to dramatic job losses at the TV stations themselves since mid-1989: at Ten 25 per cent of network staff have lost their jobs. The medium term outlook for TV network affiliates in regional Australia, servicing some 33 per cent of the Australian TV audience, is looking increasingly desperate.[4]

As networks slash production spending by as much as 40–50 per cent, the independent programme production industry, which is the major supplier of Australian commercial TV programming, is undergoing a dramatic downturn. Established producers are seeing new productions cancelled or indefinitely shelved and unemployment within the industry is mounting. Not only have actors' rates declined but work opportunities are considered to be the worst in the Australian film industry in twenty-five years.[5] Already creative personnel from actors to camera operators to directors are in or seeking overseas employment; and Australian production houses like Grundy's are in the process of establishing offshore production companies to service markets with greater production opportunities.[6] In this context coproductions become *de rigeur*, with the 'purely Australian product' (which has been so successful on British screens with *Neighbours* and *Home and Away*) being seen as too costly for 'an Australian network to shoulder'.[7]

Finally, to meet US trade pressure and the Australian government's microeconomic reform agenda, the regulation which stipulates that all TV advertisements should be Australian-made is likely to be somewhat eased. This is expected to further diminish opportunities within the Australian film industry as well as to have a negative impact upon the technological infrastructure available to the Australian film industry as a whole.

The immediate outlook for Australian TV is bleak. What happened? How did a previously profitable – and highly competitive – TV industry with minimum debt levels and expanding overseas export markets become a basket case saddled with crippling debts and a substantial production downturn despite the international success of *Neighbours* and *Home and Away?*

BACKGROUNDS: THE ENTREPRENEURIAL GAME PLAN

The Australian commercial TV crisis had its immediate origins in two unrelated governmental decisions. The first was the deregulation of the Australian financial sector which created long credit lines fuelling an investment boom in which accepted price to earnings ratios became grossly inflated. The second was the federal government's decisions to change TV ownership rules and introduce more TV to regional Australia. The ownership rules changed from a limit of two stations that any one company could own, to a limit expressed in terms of the overall share of the audience able to be reached.[8] After November 1986 a company could have access to TV stations with a cumulative reach of 60 per cent of the total Australian market (prior to the 60 per cent market share rule coming in, the highest market share available was 43 per cent – only available in theory to three companies – those which owned both a Sydney and Melbourne TV station). Accompanying this extension in the allowable market size came cross-media ownership limitations which restricted common ownership of TV, radio and the press in a particular geographical market. The catalyst immediately driving these regulatory changes was the plan to bring three commercial stations to regional TV markets. This 'equalisation' policy was to be achieved by a process of 'aggregating' adjacent regional TV markets into larger single markets. Briefly, this involved turning some thirty regional TV markets on the eastern sea-

board, where only a commercial and an ABC station (Australian Broadcasting Corporation – rough BBC equivalent) were available, into four
discrete markets where the ABC and three commercial stations would
be available. For some of the larger cities in these markets a fifth public
network, the SBS (Special Broadcasting Service – a cross between BBC2
and Channel 4), would also be made available.[9] Aggregation thus promised the integration of most regional TV markets with their metropolitan
counterparts. In short, equalisation would bring TV networking to
regional markets. And the ownership changes would enable companies
to get bigger and to exercise qualitatively greater control over the shape,
profits and definition of the TV market than was possible hitherto.

Additionally, the launch of the domestic satellite AUSSAT in 1986
promised a new TV message delivery structure. The purchase of satellite
transponders by the networks replaced per message charges on the Tele-
com terrestrial network. Australia had not had much 'simultaneous' TV
up to that point; on commercial TV it was sporting events, current
affairs programming like the weekly *60 Minutes* and some national news
segments. Like Italian commercial TV, Australian TV used videotape
delivery extensively. Whilst the same programming was aired throughout
Sydney, Melbourne, Brisbane and Adelaide (Perth and the regionals used
the same material but less of it), it tended not to be broadcast at the
same time, nor on the same day, nor in the same order.[10] The combination
of the satellite and the extended market share available to companies
now encouraged the networking of programme schedules.

Network, common ownership and a technologically advanced delivery
system seemed to offer a chance to get additional advertising revenues,
with networks controlling national advertising, having wrested that from
the advertising agencies. Ad space buyers would only do more or less
one-stop shopping, bringing added business and greater control over the
TV system, from Sydney head office right down the line to Cairns and
Perth. The networks, now national players at the pinnacle of the system,
commanding 60 per cent of the national audience, would be in a position
to dictate terms to the smaller regional market players, which would have
no alternative but to become their affiliates. The profits to be had from
this, based on American experience, must have looked promising.[11] Thus
under the new conditions companies sought to become networks, owning
four of the five largest TV markets in the country (Sydney, Melbourne,
Brisbane, Perth and Adelaide collectively making up 67 per cent of the
Australian viewing audience). Prior to the changes, networks were a
loose grouping of stations operating in the major metropolitan markets
of Sydney, Melbourne, Brisbane, Adelaide (and Perth after 1988 when
a third commercial station came on stream). These networks were dominated by the companies controlling Sydney and Melbourne licences.
Under the new conditions, the existing structural subordination of Bris-

bane and Adelaide stations could be replaced in two of the three markets of Brisbane, Adelaide and Perth with branch office control.

The cross-ownership regulation in itself was bound to spark activity in media stock as companies readjusted themselves to the new environment. Similarly, the extension in market share was bound to create a speculative environment as a premium price could be expected to be paid for such effective control over the Australian TV audience. This was particularly so in the context of 1987–8 where it appeared that the 60 per cent audience share would be raised to 75 per cent. But the regulatory background and the logic of market opportunity cannot explain the inflation of media asset values that resulted. Responsibility for that must be shared by financial deregulation and Australia's entrepreneurial business culture in the 1980s.

The prices paid for TV stations were underwritten by domestic and foreign banks eager to lend in a newly deregulated environment. Banks in Australia, fearing competition from each other and foreign banks, scrambled for market share, forgetting for a time all the rules about prudent lending and how to compete in an oligopolistic market (that is, 'compete' in an arranged sort of way so that risks are minimised and market shares become predictable). They actively sought potential debtors, bidding against each other for the rights to service bigger and bigger debts of increasingly indebted clients.

The availability of easy credit fitted all too well the public company logic of the 1970s and 1980s, which had previously been kept in check by financial regulation. This logic went something like this: 'Go into debt. Forget about developing equity and cash reserves – that only makes you liable as a takeover target by a company with long credit lines.' In this climate, publicly listed companies had to go sufficiently far into debt to stave off takeover bids from people seeking to convert equity and cash into tax benefited debt.

Aiding this logic was the common practice of Australian corporate 'raiders' to buy assets, revalue them upwards and use that revalued asset to borrow against for additional purchases. Seven and Nine's new owners, Skase and Bond, were amongst the biggest culprits here. Revaluations could even occur after asset-stripping. This revaluation was made possible by rising share values and market confidence in these players – particularly as they seemed to be the most outward looking, keen to establish not simply national, but also international profiles. These same corporate raiders also exploited the tax act to use the size of their interest on debt to minimise tax payments, thus reducing the effective rate of interest by the amount that would have been paid in taxes. Only when interest rates reached the 20 per cent level, in the context of diminishing not rising asset values, did this equation come unstuck and did it appear that it might be a financially sound practice to pay some tax.

Of additional help were Australia's lax company and securities laws, low accountancy standards and light regulation and penal sanctions. Differing state business laws do not encourage transparency. Funds and the political will were lacking for corporate investigation. Creative accountancy practices[12] could, for example, lead to public reporting of profits by companies such as Skase's Quintex group, in the 1987–8 financial year, projecting profit after tax to be higher than profit before tax.[13]

The mid-to-late 1980s saw debt financing move into TV in a *big* way. By early 1988 Alan Bond's companies accounted for 10 per cent of Australia's external debt – and were among the companies which paid little to no tax.

Further assisting corporate debt in TV was the fact that all the new proprietors were taking their initial decisions in the midst of a share market and property boom. But the share market boom ended in October 1987 – so it cannot account for the subsequent profligacy of 1988 and early 1989, although it can help account for the initial prices paid. The property market was levelling off by mid–1989, but like the real estate market in Sydney in this period, it had seemed that no matter how much was paid for a property, it would be able to be sold at a profit just down the line, leading to a form of pyramid selling.

Changes in the operating rules, combined with easy credit in a deregulated financial market and Australian corporate practice did not simply inflate TV station prices, it blew them out. The value of the Nine and Ten networks doubled overnight.[14] Speculation in TV assets reached phenomenal proportions as the three networks acquired new owners. These new owners were prepared to pay a premium for such strategic positions in the Australian TV market. The US broadcasting journal *Channels* put the prices graphically: Alan Bond's Bond Media paid $US88 per viewer for Nine; Frank Lowy's Westfield group paid $US80 for Ten; Christopher Skase's Quintex group paid $US49 for Seven.[15] In the period stretching from November 1986 to November 1987 Australia's three commercial TV networks, Nine, Seven and Ten, changed hands for an estimated $A2.5 billion. These prices made metropolitan Australian TV stations among the most expensive in the world.

The companies which bought into TV were not simply after media industry cash-flows to service interest payments to finance further corporate expansion. They were also acquiring assets which could be integrated into their other activities in complementary or 'synergistic' ways. Bond, for instance, was putting a package together that saw Bond University as a user for his satellite space (in the provision of distance education) alongside Sky Channel (a pub and club direct broadcast by satellite service) and the Nine Network. The journalism students at Bond were to get work experience at Channel Nine (thereby giving its journalism school a competitive edge over rival ones). Bond University was also a 'real estate' development whose property values could be increased by siting a university in the neighbourhood. Bond's brewing and other national companies would be benefited by the Nine Network being within the same company stable: there was scope for integrated national marketing packages, including TV programme sponsorship. Finally, TV network ownership conferred a certain prestige value which could be traded in the dealings of the company in the marketplace and with government.

Both the new network owners and the banks also believed the talk about the 'media' as a growth industry in the business of providing 'information services' and 'software' (as 1980s nomenclature came to describe the humble TV programme). Information was power. Information was a (tradable) asset. In late advanced capitalism, knowledge was power and therefore *control over knowledge was the route to greater power and wealth*. The information sector was identified as the *development* sector. So our property developers (Skase, Bond and Lowy) *moved in on knowledge*, bringing with them practices, accountancy techniques, and methods of asset development fine-tuned over years in the property trade. In short, information became property to be traded, markets were established in it. Underlying these moves appeared to be a notion that 'information' asset values could be just as unrelated to cash flow and profit levels but, none the less, just as capable of enormous capital gains as property values. It seemed that a new and immensely profitable market was developing, where property developers like Bond, Skase and Lowy could occupy strategic places. In an emerging information economy, assets were now those previously intangible things that were only profitable in circulation: the fickle audiences and consumers of entertainment and information. Getting into TV meant becoming part of the information revolution; in fact TV was a pivotal institution in this process. And it was made more important by the convergence of telecommunications and mass communications. Skase and Bond played this game to the limit. They attempted to control as much intellectual property as they could. Bond extended his interests into Hong Kong TV and British satellite television, and into knowledge production itself with a university. Skase extended his interests into US production companies, and attempted to buy up the Hollywood major, United Artists.

The Bonds, Lowys and Skases would have taken heart from the fact that during the 1980s American media stock changed hands at grossly inflated prices, and new players were entering that market with little or no media experience. Debt financing was used there too.

Also, it was commonly assumed that, by the turn of the century, there would (in the words of a Time Warner executive), be only five or six large global communications companies. Skase and Bond, at least, wanted to have a shot at becoming one of those companies. Indeed, a trend towards international oligopoly characterised the 1980s in cinema, VCR markets, publishing and cable TV. This trend is redrawing established connections within and between language markets, pushing the international book, the international TV programme (now including information and sporting programming), and, of course, that old familiar chestnut, the international film.

COMING UNSTUCK

It is clear now just how misguided this game-plan was. The TV industry was not complacent in Sydney, Melbourne, Brisbane and Adelaide. Indeed, there simply was not room for rapid increases in advertising revenues there. Australia, according to 1984 rankings, was second only to the USA in terms of advertising expenditure as a proportion of gross domestic product. Additionally, TV's total market share of advertising revenues compared favourably with equivalent market environments, Canada and the USA, where 'networking' was often held to be more advanced.

The expected benefits from national integration were also based on some questionable assumptions. First, *the national integration of advertising preceded by many years the national integration of programming*. Sophisticated national placement strategies had already evolved to get around the then relatively disconnected Australian TV system. Just because the networks were not doing the co-ordinating does not mean that efficient and effective co-ordination was not being done.

Second, national integration of programming and the move to simultaneous programming produced mixed results. The previously mixed system, wherein connection and disconnection existed side by side, permitted a degree of audience community knowledge about appropriate programme scheduling. The disconnected system accommodated the different climatic and cultural conditions pertaining in the different capitals. Subtropical Brisbane, for example, *does* go to sleep half an hour to an hour earlier than Sydney. Such programming flexibility and tailoring to local knowledges were now out. The national programming which evolved was, perforce, most critically centred on fitting somewhere between Sydney and Melbourne. Under these conditions some of the benefits of a nationally integrated system were cancelled out by the losses associated with no longer having in place locally responsive scheduling. Accompanying the loss of flexibility in scheduling was a loss of local programme production capacity and identity. The loss of both may well have cancelled out any positive response to the emergence of simultaneous national programming.

Third, the extension of additional TV services to regional Australia is proving less than a licence to print money. Regional TV companies are faced with the huge capital costs involved in building TV transmitters and signal translation facilities. Problems of signal reach have also accompanied their move onto the UHF frequency – the worst possible frequency for signal transmission over distance. The regional stations are just not able to be milked of profits as the US literature suggested they should have been. (Perhaps they can be in a decade's time! But by then cable will be around). Indeed in many cases programming is being supplied at minimal cost to regionals so as to permit them to develop the infrastructure for the network of regional stations required by aggregation.

The attempt to establish asset values unrelated to cash flows in the information sector overlooked the difference between property values and information market values. The stability and profitability of the Australian commercial TV industry was itself a product of practices, routines, cost monitoring and managed competition in the context of viewers exercising consumer sovereignty. It was not a given. Nor was it achieved by licence scarcity. Australia has had *five* well established quasi-national networks reaching 10 per cent of the viewing audience since the mid-1980s. And it has had *four* quasi-national networks since 1965.

Each of the new network proprietors had limited broadcasting experience. And this showed in their incapacity to manage costs and competition. Each used debt, not equity, to finance their takovers (replicating in part the US experience of broadcast deregulation). And this exposed them to high interest rates after 1988 and downturns in advertising revenues in 1990.

Each, when faced with considerable interest bills in late 1988, engaged in cut-throat competition in an attempt to increase market share at each other's expense. The result was not increased audience shares but the opposite. Expenditure on local programmes and imported programme costs dramatically escalated into the 1988/9 financial year: the cost of overseas programming doubled, local programme costs rose by nearly a third, and general expenditure increased by a third.[16] And this at a time of record domestic interest rates in Australia. Additionally, for at least two of these networks, Nine and Seven, management fees paid to the management team and parent company more than doubled in the same period. (Such management fees were critical to Skase and Bond increasing their own personal wealth in the context of the 'publicly listed company' of which they were chief executives).

As a result of the competition for programming, in early 1989 Australian networks entered into unprecedented output contracts with US production houses and, in the case of the Seven Network, signed an affiliation agreement with the American NBC network. Australia, with its 16.4 million people, was paying more for the broadcasting rights of *all* kinds of US TV than countries many times its population size, like the UK, Germany, Italy and Japan (of course, Australia has always paid more, per capita, than anywhere else for US programming). Additionally, it was now carrying part of the cost of developing programmes which US audiences, let alone Australian ones, would never see. These moves to integrate the Australian market with the US market came from the Australian competition for 'scarce' US programme resources – and not from the US.

The result: TV revenues, despite rising 15 per cent in 1989 (and 18 per cent in the financial year 1988–9), could barely meet the increased programming and networking costs. This left virtually no money to pay rising interest bills on debt. The consequence: receivership for Seven (the Quintex group of companies owed $A1.4 billion); losses for Ten in addition to the $A280 million loss suffered by Lowy when he sold Ten in September 1989,[17] leading, in turn, to its receivership with the collapse of its owner, Northern Star Holdings, with debts of $A455 million; and problems in meeting its $A367 million debt for Bond Media. At the time of writing, in 1990, costs are being reigned in: domestic and imported production costs have been on average halved and management fees are the subject of corporate affairs investigations.

THE SHAKE-OUT

What was left? Certainly not the ambition to be a global corporation. In its stead was the ambition to be the *Australian branch office* of a global corporation. The Ten Network, exploiting loopholes in the Broadcasting Act prohibiting foreign ownership above 20 per cent, had ceded 44 per cent of company control to foreign companies (including Thames TV, 10 per cent; *Daily Mail* & General Trust, 14.6 per cent; BT Australia, 11.5 per cent; and Murdoch's News Corporation, 4.9 per cent) in September 1989. But even this foreign shareholding was not enough to stave off receivers who were called in by the network's bankers in September 1990. In mid-1990 Bond Media executives dutifully plied the offices of US media companies seeking companies interested in an Australian junior partner. Reportedly they had a consortium lined up which included CBS, Paramount, a Paramount executive, TV New Zealand and Banker's Trust, to take up a 30 per cent stake in Bond Media, providing a much needed capital injection into the company of some $A232 million.[18] International company integration, with Australia as an offshoot on the parent's terms, was set to occur.

This integration was supported by the banks. The Australian clients to whom they had so assiduously extended credit lines were retrospectively labelled corporate 'cowboys'. They supported TV network moves to have the existing loophole permitting up to 49 per cent foreign ownership regularized. They saw such moves as a way of turning their bad debt into good debt. Their lobbying met with some early success. A lift of the foreign ownership level to 40–49 per cent was mooted by Labor before the federal election. Prime Minister Hawke was even alleged to have promised it to Nine's Chief, Sam Chisholm. Creditors saw overseas investors, like the US networks and programme production suppliers, adding a premium of somewhere between 30–40 per cent to the Network asking prices.[19] It was assumed that US and to a lesser extent UK media groups would want to keep in place the unparalleled arrangements the enterpreneurs had entered into with them, would want to keep alive their hopes of developing global perspective, and would have the added incentive of the cheaper price of money in the US market. Of course this is not how the networks and banks represented the situation. These *individuals* were prepared to bail Australia out; they did not want to interfere in Australian programmes; after all, the regulatory authority, the Australian Broadcasting Tribunal, looked after that area effectively.

The Federal government, and more particularly its new Communications Minister, Kim Beazley, faced a stark choice. The loophole could be maintained or regularised – in which case all Australian networks would quickly become 40–49 per cent foreign controlled and ultimately affiliated to the three major US TV networks, with consequences for the kind and nature of Australian commercial programming.[20] Alternatively, there could be a return to 20 per cent foreign ownership which would leave each of the networks open to cheap takeover bids from Australian investors and leave the banks with substantial debts to write-off (an estimated $A2 billion of debt is currently being carried by the TV industry).[21] The Labor government, facing a Labor caucus on balance opposed to lifting the ownership ceiling as a means of 'bailing out' the banks and the enterpreneurs for their bad investment decisions, supported Beazley on a return to the 20 per cent ownership level. Beazley's decisions should shift some of the loss (but not all) *onto the creditors rather than the TV audience and the production industry*.

In this context, the banks should be forced to accept write-downs in the value of the media assets they supported. Indeed the effect of this ruling was immediate. Packer acquired a controlling interest in Bond Media. Similarly, the liquidators of the Seven Network will find it difficult to get the $A635 million price-tag they demanded for the network in January 1990 – and even the $A400 million reputedly offered for it then. To date the liquidator has been reluctant to see the price per earning ratio come down from the estimated 13:1 tag to the 5:1 ratio implicit in Packer's bid for Nine. The liquidator will either sell now and face a $A235 million write-down, or hold on for twelve to eighteen months in the hope of obtaining a better price. Clearly the latter choice is not in the interests of industry stability and long-term planning within the network. With the Ten Network just being placed in receivership, the prospect of two networks in long-term receivership may well force the federal government to bow to pressure to revise upwards foreign ownership limits in the interests of both industry stability and to ensure that Kerry Packer does not become the Sylvio Berlusconi of Australian TV with *de facto* control over the Ten Network in addition to his control of Nine.

The real issue is now who pays the most – the *TV industry* or *the banks* – for the corporate and lending madness of the late 1980s. If it is the industry then it is likely to be continually in hock throughout the 1990s, with little hope of recovery in the short term. In this case ongoing local production difficulties and increased US TV content can be expected. If it is the banks who accept the losses and allow the write-down of media values to which they contributed so much, then some recovery in programme capacity can be expected in the next two years.

As it stands now, the Australian TV industry management is being hit on at least three fronts: continuing high levels of debt; high interest rates; and a dramatic slow down in the rate of increase of advertising revenues (down to an estimated 6 per cent increase after a 15 per cent increase in 1989). The resulting cost-cutting has led to a marked drop in the standard and quality of TV, which is starting to acquire a frumpy, undercapitalised image. Already the Australian Broadcasting Tribunal has made concessions on Australian content levels and can be expected to make more. Such concessions are in turn having their impact. Australian programming has, since the late 1960s, been the pivot around which prime-time ratings success has been hung. Its diminution and falling quality are leaving a gap in TV offerings to the public. Cost-cutting does not just impact upon TV's standing with audiences – it also impacts upon advertisers. As national content overall becomes further diminished, and what there is of it is increasingly impoverished, no amount of marketing in the short term will be able to convince audiences that there is something worth watching on TV – and that something would anyway be American TV. At times it seems the industry and the banks have forgotten that audiences are not permanently hooked to the set, and advertising is not exclusively oriented to TV. Just as Ten's ratings suffered from the community perception of corporate failure and cost-cutting, the other networks will suffer as the news gets out. There is no cross-ownership now which could allow Fairfax, Packer or Murdoch to suppress adverse comment about TV in their newspapers, as was alleged to have happened in the past.

Now the TV industry is feeling the chill winds that swept over their film, documentary and TV mini-series cousins after 1987. A new austerity has arrived. Gone are the $1 million parties to celebrate *Neighbours* 1,000th episode. Staff, from the bottom to the top are being laid off, salaries cut, production shelved.

In this context, it is a cash-strapped Australian government which is disproportionately carrying the can for continuity in production in the film industry. The Australian government, through the ABC, the Film Finance Corporation, SBS and the Australian Film Commission is keeping alive Australia's drama production capacity in terms of mini-series, one-off drama and documentaries and, therefore, much of our international export profile. Government agencies, not the private sector as such, are committing funds to TV and cinema production. Even now proprietors like Kerry Packer would probably not contribute much in the short term. A return to a stable oligopolistic environment would see new proprietors doing just enough to maintain an edge over competitors. Packer's record, like his father's, was never one of destroying the competition – he simply wanted to maintain an edge.

THE LOST POSSIBILITIES OF AUSTRALIAN TV

So an industry which had not lost money since 1957 finally did so in 1989 and 1990. This was a remarkable achievement. TV networks were operating at a loss in an environment where advertising revenues did *not* decrease, indeed, actually increased well above inflation. Revenues have been increasing each year and at a healthy growth rate since 1980. This was *not* an industry hit by falling sales, by a recession, by diminishing returns; it was an industry hit by rising sales, an overheated economy and increasing returns.

Many possibilities have been irretrievably lost to the Australian film industry. Unlike Europe and the UK, Australian TV had so much going for it. The period 1986–90 should have been the time when Australia consolidated its share of international TV programme markets. It was so well placed. It already had a competitive TV market dedicated to producing relatively low cost TV drama and informational programming. It was used to producing popular product, geared to ratings. It was well placed to take advantage of the emerging export markets for popular TV which were opening up in Europe and the UK with the introduction of commercial TV, cable and direct broadcasting by satellite. As the older restricted and paternalistic services in the European system were being broken down, there had probably never been (apart from the beginning of the first world war) a more propitious time for Australia to get into international audiovisual export, secure a larger market niche and take advantage of what it did have.[22] Furthermore, Australia had a comparatively debt-free TV system. Apart from the capital requirements to enable equalisation and the Perth licence, a TV system was already set in place with five-channel competition in the major capital city markets. Each of the commercial licensees were either long-standing companies whose investment had been recouped many times over or were people who had not paid huge entry prices to get into the market. The existing Australian TV networks were thus well poised to take advantage of the changing profile of international TV and the development of demand for popular TV programmes.

But Australian comparative advantages did not stop there. As of the mid-1980s, the structural impediments to an effective nationally co-ordinated market in TV programmes as distinct from a nationally co-ordinated market in advertising (which was there from inception) were removed. Twenty-five years after a third commercial station came to Brisbane and Adelaide, Perth (now bigger than Adelaide) got a third licence, and equalisation was set to permit the greater integration of regional markets into the national system. For the first time it appeared that the whole of the TV system, not just the Sydney, Melbourne, Adelaide and Brisbane segments of it, would pay equally for Australian programming. At last true economies of scale were possible. Changes in the basic technological infrastructure with AUSSAT and pricing policy also dramatically reduced the cost of sending messages over distance – so long as you sent a lot of them. Australian TV had the money now, and the technological infrastructure, for an expanded and higher budget production capacity in drama and informational programming areas. Australia was, in short, 'lucky'. The trauma and investment costs of establishing and managing a competitive environment were behind it (France, Germany, Italy, Spain, even the UK, were only now moving into this era). And the final pieces, conferring additional 'economies of scale' in the national market, were now in place.

The Australian TV system was thus well poised in the international market, well able to produce a commodity capable of export into English language and European markets, capable of producing not simply more, but better quality TV, well placed to manage *on its own terms* the popular audience oriented 'internationalisation' taking place in the more profitable parts of the international TV system, and well able to develop a market niche as a medium-sized production centre.

But it is now history that this did not happen. The Australian commercial TV system managed to successfully erode its comparative advantage of a debt-free TV service and it acquired debts in excess of TV establishment costs. It diminished its production levels and production capacity. It increased production costs with no accompanying increase in standards – and then later stripped down productions with a loss in standards. It lost the possibility of managing internationalisation on its own terms and so had it managed for it. It lost a possible place as a successful medium-level international producer. Now it was just another one struggling in a difficult environment.

While Europe was struggling with more TV stations reducing advertising revenues, and new TV programmes eating into audience shares, Australia was struggling with the same number of TV stations and relatively static audience shares. Australia, awash with talk of the need for an international orientation, critically *turned inward, not outward*. Instead of managing a competitive market environment as the Packers, Fairfaxes, *Herald & Weekly Times*, and Murdoch had, the entrepreneurs engaged in a critically destructive competition which squeezed margins, lifted production costs and the price of imported programming, which led to international integration with Australian TV, not as an importer and exporter of programming, *but principally as an importer*, looking for limited coproduction opportunities. In short, Australian commercial TV was not prepared to just get on with the business of Australian TV; it had to reinvent it.

CONCLUSION

Is this Australian case a cautionary tale about too much deregulatory change occurring too quickly for an industry to handle it? Is it an example of over-blown ambitions to integrate information sectors coming unstuck? Is it an example, *in extremis*, of the 1980s culture of business in English-language markets where debt replaced equity, where leveraged buy-outs ruled, where a management culture sought resources for itself with little sense of obligation to its public shareholders or employee base, where paper profits and artful schemes of tax avoidance and minimization ruled over ethical business practice? Perhaps it is a combination of all of these. It is what happened when 'the market was left to decide', Australian-style!

NOTES

This chapter first appeared in *Screen*, 32 (1991)

1 This paper is a substantially revised version of an article entitled 'Of money and madness', in *Filmnews* (July 1990), pp. 8–11.
2 Packer's Consolidated Press converted its $A200 million in preference shares owed by Bond Media and a further $A25 million in interests and dividends into 55 per cent of Bond Media. An additional $A79 million was to be raised to pay off debt to Bell Resources.
3 Neil Shoebridge, 'Ten: now for the hard part', *Business Review Weekly*, 22 June 1990, p. 23.
4 Tony Thomas, 'Regional TV's woes', *Business Review Weekly*, 2 February 1990, pp. 54–9.
5 *Sunday Herald*, 1 July 1990.
6 Grundy's has recently set up production subsidiaries in Spain, Belgium, Luxembourg and the Netherlands; see *Screen Digest*, (July 1990), 150.
7 Terry Ohisson, chief of Crawford Productions, quoted in Guy Alcorn and Raymond Gill, *The West Australian*, 30 June 1990.
8 For an account of the politics of these media changes see Paul Chadwick, *Media Mates*, Macmillan, Melbourne, 1989.
9 Two states, Western Australia and Southern Australia, have been omitted from the equalisation plan on the grounds of their insufficient regional popu-

lation to support three commercial stations. Neither Tasmania nor the Northern Territory were considered for equalisation.

10 Tom O'Regan, 'Towards a high communications policy: assessing recent changes within Australian broadcasting', *Continuum*, 2 (1) (1989), 135–58; see also 'The background to TV networking', in Glen Lewis and Elizabeth Moore, *Australian Communications Technology and Policy*, Centre for Information Studies & AFTRS. Sydney, 1988, pp. 126–43; and 'Aspects of the Australian film & TV interface', *Australian Journal of Screen Theory*, 17/18 (1986), 5–33.

11 Gomery notes that 'One study . . . found that between 1964 and 1976 network income increased some 575 per cent (some 44 per cent per year) while payments to affiliates rose only 34 per cent (some 3 per cent per year)'; see Douglas Gomery, 'Economic change in the US television industry', *Screen*, 25(2) (1984), 63.

12 Australia has a well-known capacity for 'creative accountancy' produced by the tendency for professional groupings to be 'self-regulated' and by the state (rather than federally) based nature of much corporate affairs legislation.

13 Austin Donnelly, 'No tax – no profit', *The Independent Monthly*, May 1990, p. 19.

14 Max Walsh, *Sydney Morning Herald*, 27 April 1981, p. 23. Walsh argued that Packer and Murdoch (who sold Ten) received a gift of $A1 billion as the value of their assets rose from $A800 million to $A1.8 billion. For a discussion of these asset values see Julianne Schultz, 'Failing the public' in Helen Wilson (ed.). *Australian Communications and the Public Sphere*. Macmillan, Melbourne, 1989, pp. 68–84.

15 See Alex Ben Bock, 'Who is Christopher Skase?', *Channels* (September 1988), 46.

16 L. Wright, 'TV incurs its first loss', *Sydney Morning Herald*, 22 May 1989.

17 Candice Sutton, *The Sun-Herald*, 3 September 1989, p. 6.

18 *Variety*, 30 May 1990, p. 48.

19 Tony Burchill, 'Saga of woe continues for the embattled TV industry', *Financial Review* (Australia), 8 May 1990.

20 Alan Kohler, *Sunday Age*, 13 May 1990.

21 Megan Jones, *Sunday Herald*, 29 March 1990.

22 For an excellent discussion of the opportunities Australian cinema groups deliberately eschewed in the teens of this century see Ina Bertrand and William Routt, 'The big bad combine', in A. Moran and T. O'Regan (eds), *Australian Screen*, Penguin, Ringwood, 1989, pp. 3–28.

Chapter 5

Australian cinema

An anachronism in the 1980s?

Elizabeth Jacka

The original inspiration for those who wished to found a film industry in Australia was the desire to have a cinema which could speak of the national and the local, to have films in which, in the words of an early industry campaigner; 'the workaday world is integrated with the world of one's imagination'.[1] This perhaps naive but honorable aim has suffered many vicissitudes in the period 1968 to the present as the sharks and the crocodiles and the small fry scrambled for their place in the cash flows offered by changing funding regimes, but it remains still somehow important as the *point* of all the much more visible flurry surrounding the business side of the industry, and it remains the touchstone against which one wants ultimately to make the judgement about whether the last twenty years of a government-assisted film industry have been worth all the trouble.

But as the 1980s have unfolded and the level of the internationalisation of culture and information has grown, the ideal of a national cinema has looked increasingly naive and anachronistic. At the same time, however, Australia has a formidable level of government regulation, the purpose of which is to preserve the Australian character of various forms of cultural production, including cinema. These systems are under constant attack from established media interests; and the present moment, when a major inquiry into Australian content on television is drawing to a close, seems a good time to examine critically the fate of that dream of an Australian national cinema.

THE TRADITIONAL ARGUMENTS FOR REGULATION

It is impossible to define Australian content in television.[2]

'Australian culture' is an empty box into which various people can put what suits them.[3]

In recent years art critics, cultural critics and media commentators have increasingly endorsed the above judgements on 'Australian' culture and have expended a good deal of energy demonstrating the great variety of ways in which a notion of 'Australian-ness' has been constructed in various places and for various purposes.[4] In addition, the debate around the Bicentennial has made it virtually impossible to speak about nation or national identity without intense qualification and discomfort. As has often been pointed out during 1988, the Bicentennial represents nothing that Aboriginal people feel inclined to celebrate and, for many others, its nationalistic and populist excesses have constituted a major problem.

Yet it is very difficult to see any signs of these disturbances or this sophisticated and detailed argument about constructions of Australian-ness appearing in the debates around Australian content in film and television. Here we find the same rhetorical positions that were expressed throughout the 1960s and 1970s, when the situation was profoundly different. There seems to be an ever-widening gap between cultural critique and cultural policy.

The reasons for this are easy to understand. The proponents of the regulation position feel (and rightly) a constant threat from the proponents of deregulation. In June 1988, Christopher Skase, the new owner of the Seven Network, warned the House of Representatives' inquiry into the operations of the Australian Broadcasting Tribunal that if new players were allowed into the televison industry, he would 'automatically and instantly' cut the level of Australian production back to the statutory requirement of 104 hours from the 300 hours currently being broadcast. This threat means that proponents of regulation are constantly thrust into a defensive position which militates against open and critical debate about the adequacy of the terms in which arguments for Australian content are couched. Let us examine some of these arguments briefly in order to pull out the common discourses that underlie them.

The following are a series of key passages from various official or representative policy documents that span the period 1969 to 1988 and which exhibit a remarkable consistency of rhetoric; although there are also some significant shifts:

> it is in the interests of this nation to encourage its local film and television industry so as to increase the quantity and improve the quality of local material in our cinema and on our television screens . . . our audiences are subjected to the ever-increasing sociological influence of imported material, and our writers, actors and film-makers are unable to fulfil their creative potential . . . this situation hampers Australia's efforts to interpret itself to the rest of the world.
> (Australian Council for the Arts,
> Interim Report: Film Committee, 1969)

Australia, as a nation, cannot accept, in this powerful and persuasive medium, the current flood of other nations' productions on our screens without it constituting a very serious threat to our national identity.
(Report, Interim Board, Australian Film Commission, 1975)

A healthy and vibrant domestic industry is vital in promoting our cultural identity and projecting a positive image of Australians.
(Mr Gary Punch, Minister for Arts, announcing formation of Film Finance Corporation, May 1988)

The Tribunal believes that the primary objective of any legislative and regulatory requirements for Australian program contents has been and should remain a cultural one: to ensure that television plays a role in showing Australians the realities of our own society and helps us to form a view of ourselves and our place in this world. The continued existence of a viable and highly skilled production industry is a valuable concomitant of this objective, but it cannot be the paramount concern of the Tribunal.
(Gill Appleton, *How Australia Sees Itself: The Role of Commercial Television*, ABT, Sydney, 1987)

The consistency lies in the call for an industry which can help us to form a sense of 'national identity'; the shift that occurs is that in the later passages there is less concentration on the theme of the evils or the polluting influence of foreign material. However, the notion of foreignness is never far from the centre of things: it is the covert Other in the definition of 'Australian': describing something as Australian depends on differentiating it from something which it is not.

And how is television going to play its role in constructing a national identity? According to the ABT's 1977 Report, *Self Regulation for Broadcasters*, it will be by cultivating a distinctively Australian 'look':

An Australian television service *which looks unmistakably Australian* has long been regarded as a highly desirable ideal. However, the means of ensuring the production and presentation of Australian programs of a quantity necessary to achieve *a distinctly Australian look* has proved to be a most difficult problem.[5] (my emphasis)

And how is this 'look' to be achieved? The answer differs slightly depending on whether it is film or television that is being regulated, and whether it is early or later in the period 1976–88, but basically it comes down to the number of Australian elements in the production process. For example, the ABT Program Standards define indigenous drama as 'a drama written or [adapted] by Australians, and produced and performed by an Australian crew and cast'. This is elaborated in both the 10BA Australian content certification requirements for film and in the

ABT's guidelines for part-indigenous programs (based on the 10BA criteria) to mean that in determining the level of Australian involvement the following things would be examined: the subject-matter of the film, the place where the film was made, the nationalities or residential status of the leading creative inputs, the copyright owners, the owners of the production company and the sources of finance of the film.

There are a number of consistent themes which run through these various statements; these are not necessarily consciously intended but they are an unavoidable concomitant of the discourses on which the rhetoric depends for its effectivity. These are:

- Australia is a unified entity.
- There is an essential Australian-ness which can be captured in an 'Australian look'.
- There is a difference or set of differences which marks Australia off from other nations and Australians from the people of other nations.
- These differences are more significant than the differences within Australia.
- Foreign or imported material is somehow harmful or pernicious and encourages 'cultural dependency'.
- Australians need to 'see' themselves in order to form a 'cultural identity' and become 'culturally independent'.
- If Australian nationals (or residents) have creative control over production of films/programmes, this will help to ensure the 'Australian look'.

The discourse underlying the official positions turns out, unsurprisingly, to be the familiar radical nationalist one, although we should be careful of too easily making the equation of the national and the nationalist. The extensive recent debate around Australian content has been, on both sides, long on rhetoric and the repetition of well-worn formulae and remarkably short on critical interrrogation of the terms in which the debate is couched and the underlying philosophy of a national cultural policy in the circumstances of the late 1980s and the 1990s. Even the best contribution, Gill Appleton's background paper to the ABT's 'The price of being Australian' Conference, 1987, continually makes statements which take the notion of an Australian cultural identity for granted, rather than problematising it. The following statement perfectly illustrates this tendency. 'Films like *Breaker Morant* and *Gallipoli*, and mini-series like *Anzacs*, *Bodyline* and *Vietnam* have interpreted (or more accurately, reinterpreted) our history *from an Australian*, rather than a British or American, perspective'[6] (my emphasis).

The rhetoric constantly features phrases like 'adequately reflect our way of life', 'show Australians to themselves', 'give us a more realistic view of our society (than foreign programmes can)'; and a more sophisticated and elaborated version of the same thing, for example, in Actors' Equity 1983 Submission to the ABT's Australian Content Inquiry: 'Local programs can provide Australian viewers with entertainment to which they directly relate, and enjoy because of their personal relevance, while experiencing a reflection of their own social and cultural values, hopes, fears and humour.'[7]

In all these statements there is the continual reference to 'we', 'our', 'Australian', as if these terms were unproblematic. There is also the unfortunate assumption that what the mass media (or any other cultural form) do is reflect, or show, so that if one ensures that the film or program-makers are Australian and they chose Australian subjects, then the result will be an accurate, or authentic representation of 'the Australian way of life' or 'our' hopes, fears, history, perspective, sense of humour, etc. So a realist aesthetic is combined with a unitary conception of Australia.

Now of course none of the proponents of Australian content would be naive enough to subscribe to any of these positions if confronted with them head-on. All would proclaim that of course Australia is a diverse, multicultural society, divided by race, class, gender, etc., and of course the media do not *reflect*, but rather render material in a way that is infinitely complicated by narrative, genre, representational and other codes and conventions. So I do not mean to caricature a position and then make an easy critical target of it. Rather, I am concerned to show that, although the proponents of Australian content do hold a more sophisticated position, the ways in which the debate has been formulated have been constrained by the radical nationalist discourse, in spite of its inadequacies, both because it does have such a strong rhetorical effectiveness, especially in the currently fervent nationalist-populist environment cultivated by the Labor government, and because it is the easiest one to legislate for. The problems with the radical nationalist discourse are not just that it is a bit of an embarrassment to leftists, who would like to support the notion of regulating for Australian content but resist being locked into a nationalist position that has come in for so much criticism, but also that it is so susceptible to right-wing, deregulationist critiques (especially those put about by the network owners and other powerful figures in the film and television business). For even though the favoured rhetoric of the Hawke Labor government is a national-populist one, in reality it is about anything but preservation of Australian economic independence; as Boris Frankel puts it: 'The major achievement of the Hawke government has been to destroy those institutional mechanisms (financial controls, tariff barriers, etc.) which permitted a greater political sovereignty by Australian citizens over their own resources.'[8]

THE NATIONAL AND NATIONALISM

A very sophisticated version of the argument for national cultural protection has recently been put forward, not in the context of media or film, but in the educational sphere, in the 1987 Report of the Committee to Review Australian Studies in Tertiary Education (CRASTE), entitled *Windows onto Worlds*.[9] This report, which argues for an 'Australianising' of the post-secondary curriculum, is introduced by a remarkably lively and fertile chapter called, significantly, 'Producing Australia'. It puts forward a nationalist position which at the same time attempts to take account of both the differences that exist within Australia and to avoid racism and cultural isolationism. In particular, the authors attempt a particularly ingenious redefinition of the terms 'patriotism' and 'nationalism' which they hope can recognise both the diversity and the unity of Australia as a nation-state and form the basis of seeing the 'national' as the level on which cultural protection can occur.

For them 'patriotism' is not a love of country (in the sense of nation) or a sentiment of 'my country (nation) right or wrong', but rather a love of country in the sense of a locality, a place (not just geographical but cultural):

> Patriotism refers to a love of one's country, such as the feelings which Aborigines had before they were enmeshed into European social structures, and which persist despite that system . . . patriotism extends into affection for the people who made their lives in these surroundings, hence the interest in family history and in televised dramas about our past.
>
> (p. 17)

while

> nationalism is that group of practices which helps to make or keep a country independent of foreign domination . . . nationhood is one means for giving effect to the values flowing into patriotism, of protecting the landscape and promoting our people's welfare.
>
> (ibid.)

However, this nationalism does not exclude internationalism, in fact the latter requires it, for 'internationalism rejoices in a multiplicity of independent nations . . . [it] is not the abolition of nations, but is built upon self-reliant nations which require neither chauvinism nor cosmopolitanism to cope with their country's inadequacies and achievements' (ibid.).

The report goes on to argue the importance of an Australianised curriculum in building the local knowledges and local culture that can play their part in making the national economy self-reliant. A very similar argument could be mounted for 'Australianising' our film and media culture, although it has not so far been done with such sophistication and detail.

How successful is this revamped version of radical nationalism? As one critic of the report has pointed out, the definition given of nationalism is, of course, circular.[10] Andrew Milner points out that to argue that the nation-state is necessary in order to guard the independence of the nation is to simply continue to take for granted the natural primacy of nations when, as Benedict Anderson has so persuasively argued, the nation is no more – and no less – than an 'imagined community'.[11] The concept of nation underlying *Windows onto Worlds* is modelled on the liberal conception of society composed of free and equal individuals coexisting in a peaceful system of interaction through exchange. The notion of national dependence and independence is parasitic on this model and makes sense only so long as one takes the nation as a unified, self-governing, self-sufficient entity like the liberal conception of the individual.

But how much sense does this notion of national dependence and independence mean in the present phase of multinational capitalism (if indeed it ever made sense)? It denies the reality of the way social life is organised in the last half of the twentieth century. Multinational capitalism, presently reinforced by the deregulationist impulses of Australian and other advanced capitalist governments, is *dissolving* national boundaries, and we are increasingly positioned in a world whose economic, cultural and informational organisation is transnational, not national. It is only at a formal political level that nation-states retain some identity.

Milner's response to the problems of a nationalist position is a thorough-going internationalist one. He points out nationalism's bad record – all the cases in history where it has degenerated into expansionism and racism (e.g., in Nazi Germany) or has been used simply as an ideology of the ruling class in pursuing imperialist or colonialist campaigns of invasion and conquest. This is the familiar left-wing critique of nationalism and it has its point, but Milner is too selective in his choice of historical examples, for he ignores all those cases where nationalism has been a progressive force and has been a vehicle for anti-imperialist struggles (Vietnam or, locally, the struggles around Aboriginal land-rights or American bases in Australia). He sees nationalism as the enemy of internationalism and of socialism, but as Frankel points out:

> It is not radical to be in favour of the break-up of the nation-state. The main beneficiaries of this are the large transnational corporations, and the bureaucrats eager to rationalize whole communities, regions and industries away as they sit in their boardrooms in Brussels, Tokyo, New York or Moscow.[12]

The other side of the critique of nationalism, is the one that has been more commonly voiced in Australia in recent years, especially around the Bicentennial, and that is the critique of nationalism as populism. From Bob Hawke to Alan Bond (not such a great distance after all) this is the version of nationalism that has been used to sell everything from economic policies to beer; populism takes a particular image of the national (in our case one deriving from the Anglo-Celtic, working-class, Australian legend) and uses it as a metonym for the whole nation, thus denying not only cultural, ethnic, race and class differences, but more importantly, the conflict and division that stem from them.[13] It thus acts as both a concealment of and sanction against political struggle: in the name of the national-popular it depoliticises social and economic change. This aspect of nationalism has come in for considerable analysis and criticism in recent years, but is a continuing and frightening social force, reappearing again only recently in the debate around the Fitzgerald Report on Immigration, the question of an Aboriginal Treaty and in weird manifestations like the *Heart of a Nation* movement's campaign against Japanese investment in Queensland.

Dependency theory which studies international economic, political and cultural power relations, uses a model of dependency not based on the notion of one nation dominating another, but a centre-periphery model which recognises that the world economic (and cultural) order is a network of relations and flows, with power centres located at sites that cannot be simply identified with nations, though this is usually the way in which it is rendered at the level of meaning and therefore struggle. The centre-periphery model allows the possibility of conceptualising the uneven distribution of power *within* nations and of the power alliances that exist between elements within one nation and another (the multinational companies and their local subsidiaries and the other local entities that are tied to them, to mention only the most obvious case). This perspective also enables us to conceptualise not only the intricate and many-sided relationship that exists between *economic* power relations within the complex world economic system, but also the ways in which cultural industries are both part of this economic order (they are after all *industries*) and how the directions of the flow of culture and information sustain and reinforce the power differentials within the world system.

Unless one takes this perspective one is locked into a view which is easy to caricature and to undermine. In other words, if the 'cultural imperialism' thesis is given a nationalist cast, if it is rendered as some version of 'Australia good, America bad', it is wide open to right-wing deregulationist accusations of chauvenism, parochialism and xenophobia as favouring, in Tony Ginnane's immortal words, a 'kangaroo quotient'.

Older versions of cultural nationalism – for example, those that are embodied in some of the earliest official documents arguing for national cultural protection – embody an essentialist notion of the Australian-ness that is to be exhibited in the indigenous cultural works that the policy will foster; this can be a populist version that identifies Australia with various supposed egalitarian qualities that are said to characterise its people, or other versions which, for example, identify Australia with certain qualities of its landscape or even, much more confusedly, with aspects from its traditional vanishing past, as is now the danger with some deployments in white culture of traditional Aboriginal art and artefacts.[14]

More recent versions of it attempt to move away from this essentialist notion and work more with the notion of difference, adopting a position which acknowledges all the diversity within Australia but also maintains that, in spite of this diversity, there are still significant differences between what is Australian and what is not. They acknowledge the connection between certain aspects of the Australian way of life and those in other areas of the world but argue that in Australia these things exhibit a difference which gives them a kind of Australian 'accent'. For example, *Windows onto Worlds* says 'Differences between classes and sexes . . . do exist within Australian culture, but those experiences have a specific location which distinguishes them from parallel differences in Vietnam or Spain' (p. 27). Graeme Turner uses the accent metaphor quite explicitly:

> Australia is only physically an island and . . . its history is enclosed within a larger, Western history . . . the examination of the cultural specificity of our narratives is not in any way an argument for their uniqueness but rather for a kind of Australian accent which is audible and distinctive when placed in relation to that of other English speakers.[15]

Here again we see that, in spite of efforts to move away from essentialism, in any attempt to establish *the difference* of Australia or Australian cultural artefacts essentialism returns.

THE LOCAL AND THE NATIONAL

So far I have been discussing only cultural arguments for regulation of Australian content, but of course there are a couple of different though related arguments. One is the economic argument; the other the need to safeguard employment. One of the reasons for regulating for Australian content is to help counteract the economic imbalance that exists between the scale of overseas industries, especially of course the US industry, and the local one. Product, both film and television, is much more cheaply acquired from overseas (though this is said to be changing) and without some special requirement at least on television stations to broadcast

Australian material, the economic logic of the situation would suggest acquiring all products from overseas. This argument does not of course by itself justify regulating for Australian content; it only shows why Australian production doesn't happen as it were spontaneously. A separate argument is needed to demonstrate the desirability of local content in the first place, so we are back in the cultural arena.

Of course it is only because of Australia's subordinate role in the world economic and political order and because of the dominance of, on the one hand, the huge American cultural industries (cinema, television, the music industry, etc.) and, on the other, the dominance of European (and to a lesser extent American) traditions in art and high culture (classical music, literature, the visual arts, etc.) that we even have a debate about local content and the desirability of various regulatory or other measures to safeguard it. To put the argument this way is already to be in a defensive posture. It is interesting to note that, in the case of high cultural areas like literature and the visual arts, it makes little sense to legislate *for* Australian content; instead, government policy centres on various kinds of subsidy to support the activities of writers, painters, etc. The imagined threat to Australian content comes in those areas which are industrially organised or commercially based, like film and television. The fact that it does not happen as much in the similarly structured popular music industry is related to the comparatively lower costs of production there, so that by and large Australian popular music can pay for itself in the domestic market (although the Australian music quota on radio stations was necessary to kick this off). The higher costs of television and film production made them generally unviable in the domestic market, and it is no accident that the greatest pressures against regulation turn up in this area.

One of the problems with film, especially with its huge (though seldom realised) potential for 'blue-sky' profits, is that private greed tends to overcome public purpose, and the desire to realise these dreamt-of riches (which can only be achieved in the American market) means that movies are made here whose 'souls' are trying very hard to lie elsewhere. It is quite possible to fulfil all the requirements for Australian content (or at least enough of them to satisfy the minister) and still make films which deliberately distance themselves from local concerns and place themselves somewhere else; it is often not clear where.[16]

The second argument is the need to safeguard Australian employment. This requirement is explicitly embodied in Section 114 of the Broadcasting and Television Act and it is also found in the 10BA Australian content requirements for film, though less there purely for the employment reason than because a connection is being made between Australian creative control and Australian content. The unions and associations have been active to varying degrees in ensuring that Australian production does use

Australian actors and other creative personnel as far as possible, as was discussed in the first section. However, the employment argument is in a sense also part of the cultural one. The very existence of the professions covered by the various unions (the actors, writers, directors, designers, photographers, etc.) depends on the prior existence of the various forms of cultural production, and their expansion depends on the growth of the various cultural forms.

What then can we salvage from the set of problems around the concept of the national and what are the implications for regulation of Australian content in film and television? Clearly, both the economic argument and the employment argument require a national solution; in spite of the breakdown of national boundaries caused by capitalism in its present phase, economies are still administered along national lines, even when this administration is tightly constrained by transnational forces. Thus in order to protect the film and television industry as local industries and to give employment, some national regulatory policy which protects Australian-based companies and workers is appropriate. But what of the arguments on the cultural level? What *is* the thing called 'Australian content'?

While not wanting to suggest that it is the regulations which bring this about, it seems to me that Australian content can point in one of two directions. The first is in the direction of the nationalist, the populist, the touristy – projections of a mythicised essentialist Australian image, which has a reassuring and consensualist force at home and an impact overseas that is a mixture of the spectacle of the exotic and the presentation of nostalgic myths of innocence that bring comfort to audiences caught in confusing, difficult and even violent times. As Paul Taylor says:

> Australian culture hasn't necessarily 'come of age'; rather it is the beneficiary of a world-wide loss of confidence and nostalgic yearning for lost utopias. How else can the endless cranking out of Australian landscape myths and tales of our youthful energy – that is, a perpetually young adulthood – be explained?[17]

This version of Australian content has much in common with the radical nationalist position, or perhaps flows from it; it is concerned to establish *the* difference between the culture of Australia and that of other nations. Within this framework, too, it is possible to take up an anti-American (or in former days anti-British) position. It is remarkable how often this position produces rhetoric which condemns Hollywood cinema as formulaic, mass, inauthentic, lacking artistic merit, lacking 'quality', even corrupting, in contrast with our own authentic, worthwhile and uplifting home-grown product. So underlying the postion is, in Ross Gibson's phrase, an 'Anglo-centric humanist aesthetic', and a pessimistic Frankfurt-school-inspired condemnation of mass popular culture.[18]

The other direction in which Australian content faces is towards not the national but the local.[19] A localist position recognises that the local is suppressed almost as much in American culture as it is in Australian, so that a championing of localism does not mean setting up an opposition between a national 'us' and a foreign 'them'. However, because of the industrial dominance of Hollywood, the American 'local' has more often erupted and even achieved popularity than that of other countries. Witness the Philadelphia of a film like *Birdy*, or the bizarre geographic/ psychic landscape of Jim Jarmusch's *Down By Law*, or even the very specific class/ethnic detail in a 'mass' film like *Saturday Night Fever*. The local doesn't necessarily mean the veristic, in the sense of mirroring or reflecting a society or subculture, because the local can be intensely medicated or mythologised or fantasised or transformed by generic and other operations. However, it probably does mean authentic, in the sense that what is presented in the local is recognisable as applying to a particular and specific set of circumstances and forces that operate at any given time and place, be they signs of place, accent and idiom, or more diffuse but no less vivid ways of hooking into the social unconscious or social 'imaginary' of a particular subculture. Conceiving the local in this way does not entail any particular exclusion of what is not Australian; the local in a postmodern society is a huge accretion of influences from many sources, from traditional through technological to what is sometimes called 'junk' culture:

> You might start to understand how the definition of location in Australia must nowadays take heed of the effects of transnational media, shifting spheres of geopolitical influence, and the epistemological changes brought about in citizens as a result of their increased mobility within systems of communication and information. A notion of locality can entail all these things, without negating the continuing influence of more traditional criteria of place – longitude, latitude, climate, and long-running legends, myths, histories, and economic dependencies.[20]

What I am calling the 'local', the British cultural historian and critic, Patrick Wright, calls 'Everyday Life', by which he means the concept as elaborated by the philosopher Agnes Heller:

> Everyday life is the historically conditioned framework in which the imperatives of natural sustenance (eating, sleeping . . .) come to be socially determined: it is in the intersubjectivity of everyday life that human self-reproduction is welded to the wider process of social reproduction.[21]

Wright is concerned to assert the importance of 'the national' in the organisation of everyday life, condemning the traditional left-wing critiques of nationalism as so much bourgeois ideology for assuming 'those millions who have lived, argued, hoped and died by the nation' are sheep, the nationalist wool pulled over their eyes. For him the genuine tensions and aspirations of everyday life find expression in various renditions of the nation, be they celebratory or not, and, in turn, the nation gets reconceptualised according to the vicissitudes of everyday life. Wright is particularly concerned to show that the experience or memory or representation of a shared national *past* is a particularly important aspect of a symbolism that can give meaning. As he says, 'in this respect, the nation works to re-enchant a disenchanted everyday life'.[22] It need not be the official or jingoistic version of the nation that re-enchants; it may instead be, says Wright quoting Benjamin, 'a memory as it flashes up at a moment of danger'.

This idea seems particularly relevant to a consideration of much of the mini-series output of the past few years which, apparently obsessively, reruns versions of our national past, although how much re-enchantment, subversion and a genuine sense of danger is involved is a moot point.[23]

The local has the potential to be surprising, shocking, uncontrollable and thus ultimately subversive or oppositional. Paradoxically, the most familiar things can be surprising or even shocking if never before represented, like the Melbourne street-scapes of *Malcolm*, for example, or the lacerating human emotions in something like *My First Wife*, or the absurd and embarrassing moments in *Bachelor Girl*, the sight of Bondi in *Two Friends*, or the brilliant uses of Sydney made in *Grevious Bodily Harm*.

However, clearly, the local in this sense cannot be legislated for; it will erupt unpredictably if spaces are created for it, and this is where regulation for *Australian* content re-enters the picture. For there is little chance of the local appearing in a situation where economic pressures make cultural production impossible, and once again, because of the ways national economies and regulation are organised, it is only by preserving the Australian nature of the production process that one can create the space for the local. Regulation of Australian content then is not a sufficient condition for the sort of cultural production I have discussed, but perhaps it is a necessary one.

Ironically, at this very moment of the so-called 'anniversary of the nation', Australian cinema is in a limbo, poised between a past which is a history of the attempt to found a national cinema, or perhaps only a local industry, and a future which is uncertain and only dimly imagined by those who work within this local industry. There is a loss of vision, a failure of nerve, as perhaps there is generally in society, in spite of all the surface busy-ness attached to the 'management of the economy' or the 'establishment of export markets'.

This uncertainty is born not only from the local conditions of being on a cusp between one mode of film financing and a new and untried one, but from deeper causes, not confined to Australia; causes that have to do with a breakdown of a firmly left-liberal progressivist framework, which animated much of the film and other cultural activity of the 1970s and early 1980s.

The dream of a cinema that could illuminate us to ourselves and could create John Hinde's 'seminal audience' seems even more remote now than it was in the 1970s. The current industrial and policy regime is so firmly centred on the dollars and cents aspect of the business, and, day by day, the prospects of the Film Finance Corporation making any real difference to the picture of the last four years also decline.

In *The Screening of Australia*, Susan Dermody and I concluded that Australian cinema revealed itself as a:

> peculiarly inhibited cinema, enclosed by its second-world, second-cinema contradictions . . . organised into a restrictive force field of aesthetic choices by its government patronage, its mythos of commerciality, and the dictum that the cinema shall be the philosopher's stone in Australia's quest for national identity.[24]

There's little about this judgement that I'd want to change, except perhaps that the stronger commercial turn evident in the feature films has meant that the restatement of the 'national identity' question has been far less insistent – except of course in the mini-series, with its almost obsessive retelling of various parts of the nationalist legend.

As we've seen, in spite of the existence of policies to 'preserve Australian content', there has been remarkably little use made of the space thus opened up to register many of the most interesting and challenging facets of contemporary life. One of the striking things about Australian cinema is its relative lack of engagement with contemporary social and political issues or circumstances. This is not to demand that an entertainment cinema ought to have any obvious documentary or educational purpose. It is rather a matter of noting that there is remarkably little sign in our films of the huge conflicts, changes and threats that have engulfed the whole planet during the grimly right-wing 1980s – the ecological crises, the nuclear threat, the rejection of the welfare state, the growth of a radical right, the eclipse of the supremacy of the US economy, our changing relationship with Asia; let alone any of the issues closer to home – the increasing hold that multinational and finance capital exerts over our economy, private greed, crime, corruption, poverty, racial and ethnic conflict, the connections between government and big business.

These issues, and the conflict and social disruption they cause, are neither dealt with in oblique and metaphorical ways as they are, for example, in Hollywood cinema – our cinema is too gentle and well-bred for that; nor are they dealt with directly, except for a mere handful of films, and these are often obscure, low-budget, eccentric – long may they live!

When Australian cinema does register the dislocations of contemporary life, it is on the personal level, as we've seen – witness the countless films about mid-life crisis, broken marriages, separations from children – but there is little sense of the other and perhaps more momentous issues and forces that shape our lives and give rise to the sense of personal insecurity that motivates these films.

Perhaps it is naive or anachronistic to look to cinema, at least in Australia, for a sense of engagement with contemporary life and with a 'seminal' audience. It could be argued that the centre of a lively popular culture has moved to other areas, like television, sport and talkback radio, where of course it always was. Perhaps the dream of a vital national cinema was always just a middle-class illusion. But it's always too soon to call the cinema dead. In the late 1980s, the intersection of cinema with television and video does give it new life, and new means of propagation and dissemination.

Thus it is still appropriate to regret the fact that the complex set of discourses and institutions that constitute the space in which cinema exists is deeply inimical to ideas, controversy or aesthetic adventurousness. The relentless pursuit of the 'popular', the 'commercial' (perennially unsuccessful as we have seen) drives almost everything else out. Nevertheless, there are flickering signs of life here and there; if only the next period can avoid some of the cynical calculation of the last four years, Australian cinema may again attain the status of a popular event that really connects with a local audience.

NOTES

This chapter first appeared in Susan Dermody and Elizabeth Jacka (eds), *The Imaginary Industry: Australian Film in the Late Eighties*, AFTRS Publications, Sydney, 1988.

1 Tom Weir, 'No daydreams of our own: the film as national self-expression', reproduced in Albert Moran and Tom O'Regan (eds), *An Australian Film Reader*, Currency Press, Sydney, 1985, pp. 144–9.
2 Tim Rowse and Albert Moran, 'Peculiarly Australian – the political construction of cultural identity', in S. Encel and L. Bryson (eds), *Australian Society: Introductory Essays*, 4th edn, Longman Cheshire, Melbourne, 1984, p. 231.
3 ibid., p. 290.
4 For example, Ross Gibson, *The Diminishing Paradise*, Sirius Books, Sydney, 1984; Ross Gibson, *Camera Natura* (16mm film); Ross Gibson, 'Paranoid critical methods', *Art and Text*, 26 (September–November 1987), 58–66; Paul Carter, *The Road to Botany Bay*, Faber & Faber, London, 1987; Richard White, *Inventing Australia*, Allen & Unwin, Sydney, 1986.
5 ABT, *Self-Regulation for Broadcasters*, July 1977, p. 29, quoted in Michael Wilcox, 'Part-indigenous drama: coproductions', ABT Discussion Paper, 1988, p. 3.

6 Gill Appleton, *How Australia Sees Itself: the Role of Commercial Television*, ABT, 1988, p. 11.
7 Actors' Equity of Australia, Submission to the Australian Broadcasting Tribunal, September 1983, p. 3.
8 Boris Frankel, 'National chauvinism and abstract internationalism', *Arena*, 82 (Autumn 1988), 140,
9 The committee consisted of Dr Kay Daniels, Associate Professor Bruce Bennett and Humphrey McQueen.
10 Andrew Milner, 'Cringeing and whingeing: imperialism, nationalism and cultural critique', *Arena*, 81 (1987), 65.
11 Benedict Anderson, *Imagined Communities; Reflections on the Origin and Spread of Nationalism*, Verso, London, 1983, p. 15 and *passim*.
12 Boris Frankel, p. 141.
13 These themes have recently been explored in Verity Burgmann's and Jenny Lee's *A People's History of Australia Since 1788*, Penguin, Melbourne, 1988. See especially the introduction to one volume in the series, *A Most Valuable Acquisition*, McPhee Gribble/Penguin Books, Melbourne, 1988.
14 See Richard White, *Inventing Australia: Images and Identity 1688–1980*, ch. 6 and *passim* for a discussion of the populist version of national identity; for a critique of the identification of the Australian 'soul' with its landscape see Ross Gibson, 'Paranoid critical methods', 58–66; on the dangers of what she calls 'mythologisation of the native and the phantasm of origins', see Nelly Richard, 'Margins and institutions: art in Chile since 1973', *Art and Text*, 21 (1986), p. 85. A recent theoretically aware analysis of Australian culture, which nevertheless lapses at points into an essentialist populism is John Fiske, Bob Hodge, Graeme Turner, *Myths of Oz*, Allen & Unwin, Sydney, 1987; see in particular pp. 174–86.
15 Graeme Turner, *National Fictions: Literature, Film and the Construction of Australian Narrative*, Allen & Unwin, Sydney, 1986, p. 8.
16 Some films that arguably fall into this category are those animation films produced in Australia by the Yoram Gross and Burbank studios which are largely intended for foreign TV and video markets, and some of the thriller and other genre films, like *The Time Guardian*, which have come out of the Ginnane stable, or the Judith West Kung Fu movies, *Day of the Panther* and *Strike of the Panther*. Most of these received funding under 10BA.
17 Paul Taylor, A culture of temporary culture', *Art and Text*, 16 (1984), p. 95.
18 See Gibson, 'Paranoid critical methods', 64–5.
19 I should emphasise that by 'local' I do not mean what is meant by 'regional' in the current arguments around networking in television and the threat this is supposed to constitute to regional television. While geographical region is part of what is meant by local, clearly the preservation of the autonomy of regional stations does little or nothing by itself to ensure the kinds of cultural expression I am interested in. As Kim Williams pointed out in his Ian McPherson lecture at the 1988 Sydney Film Festival, networking would only make official a situation that already exists, since regional stations are almost totally dependent on the metropolitan stations for program supply.
20 Ross Gibson, 'Paranoid critical methods'. See also Meaghan Morris's brilliant article on *Crocodile Dundee*, 'Tooth and claw', *Art & Text*, 25 (1987), for a detailed argument about the complexly syncretic nature of Australian culture, and an analysis of the various rhetorical positions that have been taken in cultural debate around the notion of imported culture.

21 Patrick Wright, *On Living in an Old Country: The National Past in Contemporary Britain*, Verso, London, 1985, p. 6.
22 Ibid., p. 24.
23 See Stuart Cunningham, 'Kennedy-Miller: house style in Australian television', in Dermody and Jacka (eds) *The Imaginary Industry*, pp. 177–200.
24 *The Screening of Australia*, vol. II, pp. 231–2.

Part III

Cultural Studies and the Analysis of Culture

The essays in this section share a primary objective; they take issue with particular aspects of what they consider to be cultural studies' orthodoxies. While none of the essays in this collection would see their relation to a 'cultural studies tradition' as unproblematic, those in this section are especially clear examples of a critique that speaks from outside and against prevailing points of view. In Stuart Cunningham's essay, the speaking position is explicitly grounded in Australian conditions; in both Virginia Nightingale's and Ian Hunter's pieces, there is more of an appeal to an academic disinterestedness and the critique is more corrective than polemic. All three demonstrate the usefulness of critiques proceeding from 'south of the west' to offer new perspectives on familiar themes.

Stuart Cunningham's recent book, *Framing Culture*,[1] has been an important intervention within cultural and media studies in Australia. In it he presents the strongest critique possible of contemporary trends in cultural studies in order to foreground the centrality of considerations of cultural policy within the broad area of cultural criticism. In this essay, Cunningham presents an abbreviated and possibly more polemical version of the arguments of *Framing Culture*, arguing for the potential of policy studies to bridge the 'yawning gap' between a 'semiotics-based cultural studies' and a vocationally-based communication studies in Australian tertiary institutions. He is critical of the dominant traditions of European cultural studies – those organised around 'theories of representation', 'new understandings of the audience or the "progressive text" ', or 'notions of subcultural resistance'. He is also critical of the anti-statist ethic within this tradition, an ethic he finds 'inappropriate in virtually any context outside the First World, including Australia'. What he argues *for* is a shift towards 'rhetorics' of 'access, equity, empowerment and the divination of opportunities to exercise appropriate cultural leadership'. Cunningham's aim is ultimately to increase the public purchase of cultural studies knowledges, and to insist on a more vocationally oriented pedagogic responsibility within the teaching of cultural studies courses.

There are familiar notes struck in Cunningham's argument, perhaps, and indeed he refers to the work of Geoff Hurd and Ian Connell as being similarly motivated. However, Cunningham's is a particularly uncompromising and thoroughgoing critique of contemporary cultural studies that is not easy to dismiss. At the very least, in the specific examples he provides of cultural policy debates to which cultural studies has made inadequate contributions, Cunningham presents a compelling challenge to cultural studies' claims to be a critical practice.

Ian Hunter, too, presents a challenge to orthodox understandings of the practice and goals of cultural studies. In 'Settling limits to culture', Hunter provides a rare example of dissent from the conventional narratives of the development of British Marxist cultural studies. He accuses cultural studies of 'systematically' misunderstanding its relation to Romanticism, attributing to Romanticism 'a far narrower conception of culture than it in fact held, and . . . misconstruing the sense in which this conception was aesthetic and ethical'. Furthermore, the totalising view of culture and the self usually attributed to Romanticism is one still apparent within cultural studies practice, no matter how submerged beneath its supposed rejection of a Romantic aesthetics. Hunter challenges those accounts of cultural studies which might see it emerge from, say, Leavisism, and go on to leave it behind; indeed, his description deliberately emphasises the continuing similarities in the role of the critic within both intellectual traditions when he talks of cultural studies as 'an aesthetico-ethical practice aimed at forming the exemplary persona of the cultural critic'.

Hunter's view of the idea of culture is at once more radical and more modest, to 'restrict this concept of culture to the specialised practice of aesthetico-ethical self-shaping in which it has pertinence'. This means concentrating on organisational structures, on the administration of culture through specific institutions at specific historical conjunctures, and on a much more limited understanding of the term 'culture' itself: 'as a signpost pointing in the general direction of a patchwork of institutions in which human attributes are formed and which, having no necessary features in common, must be described and assessed from case to case.' If it seems that this might be accomplished by way of the notion of articulation, Hunter sees this idea, too, as totalising and circular rather than contingent and dialectical. In a movement towards an interest in governmentality, in the administrative practices and institutionalised 'forms of calculation' that we can also see in Tony Bennett's work, Hunter stresses the need to focus on 'the differentiated array of organisational forms in which cultural interests and capacities are formulated' as the location of a properly conceived politics for cultural studies.

The totalising momentums in cultural studies concern Virginia Nightingale as well, although in her case it is cultural studies' appropriation of ethnographic methodologies from the disciplines in which they were developed, and their subsequent deployment. Nightingale deals with what are customarily seen as the central texts in cultural studies canon of audience ethnographies: the work of Morley and Brunsdon, Morley, Hobson and Ang as well as the Australian variant in Tulloch and Moran's study of *A Country Practice*.[2] She reveals how cultural studies use of ethnography has been particularly piecemeal, separating the methodology from its designed function in order to make use of its techniques and practices. The essentially descriptive strategy of ethnography is misguidedly deployed as an interpretative technique, often involving 'a co-opting of the interviewee's experience of the text by the researcher, and its use as authority for the researcher's point of view.' Further, Nightingale raises questions about the function of ethnography within a developing tradition of cultural studies methodologies. She places the movement towards ethnographic research in television as in one sense a backward move, literally, into a cultural studies history that relied on different kinds of ethnography – that is, those concerned with distributions of social power rather than audience responses to texts. The reason for that move lies precisely in its potential to 'assert a . . . continuity' betweeen a cultural studies preoccupied with media text analysis and such originary subcultural work as that of Paul Willis.

Like Cunningham and Hunter, Nightingale too has a programme to suggest. Hers concerns what she calls 'Mixed-genre' research, 'research which integrates the study of audience discourse and data obtained from audience observation with qualitatively different observations and materials about television texts, production, distribution and industries'. A method of 'triangulation' is recommended where 'the nature of the problem under investigation' is subjected to a 'multi-method approach'. Within such a programme, ethnography does have its place; what Nightingale provides is a usefully suggestive account of what that place might be.

NOTES

1 Stuart Cunningham, *Framing Culture*, Allen & Unwin, Sydney, 1992.
2 John Tulloch and Albert Moran, *Quality Soap: A Country Practice*, Currency Press, Sydney, 1986.

Chapter 6

Cultural studies from the viewpoint of cultural policy

Stuart Cunningham

As cultural studies moves into a phase of consolidation and some respectability, it is being questioned from three broad directions. In placing these on a left-to-right continuum, I am mindful that one of the things at stake in the current climate is the viability of just such a political set. We might well remember the wonderful caveat issued by Jean-Luc Godard and Anne-Marie Mieville in *Numéro Deux*: 'This is not a film of the left or right, but a film of before and behind.'

To the left is a position that seeks to question the orthodoxies of academic cultural studies in the name of a more authentic critical and political practice, or in the name of a more thoroughgoing deconstruction or postmodernism. This position can invoke the powerful trope of recalling cultural studies to its origins as a brave intervention in established literary and social science orthodoxies.

Meaghan Morris's 'Banality in cultural studies',[1] for example, attacks the wilful calling into being of progressiveness in texts, and resistance in audiences – a cheerful populism that often collapses criticism into little more than fandom. She also suggests that the critical stances of the traditional humanities disciplines have not been so clearly dispelled as might once have been imagined.

On the right, emerging from the social sciences, is a position that views the recent sea changes in Eastern Europe and the USSR, the longer-term global shifts toward internationalisation and the collapse of movement politics of various kinds as calling into question the continuing relevance of the neo-Marxist 'motor' of cultural studies. From this perspective, the anti-capitalism, anti-consumerism and romanticisation of subcultural resistance embodied in the classical texts of cultural studies are no longer adequate responses to the big questions confronting the articulation of politics and culture in modern Western societies.

With these political reassessments has come a revaluation of empirical detail, aligned with a piecemeal approach to the articulation of ideology and culture. There is a 'beyond ideology' flavour about much of this work. John Kelly's[2] discussion of Stuart Hall's key text on left renewal in Britain, *The Hard Road to Renewal: Thatcherism and the Crisis of the Left*, is a frontal attack on a politics of grand theory that lacks credible empirics. With rhetorical naivety, Kelly poses the ultimate empirical question: 'How does Hall *know* any of these things?' (my emphasis).

The ranks of apostates from neo-Marxist orthodoxies have swelled, especially in Britain (though in the US cultural studies is still on a growth surge, and substantial questioning of the assumptions of the field from within will not come very soon or very readily). It seems that something more than a faddish search for The Next Thing is afoot.[3]

There is also a 'centrist' policy orientation. This approach seeks to position the perspectives of cultural studies within fields of public policy where academic critical protocols do not have priority. Like the 'left-humanities' position, it is aware of the limits of academic discourse. While seeking to respond to the same global concerns as the 'right-social-science' position, it is not as concerned to discredit the foundational posture of cultural studies, if that posture is distilled down to the central Enlightenment values of liberty, equality and solidarity.[4] Indeed, it seeks to revivify these core values as the central motor of reformism that can be appealed to in the public sphere of contemporary Western societies. This is the position that I wish to advance as a way forward for cultural studies.

What relations should exist between cultural studies and cultural policy? I employ the term cultural studies (or cultural criticism) as a convenient shorthand for work that treats film, the arts, media and communications, as well as lived, everyday cultures, and is driven by the major strands of neo-Marxist, structuralist, poststructuralist and postmodernist thought. Cultural policy embraces the broad field of public processes involved in formulating, implementing and contesting governmental intervention in, and support of, cultural activity.

The commonsense reaction to my question, one likely to be offered by most of those outside the academy who might be inclined to consider it, would be that the former serves as a kind of 'handmaiden', developing rationales for those engaged in public policy. Theory, analysis and commentary should undergird practice; practice implements theory. On closer inspection, however, the relations are far less harmonious than this model suggests. Indeed, in many ways, contemporary practices flatly contradict received wisdom.

Cultural studies, from the viewpoint of cultural policy, is rather like the curate's egg – good in parts – but even the good parts mightn't be very good. Liz Jacka wrote recently of the 'widening gap between cultural critique and cultural policy'.[5] Taking my cue from this, I want to canvass some recent issues in Australian cultural and communications policy where practical opportunities for cultural analysis have been forgone, or worse.

AUSTRALIAN CONTENT ON TELEVISION

The Australian Broadcasting Tribunal's exhaustive inquiry into Australian Content on Commercial Television concluded its main considerations in December 1989 with the introduction of a new Television Program Standard. The inquiry ran for about five years, with a break of three years in the mid–1980s.[6]

One of the members of the tribunal, Julie James-Bailey, commented that during the inquiry there was virtually no input from academic cultural critics and analysts.[7] There *was* one such contribution, however, from John Docker, who employed an array of contemporary theory to attack the legitimacy of regulation of Australian content on television.[8] Docker argued that regulation actually means the imposition of (British) high-cultural values onto popular cultural forms whose appeal is indifferent to national variations and registrations. What viewers actively embrace in television culture, according to Docker, is the carnivalesque overturning of statist official culture and the celebration of working-class values and interests. These values and interests are transnational, and subvert state interventions to preserve national registrations of popular cultural forms.

It is probably just as well that Docker's arguments had no effect on the outcomes of the inquiry. But it is alarming that Docker's was the only significant contribution that presented any of the theoretical issues that have concerned theorists, critics and historians for decades. Docker's view of popular television and its audiences may be idiosyncratic, but it is, in Graeme Turner's words, 'directly licensed' by current strands of cultural theory.[9] To applaud Docker's irrelevance could be tantamount to applauding the irrelevance of critical and theoretical input to the policy-making process in general.

ADVERTISING AND NATIONAL CULTURE

The tribunal's inquiry addressed Australian content provisions covering all television programming, including advertising. The regulations for television advertising are different from those for other programme material. They are directed at prohibiting more than 20 per cent of any advertising being produced overseas, unless Australian crews travel overseas to obtain the footage. They constitute a very high level of protection for local content, and, because they have been in place for thirty years, they have been extremely influential in underwriting the television advertising industry in Australia.

The inquiry into foreign content in advertising has operated virtually as a sidelight to the main act. It is not hard to see why. Advertising is the unworthy discourse, as far as both criticism and policy are concerned. If there has been an outstanding consensus among critics of various persuasions it is that advertising panders to patriarchy and consumerism. This consensus sits comfortably with moves to deregulate a 'blatantly' protected industry. Regulation against foreign advertising content has been the subject of concerted attack from industry – primarily from transnational advertisers – as well as high-level economic rationalist sources of advice to government. A recent report by the Industries Assistance Commission (now the Industry Commission) attack the 'virtual embargo' on foreign-produced ads: 'the sector enjoys an extremely privileged position relative to nearly all other economic activity in Australia'.[10]

The main rationale for continued regulation has been the argument that advertising has a role in the formation of national cultural identity. The argument for making a positive connection between advertising and national culture can be mounted in two basic areas. From the viewpoint of policy, the weaker argumemt is the appeal to the effects of deregulation in the area of advertising on the drama production industry. It is clear that drama production could not have developed its present scope and depth without the industrial infrastructure of the Australian advertising industry. Evidence for this link is widely accepted, and pieces of it are often cited in film and television histories.[11] For this reason, if for no other, deregulating television advertising would have major cultural consequences.

The central argument, however, has to grasp the nettle – the positive contribution advertising itself may make to national culture. In its present forms, cultural studies is spectacularly unsuited to this task.

Two main patterns of criticism have remained foundational to the cultural critique of advertising. The first is diachronic, focusing on the history of advertising as an agent of American cultural imperialism. Jeremy Tunstall's *The Media are American* and Mattelart and Dorfman's *How to Read Donald Duck* established the parameters of this pattern, and the general critical perspective on advertising has never seriously deviated from it. The other pattern is synchronic; informed by the early semiotic guerrilla tactics of Roland Barthes's *Mythologies*, it focuses on the cultural reproduction of dominant ideological values embedded in bourgeois culture. In spite of an increasingly strong emphasis on feminism, the cultural studies approach to advertising, both in critical writing and in curricula, has not advanced significantly beyond the works of Barthes, Tunstall and Mattelart and Dorfman in the 1950s to 1970s.

Under the umbrella of the tribunal's content regulation, Australian television advertising has developed a strong grammar of national imaging that parallels film and television fiction, but has a considerably greater permeation of the mass market. Advertising occupies an average of about three and a half hours a day on each commercial metropolitan television station, compared to recent Australian drama content of about two hours a week. By dint of repetition, saturation coverage across the most popular

networks, and sophisticated textual strategies that increasingly link programmes with their commercial 'environment', advertising must be seen
as having considerable cultural valence.

Such indicators of cultural permeation, though crude and problematic
from a critical perspective, are important in policy formulation. The real
issue is: to what extent can a positive character be imputed to them?
This is not simply a question of putting the Mister Sheen gloss on what
the critic has regarded as a tawdry business. It is a matter of evaluating
the contribution of television advertising in terms that are not just a
matter of marking ideological ticks and crosses. It is to describe the
impress and influence of advertising in terms that accept that its ideo-
logically regressive elements – its sexism, its chauvinism, its rowdy populism – are bracketed within a more neutral, descriptive cultural and
audiovisual history.

Such a history would focus on the central role that advertising has
played in the development of a popular audiovisual 'grammar' of national
identity during the 1970s and 1980s. The so-called 'new' nationalism of
this period was most visibly expressed in advertising campaigns despite
the large claims made for the contribution of film and television drama.
These campaigns were at key moments explicit attempts at social engineering – for instance, the 'Life. Be In It' campaign and the 'Advance
Australia' campaign of the late 1970s and early 1980s. This is clear in the
published aims of 'Advance Australia': 'To heighten community and
public awareness and pride in Australian skills, achievements and potential. To highlight the role of individual enterprise in the economy. To
encourage improvements in quality design, marketing and other characteristics of Australian identity.'[12] This advertising campaign, and others
that came in its wake, sought to redress what attitudinal research had
identified as a widespread lack of 'pride in country' and support for
Australian manufacturing.[13]

This kind of public-service advertising has had its counterparts in purely
commercial campaigns, which over the last fifteen years have invented a
popular audiovisual grammar of nationalism. Prestige national advertising
campaigns now routinely incorporate this established repertoire of Aus-
tralianist tropes. The fact that this repertoire is used for evidently contradictory purposes, from promoting health to flogging beer and tobacco,
and utilises images that range from the unacceptably sexist to the innovative, even progressive, simply registers the modularity of advertising's
nationalism.

There is very little substantial critical appraisal of this enormous port-
folio of material, and what there is does little to articulate a position
sensitive to the policy issues. There are critical exercises of the traditional
kind, such as Stephen Alomes's less than trenchant putdown of the course
of Australian nationalism ('from jingoism to jingle-ism') in *A Nation at*

Last?, or Tim Rowse's critique of television populism in the 'humanity' ads.[14] But the 'sophisticated theory of consumption' called for by Kathy Myers in Britain,[15] or the magisterial descriptivist account of 'advertising as social communication' given by William Leiss, Stephen Kline and Sut Jhally in North America,[16] have no Australian counterparts. Such approaches must be applied to the question of Australian national identity in advertising if we are to advance beyond reflex ideological critique and begin to address urgent and practical policy issues.

FEMINIST CULTURAL THEORY AND BUREAUCRATIC REFORMISM

Australia lags behind Canada and some Scandinavian nations in implementing strategies to modify sexist representations in the mass media, but in the last few years there have been significant initiatives here. The Office of the Status of Women has acted as the co-ordinating secretariat for a body called the National Working Party on the Portrayal of Women in the Media, a body consisting of representatives of the advertising industry, community groups and government departments.

To my knowledge, little or nothing arising from feminist scholars' sophisticated repertoire of theories of representation has been brought to bear on questions of bureaucratic reformism. Indeed, the most willing and effective advocates of institutional change use 'outdated', reflectionist and empiricist research to drive evidence for change, and a liberal humanist feminism to ground their campaigns.

It is not hard to see why advanced feminist theories of representation have weighed so lightly, despite the considerable body of literature that has been developed around exactly the sorts of questions that animate reformist policy initiatives. As Leiss, Kline and Jhally argue, 'representation' critiques of advertising have been subjective, non-quantitative, and have reduced the specificity of advertising to a generalised social critique.

From the viewpoint of policy, such critiques depend to an unacceptable degree on methods that are difficult to replicate without a high level of interpretative training. Semiotic method is powerful and convincing in the hands of a Barthes or a Williamson, but there has been a lot of obfuscated and redundant 'normal science' in the area. Representation critiques also depend too heavily on extrapolated pertinence – the findings are not underwritten by content analysis based on accepted sampling techniques. And they are guilty of simply using advertising, because it is arguably the most visible and most insistent form of commercialism, as a springboard into a generalised critique that is of little use within the protocols of piecemeal reformism. For all these reasons, representation accounts have been of little value in policy calculation, even for those predisposed to accept the assumptions from which they stem.

MEDIA OWNERSHIP AND CULTURAL POWER

Cultural studies has increasingly moved away from the orthodox political economy model's concern with questions of ownership and control of the mass media. The cultural power that is interesting now resides with audiences and, to a lesser extent, producers of media content itself. Set over against these interests are what appear to cultural theorists as rather hackneyed and predictable arguments for greater diversity and less concentration of media ownership. The calls of a David Bowman, a Paul Chadwick or an Eric Beecher appear hackneyed and predictable because they are voiced within very narrow terms of cultural debate, and partake of what Walter Benjamin memorably called 'left-wing melancholy'. This miserabilism, this prophetic nay-saying, is something that cultural studies is now resolutely rejecting.

The exercise of political and cultural power through media control, however, remains one of the key blind spots of public policy in Australia. There is considerable evidence that the issue cuts through established party and factional allegiances and is beginning to create intolerable anomalies for public policy.

This issue will certainly not go away in a postmodernist flush of audience sovereignty. Indeed it will increase in centrality as media converge and narrow their focus ever more powerfully toward precise demographic and psychographic fine-tuning. Not only that, but the current theoretical fashion for championing the active audience finds an ironic echo in the rhetoric of consumer sovereignty that is offered by media owners and deregulators.

Unambiguous economic and political power will increasingly be translatable into unambiguous cultural power. Those who are best positioned to benefit from enhanced technologies of audience targeting, from the convergence of media of carriage, and from pro-competitive public policy parameters, are precisely those who now exercise enormous power through control of the traditional media. Unless it allies itself with social-democratic advocates of media reform, cultural studies could well become irrelevant in the near future.

NOW, JUST WAIT A MINUTE!

The 'handmaiden' model is easy picking for those inside the academy. Most people trained in the politics of cultural studies would view their primary role as critics of the dominant political, economic and social order. When we as cultural theorists do turn our hands to questions of policy, our command metaphors of resistance, refusal and opposition predispose us to view the policy-making process as inevitably compromised, *ad hoc*, incomplete and inadequate, controlled by people who are inexpert and ungrounded in theory and history, or who wield gross forms of political power for short-term ends. These people and processes are then called to the bar of an abstrusely formulated cultural idealism. Critical idealism would retort that mine is the mealy-mouthed voice of liberal bourgeois compromise.

A more reflective critique of the position I am advancing would raise the issue of the long-term leavening effect of critical idealism. Tomorrow's public debate and potential consensus may well issue from today's utopian, abstruse, left-of-field thinking. The clearest example of this is the 'sourcing' of femocrat reformism by feminist movement politics. Similar sourcing relationships hold between the environmental movements and green politics, or between ethnic advocacy and official discourses of multiculturalism. A more pragmatic variant of the same objection is that, if cultural studies doesn't hold to the humanities' traditional critical vocation, who will – particularly in the wake of the breakdown of more broadly based social movements?

These objections seem reasonable, so I want to respond to them carefully. First I do not wish to discount the model of prophetic critic, a role that is the essential prerequisite of critical practice. It is, however, rather disingenuous for the academy to don this mantle, as a great deal of the critical work performed within the academy cannot plausibly claim such prophetic status. The most effective public intellectuals on issues of culture in the Australian polity are not vanguard theorists, but those who work within the terms of a given (and, one might readily concede, narrow) set of public-interest, liberal-democratic and social-democratic norms. Vanguard theory, on the evidence we have to date, is less than likely to translate into prophetic criticism.

The second response proceeds from the first. To get to the nub of the problem: what is cultural studies' understanding of its political vocation? What is its vision of a better, more just, equitable, participatory, cultural order? What measures are cultural theorists and analysts taking to have this vision articulated widely? What alliances are we forming with cultural activists and policy agents and players? To what extent are we informing ourselves about the historical, existing and emergent policy agenda, and identifying where we might fit?

In an interesting interchange between John Fiske and an unnamed interlocutor, published in Fiske's *Reading the Popular*, Fiske asserts that 'internal or semiotic resistance . . . is an essential prerequisite of social change'.[17] This statement brings to the fore the politics of Fiske's influential model of resistive populism. The resistive strategies imputed to consumers of popular culture, by definition, are never mobilised into organisations that might seek to influence change in any institutional arrangement or professional practice by which cultural meaning is produced and delivered. The resistance Fiske champions actually undermines the strategies of organised reform movements because it sets itself against ideal standards of professional media practice and against empirical audience measurement. Both are essential if reformism is to gain some purchase in public policy processes.

The missing link is a social-democratic view of citizenship and the trainings necessary to activate and motivate it. A renewed concept of citizenship should be increasingly central to cultural studies as it moves into the 1990s. Political science, government, sociology, journalism, organisation studies, to say nothing of traditional professional trainings such as law, all have particular mobilisations of citizenship embodied in their curriculum. Despite this, the emerging evidence for an attention to citizenship in cultural studies signifies an important advance. It demonstrates that cultural studies is coming to terms with its neo-Marxist heritage as it realises that other political postures can be as radically reformist as neo-Marxism without employing a totalising and confrontational rhetoric. For this reason, the perspectives of Australian social-democratic thinkers like Hugh Stretton in social theory, Donald Horne, Peter Wilenski and H. C. Coombs in cultural and communications areas, or Francis Castles in economics, should assume as great an importance for rethinking the vocation of cultural studies as the international fathers (and mothers) of the discipline.

Replacing shop-worn revolutionary rhetoric with the new command metaphor of citizenship commits cultural studies to a reformist strategy within the terms of a social-democratic politics, and thus can connect it to the wellsprings of engagement with policy. Even though, as Ham and Hill show,[18] the policy process in modern capitalist states has arisen within a liberal pluralist problematic, it need not be limited by liberalism's underdeveloped ideas of power and of the necessity of struggle for access to decision-making processes.

This concept of citizenship does not by any means imply a politics of the status quo – a sort of primary-school civics. Donald Horne uses it to advance his Lockean notion of the 'cultural rights' of the citizen in modern social democracies. Graham Murdock and Peter Golding use it to invite thinking about information poverty in our age of increasingly privatised communications. It is also being employed to pose questions about new forms of citizenship that may embrace larger units than the individual nation-state, such as the emergent European community. Similarly, in a 1984 report to the French Ministry of Culture, Mattelart, Delcourt and Mattelart proposed a linguistic-cultural transnational community – a 'latin audio-visual space'.[19] Such concerns have been abroad for decades in the continuing debate in Unesco concerning the New World Information and Communications Order (NWICO).

Third, the greater proportion of cultural studies work is performed within academic arrangements that either prioritise vocational training or seek to marry a liberal arts education with gestures toward such training. These institutional orientations will become more established, if not necessarily accepted, under current government policies. Pragmatically then, there are powerful reasons to review the current state of cultural studies.

The calls to introduce a policy orientation into cultural studies have become louder in recent years.[20] We hear that cultural studies remains fixated on theoretical and textual orientations that provide little to equip students with knowledge and skills for citizenship and employment in the 1990s. The gap between textually based studies and policy cannot be bridged merely by further refinements in theories of representation, in new understandings of the audience or the 'progressive text', or in notions of subcultural resistance.

Indeed, two British cultural studies 'apostates', Geoff Hurd and Ian Connell, have argued that cultural critique, as a governing educational model, has actively deskilled students:

> While we accept there is a need for cultural appraisal and reconstruction, we would also suggest that the predominant view of the cultural organisations within cultural studies has been misleading and that criticism has been placed before understanding. In short, cultural studies has been critical of enterprises whose modes of operation and social significance it does not properly comprehend.[21]

Questions of policy do circulate at the margins of the traditional core curricula of cultural studies. In Trevor Barr's words, moving those marginal interests toward the centre of the curriculum ultimately has to do with 'political empowerment'.[22]

A focus on policy, if extended to both types of communications curricula – semiotics-based cultural studies on the one hand, and business communication, journalism, public relations, marketing and advertising on the other – has the potential to bridge the yawning gaps between these traditions. Its integration into liberal arts and media production programmes would encourage a firmer grasp of the social and vocational implications of cultural struggle as embodied in governmental and industrial processes. On the other hand, its integration into industry-driven courses would draw students into a broader appreciation of the politics and ethics of their vocations and the reasonable legitimacy of state intervention.

Finally, many of our protocols are disabling because they take scant account of the local conditions in which theory must be developed. It might seem a truism to state that different emphases should emerge in cultural studies in different parts of the world. Because Australia is a net importer of ideas as much as goods and services, it is crucial for an Australian cultural studies to be self-critical about its agenda, lest the agenda be set, by default, elsewhere. I can't put it better than the report of the Committee to Review Australian Studies in Tertiary Education, which said Australianising tertiary education would prevent the intellectual cringe that slides 'between a vacuous cosmopolitanism and an apologetic provincialism'.[23]

To Australianise is not to call for a form of intellectual tariff blockade. On the contrary, it implies a much stronger and more perspicacious engagement with imported traditions. And it in no way implies an a priori defence of the status quo, or a rejection of the possible benefits flowing from greater internationalisation of inquiry. It does suggest that an Australian cultural studies engaging with policy issues that affect the future of Australian culture would involve reconceptualising certain general theories, upgrading the focus on regulation as a positive underpinning of cultural production, and rethinking the politics of culture in a non-British, non-North-American setting.

Importing British cultural studies has meant privileging subcultural resistance to a repressive and class-defined state. This has much to do with Thatcherism's far-reaching influence on the agenda of the British left, the anti-statist tone of much cultural studies and the subsequent search for positive markers of the intrinsic subversiveness of everyday life. The libertarianism implicit in this approach might find a greater echo in the United States (where the state has willingly abetted rather than mollified economic and cultural imperialism) than it ever should in Australia, or for that matter many other countries where state regulatory activity has struggled to achieve an equitable flow of economic and cultural goods and services.

Consider the perennial issue of the nation as an illustration of the importance of localism in intellectual work. The ascendant current of macro-level thought in cultural studies today lays to rest the nation-state and invites practitioners to link opportunities for internationalism with a renewed communalism. This may be appropriate for cultural thought in the present European context, but it is inappropriate in virtually any context outside the First World, including Australia.

There are high stakes involved in the arguments for internationalism and community against the nation. All the major cultural industries in Australia (film, television, the major arts and the many community-based arts programmes sponsored by the Australia Council) derive their policy justification from their being national in scope. It is too early, if indeed it will ever be politically strategic, to pit the internationalist-communalist position against the nation in Australia.

Ultimately, despite a byzantine tripartite system of government that makes Australia one of the most 'governed' countries in the world per capita, it is at the national level that debate on cultural futures has to be staged. The future of cultural production is unavoidably bound into the future of national cultural policies. In terms of the intellectual resourcing of policy development, and in the myriad ways that local, state and subcultural sites of activity depend on national provision and support, the national arena will remain the engine room for cultural policy initiatives. For its part, cultural theory must take greater stock of its potential negative influence on progressive public policy outcomes and, if it is to orient itself in a more valuable way toward policy imperatives, must attend to the tasks of consolidating the legitimacy of policy rhetorics that sustain a national cultural infrastructure.

IMPLICATIONS AND CONCLUSIONS

Is it possible to regard a policy orientation within cultural studies as simply an add-on element, one more offering in the interdisciplinary smorgasbord? I don't think so. I have suggested that the political rhetoric undergirding cultural studies would have to be re-examined. This alone would indicate a more thoroughgoing review of the cultural studies enterprise than the smorgasbord model would permit.

Nothing in what I have said should be taken to indicate a less critical vocation for cultural studies. What would count as the critical vocation, however, would change. A cultural studies that grasps and sustains links with policy will inquire across a greatly expanded field, but with methods far less totalising and abstract, far more modest and specific, than those to which we are accustomed.

To treat cultural policy adequately from a critical perspective, it is necessary to appreciate the combined impact of economics, administrative law, cultural history, entertainment financing, government and parliamentary procedures on the development of public policy. This means a more subtle and context-sensitive re-education in the roles of the state in mixed capitalist economies, away from monolithic and wooden grand theories inspired more by critical purism than by the requirements for piecemeal reformism. Critical policy research thus implies more, rather than less, critical understanding than is found in the traditions of cultural criticism developed exclusively within humanities-based disciplines, and a significantly greater sensitivity to the extra-academic contexts within which such research must circulate for it to exercise its potential leavening function.

In summary, then, a policy orientation in cultural studies would shift its 'command metaphors' away from rhetorics of resistance, oppositionalism and anti-commercialism on the one hand, and populism on the other, toward those of access, equity, empowerment and the divination of opportunities to exercise appropriate cultural leadership. It would not necessarily discount critical strategies and priorities, but may indeed enhance and broaden them. It is not a call simply to add another 'perspective' to the academic sideboard, but would necessitate rethinking the component parts of the field from the ground up. It offers one major means of rapprochement across the critical/vocational divide that structures the academic field of cultural and communication studies. Finally, it would commit us to a genuine localism, against the abstract theoreticism that usually passes as the currency of international academic exchange.

NOTES

This chapter first appeared in *Meanjin*, 50 (2/3) (1991).

1 Meaghan Morris, 'Banality in cultural studies', in Patricia Mellencamp (ed.) *Logics of Television*, British Film Institute, London, 1990.
2 John Kelly, 'Iron lady in a nanny's uniform', *Times Higher Education Supplement*, 840, 9 December 1988.
3 See, for example, the British journal *Screen*'s new editorial policy (in 31(1)), debate in that and other recent issues, and Richard Collins, *Television: Policy and Culture*, Unwin Hyman, London 1990.
4 See Manuel Alvarado and John O. Thompson (eds), *The Media Reader*, British Film Institute, London, 1990. See also Fred Inglis, *Media Theory: An Introduction*, Blackwell, Oxford, 1990.
5 Elizabeth Jacka, 'Australian cinema – an anachronism in the '80s?', in Susan Dermody and Elizabeth Jacka (eds), *The Imaginary Industry: Australian Film in the Late '80s*, Australian Film, Television and Radio School, Sydney, 1988, p. 118.
6 For discussion, see my 'Figuring the Australian factor', *Culture and Policy*, 2(1) (1990).
7 Julie James-Bailey, 'Communicating with the decision makers: the role of research, scholarship and teaching in film and media studies', Staff Seminar, Griffith University, 20 October 1989.
8 John Docker, 'Popular culture versus the state: an argument against Australian content regulation for TV', unpublished, attachment to Federation of Australian Commercial Television Stations (FACTS) submission to ABT Inquiry into Australian Content on Commercial Television, 16 August 1988 (Document D020B, ABT Inquiry File). A shorter version is published as 'Popular culture versus the state: an argument against Australian content regulations for TV', *Media Information Australia*, 59 (1991). For further discussion, see Stuart Cunningham, Jennifer Craik, Tony Bennett and Ian Hunter, 'Responses to Docker', *Media Information Australia*, 59 (1991).
9 Graeme Turner, ' "It works for me": British cultural studies, Australian cultural studies, Australian film', in L. Grossberg *et al.* (eds), *Cultural Studies*, Routledge, New York, 1992.
10 Industries Assistance Commission, *International Trade and Services*, Report no. 418, AGPS, 30 June 1989, p. 202.
11 Graham Shirley and Brian Adams, *Australian Cinema: The First Eighty Years*, Angus & Robertson/Currency Press, Sydney, 1983; Albert Moran, *Images and Industry: Television Drama Production in Australia*, Currency Press, Sydney, 1985.

12 Phillip Lynch, 'Advance Australia', *Bulletin*, 2 February 1982.
13 Gary Sturgess, 'The emerging new nationalism', *Bulletin*, 2 February 1982.
14 Stephen Alomes, *A Nation at Last? The Changing Character of Australian Nationalism 1880–1988*, Angus & Robertson/Currency Press, Sydney, 1983; Albert Moran, ' "Peculiarly Australian" – the political construction of cultural identity', in Sol Encel and Lois Bryson (eds), *Australian Society*, 4th edn, Longman Cheshire, Melbourne, 1984; Noel King and Tim Rowse, ' "Typical Aussies": television and populism in Australia', *Framework*, 22–3 (Autumn 1983).
15 Kathy Myers, *Understains – the Sense and Seduction of Advertising*, Comedia Publishing Group, London, 1986.
16 William Leiss, Stephen Kline and Sut Jhally, *Advertising as Social Communication: Persons, Products and Images of Well-Being*, Methuen, Toronto, 1986.
17 John Fiske, *Reading the Popular*, Unwin Hyman, Boston, 1989, p. 179.
18 Christopher Ham and Michael Hill, *The Policy Process in the Modern Capitalist State*, Harvester Press, Brighton, 1984.
19 Donald Horne, *Think – or Perish! Towards a Confident and Productive Australia*, Occasional Paper no. 8, Commission for the Future, June 1988, and *The Public Culture*, Pluto Press, Sydney, 1986; Graham Murdock and Peter Golding, 'Information poverty and political inequality: citizenship in the age of privatised communications', *Journal of Communication*, 39 (3) (Summer 1989), 180–95; Aramand Mattelart, Xavier Delcourt and Michele Mattelart, *International Image Markets*, Comedia, London, 1984,
20 For example, Toby Miller, 'Film and media citizenship', *Filmnews* (February 1990); Trevor Barr, 'Reflections on media education: the myths and realities', *Metro Media and Education Magazine*, 82 (Autumn 1990); Tony Bennett, 'Putting policy into cultural studies', in L. Grossberg *et al.* (eds), *Cultural Studies*, Routledge, New York, 1992.
21 Geoff Hurd and Ian Connell, 'Cultural education: a revised program', *Media Information Australia*, 53 (August 1989), 23–30.
22 Barr, 'Reflections on media education', p. 16.
23 *Windows onto Worlds: Studying Australia at Tertiary Level*, AGPS, Canberra, 1987, p. 18.

Chapter 7

Setting limits to culture

Ian Hunter

Let me begin to situate the argument that follows by juxtaposing two texts. The first is drawn from Engels's letter to Schmidt in which he expounds some of the central tenets of historical materialism, paying particular attention to the formation of the 'ideological outlook'. According to Engels all attempts to reflect on society are distorted by interests arising from particular positions in the division of labour and as a result:

> Economic, political and other reflections are just like those in the human eye: they pass through a condensing lens and therefore appear upside down, standing on their heads. Only the nervous apparatus which would put them on their feet again for presentation to us is lacking.[1]

The remark is, of course, well known, not least because the letter in which it occurs contains Engels's much-cited criticism of economism: his insistence on the 'relative autonomy' of the superstructure. It is possible, however, to bypass this familiar context of discussion – to approach the famous text from an unfamiliar angle – by comparing it with a parallel but different attempt to deploy the human nervous system as an analogue for the social system.

Written some sixty years before the Engels letter, James Kay-Shuttleworth's *The Moral and Physical Condition of the Working Classes of Manchester in 1832* begins with a striking analogy in which the author compares the 'animal structure', which possesses the faculty of a unified sensorium to monitor threats to its well-being, with the social structure, which possesses no such faculty.

> Society were well preserved, did a similar faculty preside, with an equal sensibility, over its constitution; making every order immediately conscious of the evils affecting any portion of the general mass, and thus rendering their removal equally necessary for the immediate ease, as it is for the ultimate welfare, of the whole social system.

The market is neither sensitive nor perceptive enough to compensate for this lack and as a result:

> Some governments have attempted to obtain, by specific measures, that knowledge for the acquisition of which there is no natural faculty. The statistical investigations of Prussia, of the Netherlands, of Sweden, and of France, concerning population, labour, and its commercial and agricultural results; the existing resources of the country, its taxation, finance, etc., are minute and accurate.[2]

Applied to the moral and physical condition of the populace, Kay-Shuttleworth argued, such measures would link the incoherent parts of the social body to metropolitan points of knowledge and political intervention.

We can sharpen the comparison by looking at how each writer specifies the actual processes of co-ordination and development figured forth in the metaphor of the nervous system. For Engels these processes are identified with the general movement of history powered by the economic division of labour and classes. (He does not here distinguish between the latter.) If the division of labour has created the fragmentation of class interests that prevents a true reflection of society, then, Engels argues, this same division will eventually restore a true point of view through the processes of contradiction and overcoming that drive history towards totality.

> As to the realms of ideology which soar still higher in the air – religion, philosophy, etc. – these have a prehistoric stock, found already in existence by and taken over in the historical period, of what we should today call bunk. These various false conceptions of nature, of man's own being, of spirits, magic forces, etc., have for the most part only a negative economic element as their basis; the low economic development of the prehistoric period is supplemented and also partially conditioned and even caused by the false conceptions of nature. And even though economic necessity was the main driving force of the progressive knowledge of nature and has become ever more so, it would surely be pedantic to try and find economic causes for all this primitive nonsense. The history of science is the history of the gradual clearing away of this nonsense or rather of its replacement by fresh but always less absurd nonsense. The people who attend to this belong in their turn to special spheres in the division of labour and appear to themselves to be working in an independent field. And to the extent that they form an independent group within the social division of labour, their productions, including their errors, react upon the whole development of society, even on its economic development. But all the same they themselves are in turn under the dominating influence of economic development.[3]

We shall see that it is this model of contradiction and development towards totality – itself much broader than the Marxist version employed by Engels – that defines the idea of culture. Engels identifies the 'nervous apparatus' that will overcome the incoherence of the division of labour and synthesise a true perception of society with the cultural realisation of 'man'.

Kay-Shuttleworth, on the other hand, while he might agree with Engels that the 'social nervous system' is an historical artefact, does not identify its formation with the historical development of man or society. Far from it. As far as Kay-Shuttleworth is concerned the most important thing about the knowledge required to monitor and regulate the disparate parts of the 'social body' is that no natural faculty exists for its acquisition. Neither is the formation of such a faculty governed by the historical alienation of reason and the promise of its overcoming in true vision or the total point of view. Instead, it can only be produced in a practical and piecemeal fashion by the implementation of 'specific measures' – in fact, measures that had been adopted to formulate and resolve limited social and cultural problems.

> The introduction into this country of a singularly malignant and contagious malady [cholera], which, though it selects its victims from every order of society, is chiefly propagated amongst those whose health is depressed by disease, mental anxiety, or want of the comforts and conveniences of life, has directed public attention to an investigation of the state of the poor. In Manchester, Boards of Health were established, in each of the fourteen districts of Police, for the purpose of minutely inspecting the state of houses and streets. These districts were divided into minute sections, to each of which two or more inspectors were appointed from among the most respectable inhabitants of the vicinity, and they were provided with tabular queries, applying to each house and street.[4]

Kay-Shuttleworth could not find the required synthetic faculty in 'man' or 'society'. Instead, he saw it emerging from the network of medical, penal, legal and assistantial institutions which had projected a grid of norms and surveillance over the nineteenth-century city. This was not a paradigm of consciousness or a 'mentality', but a material achievement produced by equipping individuals with specific techniques of observation and recording, deploying them in particular patterns, linking them with relays of information and command. In this grid the techniques of statistical recording and analysis could produce a delimited normatively-oriented social knowledge. In short, it was not to culture – with its promise of total development and true reflection – that Kay-Shuttleworth looked for a means of assessing and intervening in social and cultural development. He found it instead in the regions of organised intelligence framed by the always limited norms and techniques of an historically specific array of institutions.

However, the circumscribed character of this knowledge notwithstanding, Kay-Shuttleworth was able to find – in the statistical correlations linking illiteracy, incarceration, domestic economy, mortality, attendances at church and gin-shop and so forth – a blueprint for the state's intervention in the education of the popular classes. In fact, as the first permanent secretary of England's fledgeling educational bureaucracy, he played the leading role in the establishment of popular education as a uniform formative regime aimed at equipping the popular classes with the cultural attributes of a citizenry.

Why then are we predisposed to ascribe thinkers like Engels and his more famous partner – or, for that matter, prophets of culture like William Morris or Matthew Arnold – central roles in the process of cultural development, and to consign administrative intellectuals like Kay-Shuttleworth to the relative obscurity of educational history? Why is it that whenever the administrative intellectual appears in more general accounts it is with that mixture of condescension and veiled contempt reserved for those who have failed the great tasks of history through their lack of vision or their 'reformist' complicity with repressive forces? Isn't it because we are still prepared to treat Engels and the others as voices for a process of development which – whether through the conflict of classes or the antagonism of thought and feeling – sees to 'man's' cultural realisation regardless of the particular 'machinery' required to operationalise it? Isn't it because we are still wedded to criteria for the assessment of cultural development – the criteria of complete development and true reflection – that appear to synthesise and transcend the differentiated array of actual norms (for scholarly aptitudes, conduct, ethical bearing, health, civic responsibility, etc.) operative in the practical formation of cultural attributes? In short, isn't it because – the much-vaunted materialist turn in cultural studies notwithstanding – our attempts to investigate the organisational specification and formation of cultural attributes are conducted in the shadow of the concept of culture? – in the shadow of the model of a single general process of contradiction, mediation and overcoming at whose end lies the 'fully developed' human being?

It is the argument of this article that this is indeed the case. I argue that the conceptions of complete development and total point of view underlying both Marxist and non-Marxist cultural studies are unintelligible in their presented forms. Cultural interests and attributes, it is argued, can only be described and assessed relative to delimited norms and forms of calculation;[5] that is, those made available by the actual array of historical institutions in which such interests and attributes are specified and formed. Clearly such an argument entails setting limits to the concept of culture and cultural development. It also requires calling into question those mechanisms – the division of classes, the antinomies of the human subject – long held to be responsible for 'man's' cultural realisation. Only then, it is argued, will we be in a position to engage with the inescapably differentiated, limited and contentious forms of calculation and assessment in which cultural interests and attributes are formulated and operationalised.

THE MATERIALIST TURN

Man knows objectively insofar as his knowledge is real for the whole of mankind *historically* unified in a unitary cultural system; but this process of historical unification takes place with the disappearance of the internal contradictions which are the condition for the formation of groups and the emergence of ideologies which are not concretely universal but are rendered immediately short-lived by the practical origin of their substance. There is, therefore, a struggle towards objectivity (towards being free from partial and fallacious ideologies) and this struggle is itself the struggle for the cultural unification of mankind. What the idealists call 'spirit' is not a point of departure but of arrival, the totality of superstructures in development towards unification which is concrete, objectively universal, and not just a unitary presupposition, etc.[6]

These remarks by Gramsci are exemplary. Not only do they recapitulate Engels's remarks on ideology and culture, they also exemplify the two forms in which culture continues to haunt us: as the reconciliation of certain partial and instrumentally determined oppositions in the direction of totality; and as the rational recovery of the historical forms which have made consciousness possible while eluding it. These are the figures through which the humanities academy presumes to measure cultural development and it is in terms of their negative forms – incompleteness and the unconscious – that a wide variety of social, cultural and political assessments continue to be made. They also represent the twin figures of 'man's' cultural realisation that are unintelligible, I suggest, in their presented forms. Far from being the general imperatives of cultural development, the conceptions of many-sided development and true reflection that coalesce in the idea of culture are in fact products of a specialised instituted domain of aesthetico-ethical practice and speculation, and have no particular pertinence or force outside this domain.

No doubt this proposition will seem incongruous in the present context. After all, wasn't it thinkers like Gramsci and Lukács – and in the English context Raymond Williams and Edward Thompson – who broke down the aesthetic and ethical walls in which the Romantics had imprisoned culture? And wasn't it this materialist turn in cultural studies that freed culture from its high-cultural understanding as art, insisted that it be construed in terms of 'the way of life as a whole', and acknowledged its social determination and political function? In my view, both these questions must be answered in the negative.

Part of the problem is that the Marxist tradition has systematically misunderstood its relation to Romanticism by attributing to the latter a far narrower conception of culture than it in fact held, and by misconstruing the sense in which this conception was aesthetic and ethical. If we look at Schiller's *On the Aesthetic Education of Man*, for example, it is immediately apparent that culture is indeed identified with the totality of social relations and moreover, that its current fragmentation is viewed as a product of the division of labour.

> It was civilization [*Kultur*] itself which inflicted this wound upon modern man. Once the increase of empirical knowledge, and more exact modes of thought, made sharper divisions between the sciences inevitable, and once the increasingly complex machinery of State necessitated a more vigorous separation of ranks and occupations, then the inner unity of human nature was severed too, and a disastrous conflict set its harmonious powers at variance.[7]

At the level of the person this division allows for the overdevelopment of one capacity which 'not infrequently ends by suppressing the rest of our potentialities'; while at the level of the state there arose

> an ingenious clock-work, in which, out of the piecing together of innumerable but lifeless parts, a mechanical kind of collective life ensued. State and Church, laws and customs, were now torn asunder; enjoyment was divorced from labour, the means from the end, the effort from the reward. Everlastingly chained to a single little fragment of the whole, man develops into nothing but a fragment . . . he never develops the harmony of his being, and instead of putting the stamp of humanity upon his own nature, he becomes nothing more than the imprint of his occupation or of his specialized knowledge.[8]

If Schiller anticipates Engels and Gramsci in blaming the division of labour for the fragmentation of ideologies that removes man from his true being, then he similarly accepts the historical necessity of such fragmentation and contradiction as the means by which culture produces the complete development of man and society.

> If the manifold potentialities in man were ever to be developed, there was no other way but to pit them one against the other. The antagonism of faculties and functions is the great instrument of civilization

– but it is only the instrument; for as long as it persists, we are only on the way to becoming civilized. . . .

One-sidedness in the exercise of his powers must, it is true, inevitably lead the individual into error; but the species as a whole to truth.[9]

These remarks from Schiller – and we could have taken them just as easily from Fichte or Hegel – indicate that, far from identifying culture with high art, the Romantics treated it as a general process whose task was to synthesise the social and personal divisions brought about by civilisation. Furthermore, particular knowledges are treated in the manner of ideologies as imprints 'of [man's] occupation or of his specialized knowledge'. Finally, culture as the point of synthesis promising to restore a total point of view is not treated as an ahistorical realm of ideal values; it is in fact identified with the dialectical movement of history itself which by mediating the social and intellectual antinomies progressively unfolds man and society towards their complete forms.

No doubt it will be objected that, regardless of the breadth and complexity of the Romantic conception of culture, it remained rooted in a fundamentally idealistic conception of mind or the 'World Spirit'. Hence although it may have seen the problems of ideology and the division of labour it could not analyse their cause – the alienation of labour under capitalism – or conceive of their overcoming through socialist cultural politics. Failing to grasp the material conditions underlying the dialectic of culture and ideology, and failing to align itself with the only class capable of making these conditions the stake in a conscious political struggle, Romanticism lapsed into 'palliative' aesthetic and ethical activities.[10] But this objection – which has become canonical – is beside the point, for two broad reasons.

In the *first* place, it is arguable that Romantic aesthetics is not in fact a *theory* of culture and society and hence cannot be dismissed as a failed or inadequate theory of culture and society. Perhaps this statement seems contradictory given the previous citations from Schiller; but consider the way in which he actually specifies the character of culture. After describing the division that civilisation has inflicted on human nature in the form of two drives – the 'sensuous drive [which] proceeds from the physical existence of man . . . [and whose] business is to set him within the limits of time, and to turn him into matter' and the 'formal drive [which] proceeds from the absolute existence of man, or from his rational nature, and is intent on giving him the freedom to bring harmony into the diversity of his manifestations, and to affirm his Person among all his changes of condition'[11] – Schiller characterises the action and function of culture in these terms:

To watch over these, and secure for each of these two drives its proper frontiers, is the task of culture, which is, therefore, in duty bound to do justice to both drives equally: not simply to maintain the rational against the sensuous, but the sensuous against the rational too. . . . The former it achieves by developing our capacity for feeling, the latter by developing our capacity for reason.[12]

What is important about this dialectical action of culture for our argument is that it does not flow from the nature of the subject or society.

> But the relaxing of the sense-drive must in no wise be the result of physical impotence or blunted feeling, which never merits anything but contempt. It must be an act of free choice, an activity of the Person which, by its moral intensity, moderates that of the senses. . . . In the same way the relaxing of the formal drive must not be the result of spiritual impotence or flabbiness of thought or will. . . . It must . . . spring from abundance of feeling and sensation.[13]

In other words, what Romantic aesthetics provides is not a *theory* of culture and society but an *aesthetico-ethical exercise* aimed at producing a particular kind of relation to self and, through this, the ethical demeanour and standing of a particular category of person.

I have discussed the deployment of this exercise in some detail in another place.[14] For the present it can be said that Romantic aesthetics provided a minority of 'ethical athletes' with a means for dividing the ethical substance (into the disfiguring drives of thought and feeling, freedom and necessity, didacticism and spontaneity); and a practice of mutual modification or dialectics in which each side was successively played off against the other as a means of shaping the many-sided character. What Romanticism made available – through the idea that (the reading of) literature was always in danger of deviating into an irresponsible formalism or a moralistic didacticism, and through the idea that (the interpretation of) history was perpetually threatened with fragmentation into a narrow utilitarianism and an escapist Romanticism – was not a way of describing literature or history; it was a technique enabling the critic or historian to install the paired disfigurements in his or her own 'ethical substance' and thence to begin shaping this substance according to a practice of mutual modification. In other words, Romantic historicism and criticism provided the techniques for, and the means of inducting individuals into, a local practice of ethical self-problematisation and self-formation.[15]

What needs to be grasped is that since the Romantics, criticism and cultural (later social) history have not been knowledges in the strict sense. They have been the loci of an instituted practice aimed at producing a person possessing a certain aesthetico-ethical capacity and standing on which, it is alleged, knowledge depends. We might instantiate this analysis by drawing a final quotation from Schiller:

> It is not, then, enough to say that all enlightenment of the understanding is worthy of respect only inasmuch as it reacts upon character. To a certain extent it also proceeds from character, since the way to the head must be opened through the heart. The development [*Ausbildung*] of man's capacity for feeling is, therefore, the more urgent need of our age, not merely because it can be a means of making better insights effective for living, but precisely because it provides the impulse for bettering our insights.[16]

But we can just as easily exemplify the same dialectical formulae and the same subordination of theoretical knowledge to aesthetico-ethical capacity and standing in a modern Marxist biography of William Morris. Morris's achievement, it is alleged,

> lies in the open, exploratory character of Utopianism: its leap out of the kingdom of necessity into an imagined kingdom of freedom in which desire may actually indicate choices or impose itself as need; and in its innocence of system and its refusal to be cashed in the same medium of exchange as 'concept', 'mind', 'knowledge' or political text.[17]

Two remarks are warranted by this indicative reconceptualisation of Romantic culture as a definite aesthetico-ethical practice. On the one hand, it clarifies our earlier remark that as a recipe for ethical self-shaping, Romantic aesthetics is immune to Marxist criticisms that it is a false theory of the socio-genesis of culture. Deployed as a technique for the dialectical specification of the 'ethical substance', and as a means of shaping this substance by mutual modification, Romantic aesthetics can be neither true nor false because it exists not as a representation but as an instituted practice. But, on the other hand, this also shows why the concept of culture is unintelligible in its own terms; that is, as a *general* concept of 'man's' historical 'making' governed by the figures of complete development and true reflection. I have suggested that these figures are best seen as projections on the walls of the aesthetico-ethical practice of self-culture itself. To speak of 'complete development' simply means that one has mastered the technique of disavowing as 'utilitarian' or 'reformist' any particular norm of cultural development (such as those specified in Kay-Shuttleworth's blueprint for popular education) by making a counter-affirmation of 'feeling' or 'desire'. (The exercise must then be repeated in the reverse direction.) It does not mean that one has developed some new set of norms for cultural development and that these are in some sense summational or 'complete'. Quite the contrary: what the exercise of the cultural dialectic provides, it seems, is a technique for withdrawing from the discursive and institutional spheres in which cultural attributes are actually specified and formulated.

Consider, as exemplary of such withdrawal, Edward Thompson's dialectical commentary on Morris's conception of socialist society in relation to the Marxist tradition.

> When Morris looked forward to the society of the future, he proposed that a quarrel between desire and utilitarian determinations would continue, and that desire must and could assert its own priorities. . . . The end itself was unobtainable without the prior education of desire or 'need'. And science cannot tell us what to desire or how to desire. . . .
>
> Moreover, if socialists failed to educate desire, and to enlarge this conscious hope, 'to sustain steadily their due claim to that fullness and completeness of life which no class system can give them', then they would more easily fall victim of the 'humbug' of 'a kind of utilitarian sham Socialism'. . . .
>
> Moreover, it should now be clear that there is a sense in which Morris, as a Utopian and moralist, can never be assimilated to Marxism, not because of any contradiction of purposes but because one may not assimilate desire to knowledge, and because the attempt to do so is to confuse two different operative principles of culture.[18]

Suspended in the space between a knowledge which cannot be made definite without becoming utilitarian and a desire which cannot be known until it has been educated by history, it is hardly surprising that the 'society of the future' lacks any definite shape. Culture's conception of a complete development of human capacities is thus, paradoxically enough, empty, save for the capacity for aesthetico-ethical withdrawal itself which is of course highly specialised. It is possible to propose, then, that the Romantic conception of culture is indeed removed from the sphere of the governmental – not because of its 'idealism', however, but owing to the delimited materiality of its own distribution as a cultural practice (through the upper reaches of the educational apparatus) and hence not in a sense that can give any comfort to Marxism.

The *second* problem with the Marxist critique of Romantic aesthetics is that it is in all important respects shaped by the same aesthetico-ethical practice and discourse that shapes its target. This is not, of course, to say that Marxism and Romanticism are identical or that the former is a species of the latter. It is to say, however, that being relatively independent of the idealist ontology that it receives in Romantic aesthetics, the practice of the cultural dialectic can quite readily assume the materialist ontology of Marxism. The argument here is that replacing 'spirit' with 'labour' may make little difference to the conceptualisation of culture, as the preceding quotation from Thompson indicates. In fact it may be a sign that the conception of labour operative in Marxism is itself rooted in the aesthetico-ethical dialectic of culture.

This is a complex topic and it would be difficult to do justice to it in the available space. Fortunately for me Stephen Gaukroger has recently brought significantly new light to it. Gaukroger's argument is that Marx's conception of socialism – in particular the goal of decommodification and the overcoming of alienation – is rooted in an aesthetic conception of labour. In order to make sense of this argument it will help us to recall that, as we have seen in the case of Schiller's treatise, the meaning of 'aesthetic' was not initially confined to the sphere of art. Broadly construed, 'aesthetic' names a disposition or mode of being in which 'man' comes into his full powers not through reason alone but through a process or activity of self-making in which reason and the senses, freedom and necessity, are played off against each other. It is in this sense, Gaukroger argues, that Marx's conception of labour is an aesthetic one, assuming in fact the same schema of division, alienation, reconciliation and self-formation already seen in Schiller's account of culture. Hence in the 1840s we find Marx saying:

> It is just in his work upon the objective world, therefore, that man really proves himself to be a species being. This production is his active species life. Through this production, nature appears as *his* work and his reality. The object of labour is, therefore, the *objectification of man's species life*: for he duplicates himself not only, as in consciousness, intellectually, but also actively, in reality, and therefore he sees himself in a world that he has created. In tearing away from man the object of his production, therefore, estranged labour tears him from his *species life*, his real objectivity as a member of the species, and transforms his advantage over animals into the disadvantage that his inorganic body, nature, is taken away from him.[19]

But if this model is susceptible of a variety of investments including, as we have seen, that of 'culture', then there is no prima facie reason why 'labour' should have any particular privilege as the vehicle for 'man's' self-constitutive activity. Gaukroger points out that during the 1840s there were a number of equally plausible contending specifications of this vehicle: Bauer's claim that 'man' constituted himself through the creation of cultural forms and systems of values, and Feuerbach's argument that this was achieved through a naturalistically conceived cognitive activity.[20]

Moreover, in attempting to reconcile self-constitutive activity (characterised by the realisation of the self in products but not necessarily by the payment of wages) and wage labour (defined by the payment of wages but not necessarily by the manufacture of products) Marx is forced to posit a hybrid essence for labour: manufacturing 'productive' labour. The trouble with this outcome, argues Gaukroger, is that it produces an analysis of social and political problems (in terms of the alienation of manufacturing 'productive' labour) and their resolution (via decommodification and the overcoming of alienation) that simply fails to engage with the forms in which such problems arise and are addressable. His comment warrants a full quotation.

> This is a disaster of the first order. It would not be so bad if Marx's conception provided some basis for social and political change. But it does not do this. Indeed, in some ways it presents an obstacle to the formulation of serious social policies. In one respect, it is too specific – by tending to focus attention on industrial 'productive' labour it restricts the range of central socio-economic problems in a disastrous fashion. In another respect, however, it is too abstract. Indeed, it is arguable that Marx is not even envisaging a society, let alone providing us with an understanding of how it might be achieved. We are not being given an account of how social and political problems are to be recognised, or to be posed, or the mechanisms by which we might hope to resolve them. Rather, we are being presented with a picture of a state of affairs in which there are effectively no social problems: after all, if there is no alienation from nature, oneself, the human species, and others, what social or political problems could there possibly be?[21]

But isn't this precisely the outcome that we should expect if, as I have suggested, 'labour' in Marxism is a variant focus for the same aesthetico-ethical practice and speculation as 'culture' is in Romanticism? Again, the scope of this problem is such that I want to open it up for discussion and indicate a line of analysis rather than draw final conclusions. We certainly have warrant for saying, however, that the 'materialist inversion' that proposes to ground culture in labour by no means guarantees a way out of the aesthetic conception of cultural development or a way into the sphere of 'organised' culture. Far from it: there is every reason to suspect that Marxist conceptions of culture as a form of 'production' modelled on self-constitutive labour are in fact an optional variant of the aesthetic model of culture. If this is so then we should not be too surprised if the conceptions of complete development and true reflection thrown up by the Marxian dialectic – Gramsci's 'unitary cultural system' and total point of view – turn out to be just as vacuous as their Romantic partners, and for the same reasons. On the one hand, by disavowing the historically available institutions of cultural formation as partial expressions of incomplete historical agents (classes), the Marxist conception of culture removes itself from the actual norms and forms of calculation in which cultural interests and attributes are formulated and assessed. On the other, by continuing to employ notions of complete development and true reflection that have no purchase or pertinence outside of those (largely educational) spheres in which the aesthetico-ethical dialectic is practised, Marxist cultural studies declines to the status of a limited species of ethical self-formation and produces a knowledge that is inseparable from the ethical persona and authority of the cultural critic.

It is possible to extrapolate a number of indicative remarks on the basis of the preceding discussion, even if only to set an agenda for further discussion and investigation.

First, it should now be clear that it is quite misguided to theorise the problem of culture in terms of the segregation of art from other social activities; hence in terms of the need to reintegrate it in 'the way of life as a whole' where it might provide the model for self-fulfilling labour or the 'cultural unification of mankind'. This analysis never leaves the confines of the concept of culture itself. It takes place entirely within the conception of a 'wound' inflicted on society by the division of labour: one which only establishes certain exemplary antagonisms – between reason and the senses, aesthetic reflection and economic relations, desire and utility – in order to set the scene for their overcoming and reintegration in the empty figures of complete development: the fully developed society, true community, the many-sided personality and so on. If, however, cultural interests and attributes can only be formulated and shaped in the context of delimited norms and techniques, then the forms of their articulation and the degree of their integration must also be normative, contingent and 'organisational'. This is clearly the case with Kay-Shuttleworth's operationalisation of norms for literacy, conduct, health, grooming and sentiment in the regimen of the popular school, itself organised by definite forms of social and political calculation concerning the 'moral and physical condition' of the population. There is simply no reason why the question of art and its degree of integration with other social and cultural capacities should have any particular pertinence in this context.

Second, it becomes necessary to reject the imperative that the analysis of cultural practices and institutions should proceed according to a dialectical model, whether Marxist or non-Marxist. I have argued that the idea that subjectivity is divided by opposed utilitarian and sensuous drives, and the idea that cultural development is driven by the antagonism of class consciousness and historical determination – or ideology and 'social forces' – do not in fact function as descriptions of states of affairs. The need for state intervention in popular education and the forms this should take did not appear to someone like Kay-Shuttleworth in the form of ideas or representations generated by 'real' or 'material' forces operative at another level of being: the relations of economic production. Instead, this programme took shape on the surface of a set of quite material techniques and forms of calculation, typified by the techniques of 'moral statistics'. These were in turn dependent on definite forms of observation and normatisation which the disciplinary, assistantial and medical apparatuses deployed in the nineteenth-century city. This is not to say that these techniques of calculation were incapable of formulating economic and political interests alongside social and cultural ones. Nor is it to suggest that they operated in a hermetically sealed administrative apparatus. To the contrary: Kay-Shuttleworth took into account the economic benefits flowing from the higher levels and forms of consumption characteristic of educated populations (while quite rightly insisting that these benefits were not solely economic); and there is no doubt that a variety of non-administrative cultural practices and institutions – one can mention those of Christian pastoral care in particular – entered into the governmental programme for popular education. It is to say, however, that when these diverse interests and practices entered the programme they did so as the product of definite and limited forms of reasoning deployed in specific organisations: churches, political parties, statistical and philanthropic societies, etc. They were not the emissaries of a different domain of being (the material or economic) and its inhabitants (social classes) which they might represent more, or less, adequately depending on their degree of dialectical development, the extent to which they had reflected back on the economic and transformed it. The idea that they were – the idea that cultural technologies like the school system are shaped by a general movement between social consciousness and social position, and that in this movement the constraints placed on consciousness by position must be continuously played off against the promise of the totalisation of positions made by consciousness – these are signs that the attempt to describe a particular cultural technology is being forced to pass through an aesthetico-ethical practice targeted on the formation of a special ethical personality. Ever since the time of Schiller we have been told that our description of culture is insufficiently dialectical; now the great challenge is to escape the gigantic ethical pincers of the dialectic and to describe cultural technologies as 'motley' or non-oriented ensembles of norms, practices, techniques and institutions.

Third, strict limits must be established for the concept of culture itself and for its theoretical uses. Consider the following remarks in which Raymond Williams recapitulates the theme of culture as a general organon for all forms of human development in his account of 'a process of general growth of man as a kind'. According to this account the generality of this process of growth is reflected in the universality of the 'meanings and values' to which it gives rise.

We are most aware of these [meanings and values] in the form of particular techniques, in medicine, production, and communications, but it is clear not only that these depend on more purely intellectual disciplines, which had to be wrought out in the creative handling of experience, but also that these disciplines in themselves, together with certain basic ethical assumptions and certain major art forms, have proved similarly capable of being gathered into a general tradition which seems to represent, through many variations and conflicts, a line of common growth. It seems reasonable to speak of this tradition as a general human culture, while adding that it can only become active within particular societies shaped, as it does so, by more local and temporary systems.[22]

But is this 'clear' or 'reasonable'? I have argued that cultural interests and capacities can only be formulated and assessed in the context of definite normative and technical regimes (such as those provided by legal, medical, educational, political, sexual and familial institutions) and that these can only be combined according to equally normative and 'organisational' programmes (such as that assembled around the campaign for popular education). If this is the case then there is no reason to think that such regimes and programmes are founded on 'more purely intellectual disciplines' or the universal aesthetic and ethical forms of a 'general human culture'. Cultural studies has been driven by the imperative to expand the aesthetic concept of culture – the dialectic, the goal of complete development – to all social activities and relations, so that aesthetic fulfilment can be both superseded by and extended to 'the way of life as a whole'. In the light of the preceding discussion it is possible to formulate a quite different imperative: to *restrict* this concept of culture to the specialised practice of aesthetico-ethical self-shaping in which it has pertinence and to begin to chart the limited *degree* of generality it has achieved as a technique of person-formation in the educational apparatus. Only then will it be possible to propose a more appropriate understanding of the term 'culture': as a signpost pointing in the general direction of a patchwork of institutions in which human attributes are formed and which, having no necessary features in common, must be described and assessed from case to case.

Finally, it is necessary to abandon the ethical posture and forms of cultural judgement invested in the concept of culture as complete development and true reflection. While it may be possible to withhold assent from any actual organisational intervention in the formation and regulation of cultural attributes – denouncing it as utilitarian in relation to the possibilities of desire or as ideological ('partial and fallacious') in relation to the historical development of a unified culture – such criticisms only make sense as elements of a highly specialised ethical exercise, as is shown by their dialectical form. I have argued that, outside this special sphere, the practice of playing off utility and desire, ideology and culture, produces conceptions of complete development emptied of all content. In fact these conceptions of cultural development are for all practical purposes unintelligible because they are produced by a practice of withdrawing from the actual norms and techniques used in the institutions of cultural formation. The type of judgement produced under these circumstances can be illustrated easily enough in Coleridge's remark that:

> civilisation is itself but a mixed good, if not far more a corrupting influence . . . where this civilisation is not grounded in cultivation, in the harmonious development of those qualities and faculties that characterise our humanity. We must be men in order to be citizens.[23]

But it can be seen just as readily in William Morris's claim that socialism 'is not change for the sake of change, but a change involving the very noblest ideal of human life and duty: a life in which every human being should find unrestricted scope for his best powers and faculties'.[24] It is precisely these conceptions of the 'unrestricted scope' of the forms of ethical development and assessment and the many-sided development of human faculties – which Coleridge invested in a cultivated elite and Morris in the 'practical experience' of the working class – that must be abandoned. If, as has been argued, the formulation and assessment of cultural interests and attributes is the product of instituted – hence inescapably differentiated and delimited – norms and forms of calculation, then it is meaningless to propose as a political programme the 'unrestricted' development of such interests and attributes. It may not be necessary to directly invert Coleridge's remark that 'We must be men in order to be citizens'; but it is necessary to say that the normative and technical interventions through which the apparatuses of health, penality, education, welfare and the law have sought to form the cultural attributes of a citizenry set inescapable limits to our understanding of what men and women can be. Not until the investigation of culture is carried out within these limits will it be able to engage with the specific and differentiated organisational rationalities in which various cultural interests and attributes are formulated and assessed.

'ARTICULATION'

Given the fairly general character of the preceding argument let me conclude it by offering some more historically focused remarks. I will do so by looking at a variant of cultural studies that may seem to avoid the worst of the problems identified above. This is a variant developed in the name of Gramsci and one, so it is argued, that avoids the pitfalls of attempting to analyse ideology and culture in terms of pre-given (class) interests and destinies but nonetheless manages to retain them as general terms of cultural and political analysis.

It has been argued that the key to the achievement of this theoretical balancing act lies in the concept of articulation. According to Stuart Hall this concept is the bearer of an important double meaning. First, 'articulate' 'means to utter, to speak forth, to be articulate. It carries the sense of language-ing, of expressing, etc'. Second, it means to link up or connect two or more discrete elements. 'An articulation is thus the form of the connection that *can* make a unity of two different elements, under certain conditions. It is a linkage which is not necessary, determined, absolute and essential for all time.'[25] So, when one speaks of the articulation of social groups and forces to or by particular ideologies the double meaning makes it possible to achieve an important theoretical reconciliation. On the one hand, the second (contingent linkage) sense 'enables us to think how an ideology empowers people, enabling them to begin to make some sense of intelligibility of their historical situation, without reducing those forms of intelligibility to their socio-economic or class location or social position'. On the other hand, the first (expressivist) meaning, though decidedly in the background, maintains the possibility that an ideology may indeed be a vehicle expressing the interests and values of particular social forces or groups:

> In that sense, I don't refuse the connection between an ideology or cultural force and a social force; indeed, I want to *insist* that the popular force of an organic ideology always depends upon the social groups that can be articulated to and by it.[26]

So if, in the first instance, the cultural interests and attributes of particular groups are the product of ideologies which they adopt in a contingent and practical fashion then, in the second, the 'popular force of an organic ideology' is the product of the interests and attributes of the social groups expressed by it. No doubt it is this looming circularity that leads Hall to take refuge in an all-too-familiar sanctuary: 'The relationship between social forces and ideology is absolutely dialectical. As the ideological vision emerges, so does the group.'[27] It is this 'dialectical' concept of articulation that is supposed to show the superiority of Gramsci's theory of culture and ideology over conventional Marxist versions. Gramsci's account, it is argued, avoids equating ideological domination with the coercive rule of a dominant class. In stressing the non-necessary articulation of classes 'to and by' ideologies it retheorises domination in terms of hegemony or the 'winning of the consent of the subordinated classes': a process of conjunctural struggle ending in the formation of a stabilised 'historical bloc' in which the subordinated classes find their interests and values detoured through those of the hegemonic class.[28]

In expanding on the 'hegemonic principle' Chantal Mouffe does little more than reiterate this circular or 'dialectical' model. On the one hand, it seems that this principle

> involves a system of values the realisation of which depends on the

central role played by the fundamental class at the level of the relations of production. Thus the intellectual and moral direction exercised by a fundamental class in a hegemonic system consists in providing the articulating principle of the common world-view, the value system to which the ideological elements coming from other groups will be articulated in order to form a unified ideological system, that is to say an organic ideology.[29]

On the other hand, it is 'by their articulation to a hegemonic principle that the ideological elements acquire their class character which is not intrinsic to them'.[30] The articulation of classes into a hegemonic system thus depends on values 'realised' through the position of the fundamental class in the relations of production. But, at the same time, this articulation is also the means by which classes acquire values and a worldview 'not intrinsic to them'. Here the idea that the class character of interests and values is both acquired yet fundamental is an effect of the speed with which class values, having been thrown out of the window of 'non-necessary articulation', reappear in the doorway as the principle of articulation itself.

The problem with this general line of analysis can be stated quite succinctly: it puts cultural and political interests and capacities (the 'system of values') on both sides of the equation – as something *formed* by ideological practices or processes of articulation which possess no necessary relation to particular classes or groups; and as something that classes and groups *must already possess* as the stake in the 'ideological struggle', as that which they seek to win consent to and hence express through ideology. At the risk of seeming insufficiently dialectical, it must be said that this theoretical oscillation is quite disabling for any attempt to develop forms of analysis of particular cultural policies and institutions. Either classes have political and cultural interests and capacities, in which case we know what it is that the ideological struggle is meant to further; or they do not – interests and capacities being shaped by a variety of forms of calculation and social organisation irreducible to class – in which case we can have no general idea of what 'the struggle' is meant to further. Indeed, under these latter circumstances the notion of a general struggle between contending classes or 'rival hegemonic principles' over ideologies or cultural meanings becomes unintelligible. Instead of appealing to the ideological articulation (in either sense) of class interests, we must look to the differentiated array of organisational forms in which cultural interests and capacities are formulated, if we are to engage with the forms in which they are assessed and argued over.

The idea that cultural and political interests and capacities somehow acquire a class character without being directly derived from class locations or social positions simply fudges this issue. In fact it is doubly disabling for any attempt to develop practical forms of cultural analysis and assessment. By proposing that such assessment need not be carried out using the norms and forms of calculation of any given cultural institution – that we must wait to see which class interests or hegemonic principle the institution is articulated to or by – it tends towards opportunism. At the same time, because it continues to hold that cultural institutions are indeed expressive of class interests or values, this conception views such institutions as self-(in)validating depending on their degree of partiality in relation to the cultural totality;[31] hence it tends towards utopianism and lack of specificity.

Consider the outcomes of this type of cultural analysis when applied to the institutions of popular education. According to Gramsci:

> The basic division of schools into classical (i.e. grammar) and trade schools was a rational scheme: trade schools for the instrumental classes, classical schools for the ruling classes and intellectuals. The development of the industrial base in both town and country led to growing need for a new type of urban intellectual: alongside the classical school there developed the technical school (professional but not manual), and this brought into question the very principle of the concrete orientation of general culture based on the Greco-Roman tradition.

After decrying this division of education into a large technocratic sector and a residual cultured sector patronised by the leisured classes Gramsci continues:

> This crisis will find a solution which rationally should follow these lines: a single humanistic, formative primary school of general culture which will correctly balance the development of ability for manual (technical, industrial) work with the development of ability for intellectual work.[32]

The general lines of this analysis have been developed in a number of ways. Some have argued that the general popular schools that actually did develop in England and elsewhere in fact continued the technical-cultural division, providing a purely instrumental education and reserving the full wealth of culture for the middle-class grammar schools. Others have stressed the role of the new popular schools in winning the consent of the popular classes to bourgeois rule. Richard Johnson, for example, has argued that the new organisation of the popular school that emerged during the 1840s – the deployment of trained teachers using non-coercive methods; the reorganisation of school architecture and discipline around the child and its teacher as a couple bonded by sympathy and surveillance; the inculcation of norms through play as well as work – was simply a more 'subtle' way of moulding working-class children to the bourgeois ethics of regularity and conformity required by industrial labour. Observing that the attributes of literacy, conduct and sentiment invested in the popular school had a moral as well as an educational basis – requiring as they did a certain normalisation of behaviour in order to be acquired and resting as they did on normative investigations of populations lacking these attributes – Johnson comments:

> What is being stigmatised in all this [investigative] literature is a whole way of life. If one lists those aspects of the working class that meet with censure, it is the comprehensiveness of the indictment that is striking. The attack covers almost every aspect of belief and behaviour – all the characteristic institutions, folklore, 'common sense' and mentalities of the class, its culture (or cultures) in the broad anthropological meaning of the word.[33]

According to Johnson, this culture was invested in the autodidactic and self-realising educational activities of working-class political and familial institutions:

> These activities were no accidental by-product of radical activity. They were organic to the movements themselves. Chartists and Owenites in particular espoused education – '*really* useful knowledge' – in much the way in which Gramsci espoused it as a latter-day 'Jacobin' and educator for Italian communism.[34]

If educational reformers like Kay-Shuttleworth criticised the working-class family as well as more conspicuous forms of radicalism:

> It was the duality of the task – re-establishing the means of hegemony and transforming the psychological world of labour – that gave particular urgency to the project. The school and school teacher must take the child from home and prepare it for work and loyal citizenship.[35]

The extent to which this analysis is carried out in terms of the aesthetico-ethical conception of culture as complete development and true reflection should be clear enough. The extent to which the analysis of popular education in terms of articulation and hegemony represents a variant form of this conception is addressed in the following remarks.

First, it is necessary to clarify some historical issues. In England and Australia at least, popular schools pre-dated the development of technical education and hence cannot be seen as some sort of (failed) attempt to compensate for this development. Neither can popular education be seen as a purely instrumental form of training, designed to prepare the popular classes for life in a 'mechanical' society while the unfettered development promised by culture was reserved for the middle classes in their grammar schools. To the contrary; as early as 1867 Matthew Arnold, in his capacity as a school inspector, had compared the 'mechanical' character of grammar-school instruction with the sincerity and 'freedom from charlatanism given to the instruction of our primary schools';[36] in F. W. Farrar's *Essays on a Liberal Education* published in the same year grammar schools were under attack for the same reasons;[37] and by the time of the Newbolt Report and Geoffrey Sampson's *English for the English* in 1921 it was the popular school – with its 'sympathetic' relations between teacher and student, its tactics of supervised freedom and correction through self-expression – that was being identified with culture and championed as a model for the reform of the grammar-school curriculum.[38]

Second, and more importantly, while it is true that the cultural capacities (of literacy, conduct, health, manners, etc.) targeted for development by the educational reformers of the 1830s and 1840s were indeed normatively based and premised on normalising techniques, this is not enough to construe them as ideological. It only appears to be so when it is assumed that these norms and techniques have been deployed at the behest of a tendentious class interest (e.g. in a disciplined labour force) and when the population they are imposed on is assumed to be shaped by a more complete process of development (working-class) culture. Neither of these assumptions is tenable, however: the first because, as we have seen, the interest in popular education, the means by which it was formulated and the norms and techniques of its implementation, were the product of forms of calculation and institutional ensembles (medical, assistantial, disciplinary, religious) irreducible to any notion of class location; the second because, to repeat the general point, if cultural interests and attributes can only be formulated and developed via definite norms and organised behaviours then it is meaningless to think of working-class norms and organisations as possessing some special privilege through some 'organic' relation to experience or the cultural totality of a 'whole way of life'.

Finally, this last point can be clarified, and the problems endemic to the concepts of articulation and hegemony specified, through the following historical observation: when the Chartists came to plan their own popular school system they drew on the same educational thinkers (David Stow and Samuel Wilderspin in particular) and the same norms and techniques (the techniques of supervised freedom and correction through play invested in a trained 'sympathetic' teacher) as utilised by Kay-Shuttleworth in his implementation of state popular education.[39] What are we to say about this? That educational ideologies are only contingently 'articulated' to particular classes, that they may therefore be struggled over, and that our judgement must therefore be contingent on which class is victorious? Such a response is surely quite inadequate to the problem. It evacuates the organisational norms, techniques and forms of calculation employed in the educational apparatus of all specificity and effect by appealing to adjudication on a higher level – class contestation.

Further, it places the analyst in a false and opportunistic position by implying that such a contest, and the assessment of its outcome, might take place independently of the sphere of organised reason in which popular education was brought within the range of thought. Are we to say, then, that by adopting the same normative forms of moral training as the state system the Chartist programme is revealed as an ideological variant of the latter, co-opted into serving the same political and cultural interests? But this response is no better than the first. It begins the regress of ethical and political fastidiousness in which all actual norms and techniques for cultural formation remain partial in relation to culture as 'the way of life as a whole'. And it places the analyst in the phantasmatic and utopian position of assuming that new techniques for assessing the need for popular education, for specifying the teacher-child couple, forms of discipline, etc., will be somehow whistled into existence by history in a form appropriate to the 'unrestricted scope' of human development.

I have presented an argument showing how such responses arise from a conception of culture which itself has the form of an aesthetico-ethical practice aimed at forming the exemplary persona of the cultural critic. This concept of culture – as complete development and true reflection – only makes sense relative to the highly specialised form of personal development made possible by this practice and cannot be applied to the analysis of cultural institutions generally. The field of cultural institutions, I have suggested, is not rich, organically interrelated or dialectically open-ended; it is relatively sparse on any given historical occasion, differentiated and limited in the range of interests, attributes and forms of assessment that it admits of. The investigation of such a field clearly entails setting limits to culture.

NOTES

This chapter first appeared in *New Formations*, 4 (Spring 1988), Routledge
  1 Frederick Engels, 'Engels to C. Schmidt in Berlin', in Karl Marx and Frederick Engels, *Selected Works* (single volume), Progress Publishers, Moscow 1965, p. 694.
  2 James Kay-Shuttleworth, *The Moral and Physical Condition of the Working Classes of Manchester in 1832*. Collected in the author's *Four Periods of Public Education*, Harvester, London, 1973, pp. 3–4.
  3 Engels, 'Engels to C. Schmidt', pp. 697–8.
  4 Kay-Shuttleworth, *Moral and Physical Condition*, p. 5.
  5 For a parallel argument with regard to political interests see Barry Hindess, ' "Interests" in political analysis' in John Law (ed.), *Power, Action and Belief*, Routledge & Kegan Paul, London, 1986. I am indebted to this article for a number of formulations.
  6 Antonio Gramsci, *The Modern Prince and Other Writings*, International Publishers, New York, 1957 pp. 106–7. It will become clear that in drawing out

quotations of this sort I am not attempting to mount a critique of the complete *oeuvre* of a particular author. Rather, I am exemplifying a discursive and ethical practice operative in a variety of authors and even in opposed traditions of analysis. The extent to which this practice exhausts the work of a particular writer is not something that I have attempted to address in this article.

7 Friedrich Schiller, *On the Aesthetic Education of Man*, ed., trans., and introduced by Elizabeth Wilkinson and L. A. Willoughby, Clarendon Press, Oxford, 1967, p. 33.
8 ibid., p. 35.
9 ibid., p. 41.
10 The central documents of this position are Raymond Williams, *Culture and Society 1780–1950*, Penguin, Harmondsworth, 1958 and E. P. Thompson, *William Morris: Romantic to Revolutionary*, Pantheon, New York, 1955–76.
11 Schiller, *Aesthetic Education*, pp. 79–81.
12 ibid., p. 87.
13 ibid., p. 93.
14 In Ian Hunter, *Culture and Government: The Emergence of Literary Education*, Macmillan, London, 1988.
15 ibid., ch. 3.
16 Schiller, *Aesthetic Education*, p. 53.
17 Edward Thompson, in the 'Postscript: 1976' to his *William Morris*, pp. 798–9.
18 ibid., pp. 804–7.
19 Stephen Gaukroger, 'Romanticism and decommodification: Marx's conception of socialism', *Economy and Society*, 15 (1986), 304.
20 ibid., pp. 308–9.
21 ibid., p. 311.
22 Raymond Williams, *The Long Revolution*, Penguin, Harmondsworth, 1961, p. 59.
23 S. T. Coleridge, *On the Constitution of Church and State*, William Pickering, London, 1839, p. 46.
24 Cited in Thompson, *William Morris*, p. 725.
25 In Lawrence Grossberg (ed.), 'On postmodernism and articulation: an interview with Stuart Hall', *Journal of Communication Inquiry*, 10 (1986), 53–5.
26 ibid.
27 ibid.
28 See Stuart Hall, 'The rediscovery of "ideology": return of the repressed in media studies', in M. Gurevitch, T. Bennett, J. Curran and J. Woollacott (eds), *Culture, Society and The Media*, Methuen, London, 1982.
29 Chantal Mouffe, 'Hegemony and ideology in Gramsci', in C. Mouffe (ed.), *Gramsci and Marxist Theory*, Routledge & Kegan Paul, London, 1980, p. 193.
30 ibid.
31 Consider Hall's claim ('Rediscovery of "ideology" ', 86) that media institutions

powerfully secure consent because their claim to be independent of the direct play of political or economic interests, or of the state, is not wholly fictitious. The claim is ideological, not because it is false but because it does not grasp all the conditions which make freedom and impartiality possible. It is ideological because it offers a partial explanation as if it were a comprehensive and adequate one – it takes the part for the whole (fetishism).

32 Gramsci, *Modern Prince*, pp. 126–7.
33 Richard Johnson, 'Notes on the schooling of the English working class

1780–1850', in R. Dale, G. Esland, and G. MacDonald (eds), *Schooling and Capitalism*, Routledge & Kegan Paul, London, 1976, p. 49.

34 ibid., p. 50.

35 ibid., p. 51

36 Matthew Arnold, *Reports on Elementary Schools 1852–1882*, ed. by F. R. Sandford, Macmillan, London, 1889, p. 131.

37 F. W. Farrar (ed.), *Essays on a Liberal Education*, Macmillan, London, 1867.

38 Henry Newbolt *et al., The Teaching of English in England*, HMSO, London, 1921. Geoffrey Sampson, *English for the English*, Cambridge University Press, Cambridge, 1921.

39 See especially the remarks on moral training and the playground in W. Lovett and J. Collins, *Chartism: A New Organisation of the People*, Leicester University Press, Leicester (1840) 1969, pp. 90–1.

Chapter 8

What's 'ethnographic' about ethnographic audience research?

Virginia Nightingale

INTRODUCTION

Cultural studies, in its current state of development, offers two overlapping methodological strategies that need to be combined, and the differences between them submerged, if we are to understand this cultural struggle. One derives from ethnography and requires us to study the meanings that the fans [of Madonna] actually do (or appear to) make [of her]. This involves listening to them, reading the letters they write to fan magazines, or observing their behaviour at home or in public. The fan's words or behaviour are not, of course, empirical facts that speak for themselves: they are, rather, texts that need 'reading' theoretically in just the same way as the 'texts of Madonna' do.

The other strategy derives from semiotic and structuralist textual analysis. This strategy involves a close reading of the signifiers of the text – that is, its physical presence – but recognises that the signifieds exist not in the text itself, but extratextually, in the myths, counter-myths, and ideology of their culture. It recognises that the distribution of power in society is paralleled by the distribution of meanings in texts, and that struggles for social power are paralleled by semiotic struggles for meanings. Every text and every reading has a social and therefore political dimension, which is to be found partly in the structure of the text itself and partly in the relation of the reading subject to the text.

(Fiske, 1987: 272)

I must confess to a perverse fascination with this quotation from Fiske's 1987 book, *Television Culture*. My fascination centres around both the understanding of 'cultural studies' presented and the terminology used to describe it. The perversity of my fascination, on the other hand, emanates from a sense of the impossibility of the task so glibly outlined, from a sense of horror at the scope of the theoretical and methodological abyss such a project presents for the serious researcher, and from my own obstinate inability to ignore the contradictions inherent in the statement.

The disquiet and bewilderment is intensified by the actual research Fiske calls on to corroborate his summary of the cultural studies project and in the gap between what is desired of the research and what is realised. This paper, then, grows out of a commitment to such a cultural studies project and to popular cultural research which recognises the importance of audience-text interactions. Nevertheless, the commitment to cultural studies is matched by an equal commitment, an obstinate commitment, to the necessity to consider the theoretical and methodological difficulties and implications of such research.

The developments in cultural studies to which Fiske refers above derive from two theoretical projects formulated most persuasively in the 1970s by Stuart Hall: the research project encompassed by the encoding/decoding model and the marrying of the 'two paradigms of cultural studies', British culturalism and the European structuralisms (Hall, 1980a and 1980b). The research initiatives inspired by these projects reference other cultural studies projects, viz. the subcultures and deviance research of the late 1960s and early 1970s as much as they reflect contemporary theoretical debates about texts, discourse, knowledge and power.

Four central characteristics of such cultural studies research are worth noting. First, the research characteristically focuses on *texts*, and specifically on high-rating television programmes or the more popular music videos as its objects of research, followed by a variety of attempts to 'read' the audience. Second, this body of research characteristically focuses on, and legitimates, the study of *popular culture*. In particular, it legitimates the study of the texts created, produced and distributed by multinational media companies as well as particular approaches to the study of the people who enjoy such commodities. Third, the research usually recognises the importance of *discourse* as the form in which cultural meanings circulate, even though cultural studies researchers appear increasingly reluctant to pursue an *analysis* of such discourse (see especially Tulloch and Moran, 1986; Buckingham, 1987). And last, the research either claims, or has attributed to it, the quality *ethnographic*. It is with this last characteristic that I will deal in this paper, even though separating the *ethnographic* from issues of *text* and *discourse* may appear to minimise the complexity of each and the importance of the interaction of all four characteristics (issues which I have pursued elsewhere, see Nightingale, 1989).

The apparently simple formula (suggested by Fiske in the quotation above) of using semiotics to study texts and ethnography to study audiences, depends for its coherence on a refusal to acknowledge the theoretical and methodological inadequacies inherent in the enterprise. Such inadequacies include:

- the possibility/impossibility of 'reading' the audience using ethnography;
- the lack of specificity as to the appropriate hermeneutic principles required to analyse letters, transcripts of interviews, personal documents, etc. compared to the sophistication of semiotic approaches to the analysis of texts produced as cultural forms within institutionalised structures;
- the lack of any justification for treating letters (for example) differently from television programmes as texts;
- the lack of justification for 'reading' the accounts people give of their television-related practices at face value, with a crudity reminiscent of the grossest content analysis, rather than with the sophistication of semiotics, psycho-analysis, discourse analysis and the other 'cultural' research methods – methods which constitute the finest achievements of cultural studies over the last twenty years;
- the apparently absolute refusal to apply principles of 'readership', particularly those which stress the recognition that meaning is as much in the reader as in the text, to the reading of research 'texts' such as interviews, letters, diaries, etc., as read by the researcher.

These inadequacies reflect a lack of resolution of two fundamental contradictions inherent in such research – contradictions about where the meaning of a text is likely to be found and contradictions about the nature of 'ethnography' and what the researchers expect of it.

The first contradiction stems from a lack of resolution of the problem of textual meaning – the supposition that the text can stand alone, separate from its 'readers', in order to be 'read' semiotically, while at the same time being dependent on its readers for its meaning. This is the fundamental contradiction which surfaced in Morley (1980) – the problem of matching two sets of incommensurable readings: the disciplined reading of the researchers (see Brunsdon and Morley, 1978) with the 'unschooled' reading of the casual viewer. In this case the meaning of the text, *Nationwide*, is considered commensurate with the reading produced by the researchers, an assumption which is in itself tenuous. Preferring to interview fans rather than casual viewers (a solution to this problem chosen by several of the studies mentioned below) fails to solve this dilemma, for what is needed is some analysis of how the programme schools/teaches its 'fan' viewers to read sympathetically (fans, by definition, *always* read sympathetically and actively) as well as some criteria to distinguish between the reading of fans and casual viewers. While Buckingham (1987) has made a start on this problem in his application of Iser's reader-response theory to the analysis of the textual invitations offered by *EastEnders*, the task is far from complete.

The second contradiction, the one on which I will focus for the rest of this paper, involves the audience, and specifically the suggestion that it is possible to 'read' an audience *ethnographically*. The contradiction for 'ethnographic' audience research seems here to be based in a confusion between 'ethnography' and 'interpretative anthropology', a confusion of the descriptive and classificatory work of ethnography with the interpretative work possible once cultures are seen as metaphors for texts (see Marcus and Fischer, 1986: 17–44). Within cultural studies, for example, this contradiction can be seen in the failure to distinguish between the 'ethnography' of Paul Willis (1977) which applies 'ethnography to projects of broader purpose and theoretical significance' (Marcus, 1986: 188) and the 'interpretative anthropology' of Dick Hebdige (1979) which draws more directly on the structuralist theories and methods of Lévi-Strauss. The audience 'ethnographies' produced in encoding/decoding research follow Willis in the use of naturalist research methods (see Roberts, 1976) but refrain from sharing his focus on broad social process, and stop short of the interpretative work needed to 'read' the audience. In this sense the studies are unfortunately compromised – drawing on interpretative procedures to understand the texts around which the audience clusters and on descriptive measures only to account for the audience. Such an account must be a non-account.

What, then, is 'ethnographic' abut ethnographic audience research? Is 'ethnographic' an appropriate description for research of this type? In attempting to answer this question, I will refer to research carried out about five popular television programmes: the *Nationwide* research (Brunsdon and Morley, 1978 and Morley, 1980); the *Crossroads* research (Hobson, 1982); the *Dallas* research (Ang, 1985); the *Country Practice* research (Tulloch and Moran, 1986); and the *EastEnders* research (Buckingham, 1987). Morley, Ang and Hobson are all cited by Fiske (1987) as examples of the use of ethnography to carry out audience research. These studies use, among them, a combination of research methods which include participant observation (Hobson; Tulloch and Moran), group interviews (Morley; Tulloch and Moran; Buckingham), letters solicited by the researcher (Ang) or written (unsolicited) to newspapers or television channels (Hobson: Tulloch and Moran), as well as informal discussions with students (Tulloch and Moran). In each case the audience component of the research complements an extensive commitment to description/ explanation of the television programme. In the work of both Hobson and Tulloch and Moran the work on the television programme is based in participant observation, and is every bit as 'ethnographic' in character as the audience research, but for some reason seldom actually described as such.

The description of this research work as 'ethnographic' describes its research techniques rather than its research strategy. The use of participant observation, observation, interviews, group interviews and personal documents are all included among the naturalistic techniques of ethnography. While the research techniques are ethnographic, the research strategy is not. Marcus and Fischer (1986: 18) have defined ethnography as:

> A research process in which the anthropologist closely observes, records, and engages in the daily life of another culture – an experience labelled as the fieldwork method – and then writes accounts of this culture, emphasising descriptive detail. These accounts are the primary form in which fieldwork procedures, the other culture, and the ethnographer's personal and theoretical reflections are accessible to professionals and other readerships.

Clearly there are differences between this definition and the 'ethnography' of the above studies. Not only do they not set out to provide an account of an 'other' culture, but in many of them the only contact with the 'other culture' is an interview or the reading of a letter. Indeed the senses in which the mass audience, or parts of it, can be seen as an 'other culture' are also tenuous. At their most 'other', the participants in the above research may be described as 'working class', but in several instances (Morley and Ang) even this distinction does not hold.

The relationship between the researcher and researched is foregrounded as problematic once the term 'ethnography' is used to describe it. The very use of the term acts as a timely reminder of the differences (of class, education, religion, gender, age, etc.) between researcher and researched, differences which are often unacknowledged, especially when the researcher is of equal or lower status than the researched, as where television executives or production personnel are concerned. Similarly, a singular lack of commitment to 'recording' or to the provision of 'descriptive detail' is evident. Transcripts of interview, accounts of interaction, are substituted for descriptive detail – in the case of group interviews or household interviews, little time is spent describing where the interview is held, whether the interviewees are interested in the discussion or not, or what interactions (verbal or non-verbal) take place within the group in deciding who will speak for the group or how the group responds to what is said on its behalf.

What occurs, then, in the absence of rigorous ethnographic observation and description, when the techniques of ethnography are divorced from ethnographic process, is a co-opting of the interviewee's experience of the text by the researcher, and its use as authority for the researcher's point of view. This can perhaps best be described as a disproportionate reliance on the authenticating quality of ethnographic data, a reliance which can be argued to constitute what Rosaldo (1986: 82) has described as 'the false ethnographic authority of polyphony', in which the researchers' voices and the voices of their interviewees are equally heard, and yet which demonstrates no sensitivity to the power relations or to the cultural differences which operate when the data is obtained. In fact, in both the *Crossroads* and *EastEnders* research, for example, there is an openly stated denial of the possibility that such factors could influence the research. The quality of the relationship between researcher and interviewee is sometimes even claimed to overcome such methodological problems (Hobson, 1982: 107; Buckingham, 1987: 158–9). The problem then is to account for the determination with which writers such as Fiske (above) describe this body of research as 'ethnographic'.

THE ETHNOGRAPHIC CONVENTION

Since description of the studies as 'ethnographic' cannot be justified by the nature of the research actually undertaken, other reasons for the use of the term must exist. One possibility is that the application of the descriptor 'ethnographic' to these studies has acquired conventional status within cultural studies as the way of referring to the empirical audience research undertaken within the field. Accordingly, the term is used not to classify the research as belonging to, or even as having any links with, ethnography, but to signify the allegiance of the research to the academic heritage, cultural studies. The term 'ethnographic' possesses connotations which include *cultural, community-based, empirical* and *phenomenal*, all of which can legitimately be applied to the encoding/decoding studies. The term 'ethnographic' can then be a way of talking about research which possesses *these* characteristics, but which is also defined by its difference from 'cultural' research which possesses *other* characteristics, such as textual studies and perhaps even psychoanalytic studies. The encoding/decoding studies can be seen as an attempt by cultural studies to colonise a new realm, the realm of audience research. In this respect the term 'ethnographic' acts to legitimate the research, to denote its cultural, phenomenal and empirical methods, and even to signify its emphasis on 'community'.

The problem is that the term 'ethnography' has other lives. It has a life within the discipline of anthropology and a life within the research traditions of symbolic interactionism, both of which affect the ways in which the encoding/decoding research is enacted and evaluated. These other lives of the term 'ethnographic' reference both historical and theoretical links with the past of cultural studies, with its past triumphs as well as its failures. The other lives of 'ethnographic' also suggest possibilities for an 'ethnographic' future for cultural studies, especially since the discipline of anthropology, particularly interpretative anthropology, is currently appropriating many of the theoretical insights from literary studies which 'met' in cultural studies in the 1970s (see Clifford and Marcus, 1986).

USING 'ETHNOGRAPHIC' TO REFERENCE THE 'CULTURAL STUDIES' PAST

A second reason for using the term 'ethnographic' may therefore be motivated by a desire to retain something, be something, achieve something it does not (at least not yet). The case for the use of the term as an attempt to 'retain' something from the past of cultural studies is obvious. During the 1970s cultural studies was characterised by an intense interest in subcultures and deviance, and drew on the 'ethnographic' research methods popularised by symbolic interactionism to pursue its ends. The term 'ethnography' was used to refer to symbolic interactionist methods (see Pearson and Twohig, 1975; Roberts, 1976; Willis, 1980/76; Grimshaw *et al.*, 1980) as it is still by symbolic interactionists (see Wartella, 1987). The use of these 'naturalistic' methods, derived from ethnography and applied to modern society, suited the reformist tradition of the deviance research and facilitated its use as a critique of capitalist processes of exploitation and domination, as demonstrated in Willis's *Learning to Labour* (1977). It is in Willis's work that this 'ethnographic' heritage comes close to producing the sort of 'social realist' research advocated by Williams (see Marcus and Fischer, 1986: 77–8).

To this British culturalist research heritage, identified by Williams and evident in Willis's work, other researchers, such as Hebdige (1979) added structuralist, interpretative techniques. As a method the combination of these heritages had shaken the phenomenal centrality of the symbolic interactionist underpinnings of cultural studies (as cultural studies researchers such as Willis had always argued it must – Willis 1980/76 and Grimshaw *et al.*, 1980) and led to the ascendance of literary and structuralist approaches, the interpretative paradigm, instead. The meeting of these two research heritages has not been achieved without struggle. Yet it is worth noting that the struggle between the two paradigms, characterised as a struggle between culturalism and structuralism by Hall (1980b), has now been played out in the terrain of many of the social sciences. The most recent example is that of anthropology, where currently exploration of the implications of 'textual criticism, cultural history, semiotics, hermeneutic philosophy and psychoanalysis' (Clifford, 1986: 4) for ethnographic practice is under way. A similar process has affected the practice of archeology as well (Hodder, 1986). In each case what begins as a critique of practice ends in a more rigorous concentration on texts, a revaluation of hermeneutic as opposed to positivist social science practices, and a greater tolerance of relativism.

In cultural studies during the mid and late seventies, the interpretative revolution resulted in an almost exclusive concentration on media texts. The study of media audiences, however, 'belonged' to positivist social science. The 'ethnographic' tradition of cultural studies had traditionally focused on how the media exploited subcultural groups or appropriated and neutralised their resistance to the dominant culture. This tradition was constructed in diametrical opposition to positivist and mainstream audience research which presupposed an 'administrative' perspective (Gitlin, 1978), and presumed the purpose of audience research to be the management of audiences. It was the hiatus between the phenomenological orientation of subcultural research and the administrative orientation of mainstream audience research which promised to be remedied by an encoding/decoding attempt to understand audiences. Using the term 'ethnographic' to describe this research initiative asserts a desired continuity between the encoding/decoding studies and the earlier subcultural research, even though the encoding/decoding studies are text-centred, not subculture-centred. That desired continuity, which the encoding/decoding studies have so far failed to demonstrate, is a desire for a quality of research which allows the particular cultural experiences of broadcast television viewers to be understood in the context of communication in capitalist society.

The work of Paul Willis (1977 especially) is still widely regarded as the model for the cultural studies ethnographic method, as it is currently being cited as the direction for cultural studies reception research (Morley and Silverstone, 1988), for symbolic interactionist 'cultural' research (Traudt and Lont, 1987: 144 and 159) and as challenging the anthropological tradition of ethnography to undertake broader and more critical research appropriate to the conditions of the modern world order in the re-evaluation of anthropology (Marcus, 1986). What Willis's work offers, as Marcus points out, is a demonstration that the cultural (in Willis's case, capitalist society) defines the particular (school nonconformity and labour conformity). Willis achieves this not by a positivist attempt to prove Marxist theory by his observations, but by invoking Marxist theory as given. As Marcus again points out, Willis's purpose is achieved by the exploration of 'the cultural' meanings of the production of labour and commodity fetishism which 'provides textual means for bringing the larger order into the space of ethnography' (Marcus, 1986: 173). Willis's adherence to the notion of cultural totality, to the structuralist project of reading the culture in its forms – the legacy of Raymond Williams – is seen by Marcus as a positive achievement for anthropology emerging from Willis's work. As Marcus puts it:

> Nonetheless, Willis does pose the challenge for the anthropological tradition of ethnography, underlain perhaps by an unattainable ideal of holism not to be taken literally, to apply ethnography to projects of broader purpose and theoretical significance, like his own. This entails the writing of mixed-genre texts, similar to those envisioned by

Raymond Williams for social realism, in which ethnographic representation and authority would be a variably salient component.

(Marcus, 1986: 188)

TECHNIQUE VERSUS STRATEGY

Nevertheless, if a continuity is *assumed* between the 'ethnographic' practice of Willis and the 'mixed-genre texts' of Morley, Hobson, Ang, Tulloch and Moran, and Buckingham, crucial differences *between* them may
be overlooked, for while encoding/decoding audience research uses the
same research techniques as Willis, their research strategies are quite
different. Willis's aim was to demonstrate the working of social process,
to explain cultural reproduction through the interlocking of education
and the labour process. This type of broad social aim, with its singularity
of focus, is missing from the encoding/decoding studies, which concentrate
on several, and more limited, aims such as explaining the popularity of
the text (Hobson, 1982; Tulloch and Moran, 1986), teaching about British
cultural studies (Ang, 1985) or demonstrating the operations by which
pleasure is encoded in the text (Ang, 1985; Buckingham, 1987). The
encoding/decoding studies use their 'ethnographic' data to achieve textually defined aims rather than to explain social process. Their strategy,
characteristically, involves a multifocus approach. They use observations,
participant observation, interviews (individual and group), personal, commercial and/or public documents which are readily available, all of which
address some aspects of the broad range of issues which litter the field
of popular culture research. The choice of research foci is usually eclectic,
drawing on the personal interests of the researcher. For example, Hobson's strategy involves interviews with and observation of selected personnel involved in the production of *Crossroads*, participant observation
(viewing the programme with women viewers), examination of letters
written to the local press when changes to the programme were proposed,
interviews with representatives of the profession and the IBA and the
use of television criticism from the daily press.

Tulloch and Moran (1986) use a broad array of interviews and observations as they follow the sequence of 'performances' of the programme
which culminate in its final performance by the audience. The notion of
'text as performance' operates as a uniting theme, but is weak as a critique
of popular culture. Ang (1985) tries to infer ideological approaches to
reading popular cultural texts from a small number of letters about *Dallas*,
taking up themes such as textual pleasure, feminism and popular culture,
the concepts of 'tragic structure of feelings' and 'melodramatic imagination' directly from textually oriented theory. Buckingham (1987) uses
interviews with the producers of *EastEnders*, programming executives,
BBC audience research findings, interviews with groups of children about

the programme, a textual analysis based on Wolfgang Iser's theory of textual invitations, newspaper coverage and observation of public sector interest groups. A recurrent trope in the research is the disparagement of the audience and the contempt for the text which is alleged to characterise television criticism even after ten years of academic work to legitimate the study of popular cultural texts. Even though the research uses the techniques of 'ethnographic' research advocated by Willis, it is then vastly different in its strategies, which so far fail to offer a satisfying critique of popular culture.

The problem is compounded in that the ethnographic strategy outlined by Willis does not address the problem of reading complex cultural forms like popular television programmes in their particularity. Reading the significance of the signs of a subculture (dress, argot, behaviour, rituals, etc.) and its relation to the cultural totality is qualitatively different from reading television and from reading people's readings of television. The direct communal authorship of the signs of a subculture is qualitatively different from the highly institutionalised, conventionalised and commercially motivated production of television. The relationship of the community to the televisual cultural form is one of appropriation rather than authorship; an appropriation of ideas authored by agents of discursive formations, as Turner (1977) has noted, an appropriation in which the operation of 'bricolage' is much more complexly articulated than in the appropriation of other objects. The professionalisation of television production and the complexity of the text as appropriated object (appropriated by the audience that is) place constraints on the reading of such appropriation which demand more sophisticated techniques of analysis than those offered by ethnography. The things people say about television cry out, I suggest, for innovative approaches to discourse analysis combined with the now familiar 'ethnographic' techniques.

MIXED-GENRE RESEARCH

Even though the presence of the ethnographic convention in cultural studies research seems more nostalgic than progressive, other aspects of this embryonic research tradition constitute an innovation in cultural research practice. If the encoding/decoding studies are seen as first attempts at mixed-genre research, research which integrates the study of audience discourse and data obtained from audience observation with qualitatively different observations and materials about television texts, production, distribution and industries, the value of work is better appreciated.

As mixed-genre research, the work establishes an elaboration of the 'triangulation' strategy. The use of triangulation strategies is advocated when 'the nature of the problem under investigation demands a multi-method approach'. It is a characteristic of community studies, as I have argued this research to be (Nightingale, 1989). As Gorden (1987) puts it:

> Community studies must triangulate information from public records, personal documents, newspapers, direct interviews with the focal persons, participant-observation, and pure observation merely to obtain the many types of information needed to cover the complex phenomenon we call a community. Experimental studies, naturalistic communities studies, and statistical surveys can be fruitfully combined in many instances.
>
> (Gorden, 1987: 12)

The encoding/decoding model suggested discourse as the uniting focus of such triangulation, but the focus on the 'discursive form of the message', and even any notion of message, has been progressively discarded and the focus of the research, its critical edge, thus lost. The central focus, for example, in the *Nationwide* studies was on the ideology of the programme and its reflection in the verbal discourse of the audience. This centrality of focus gave way in the subsequent studies to more disjointed research strategies, leading to a lack of coherence in the research, as Craik has noted (Craik, 1987). The value of the attempts at triangulation in the studies was thus dissipated, and as is perhaps most obvious in the *EastEnders* research, the research focus fluctuates from explaining the popularity of the programme to justifying the interpretative 'work' of the audience and providing background information for teaching about the programme in school. In the *Dallas* research, by contrast, the focus is more firmly held on the 'pleasure' of *Dallas*, yet in this case the empirical research is slight (consisting of only forty-two letters, which are not analysed in their own right) and coupled with attempts to combine the letters and the programme through theoretical exegesis and description of current trends in feminism. Once again the sense in which the study coheres is tenuous, and the focus in fact fluctuates between explaining the processes by which *Dallas* is experienced as 'pleasure' and justifying feminine and feminist interest in the programme, as well as teaching about the programme.

The multiple foci of these studies, then, are used to justify the study of popular culture, to teach (often both students and the general public) about the mass media, to validate the mass television audience (or sections of it) and its interest in such programmes, rather than to engage in cultural critique or analysis. In all the studies (except Morley, 1980), the ethnographic initiative is not the central research strategy but is used only to validate the production and textual research initiatives. While the research does pioneer writing for multiple audiences, it falls short of offering any critique of cultural practice, either of production or of reception. In this sense it contrasts with the strong attraction of similar research in anthropology. Marcus and Fischer (1986: 163) correctly identify such writing within anthropology as experimentation which is likely to revitalise academic practice. As they put it:

> Writing single texts with multiple voices exposed within them, as well as with multiple readership explicitly in mind, is perhaps the sharpest spur to the contemporary experimental impulse in anthropological writing, both as ethnography and as cultural critique.

Needless to say, this position is proposed within the context of discussion of structured research strategies such as 'cross-cultural juxtapositioning'. In this regard, it seems the encoding/decoding studies have new lessons to learn from anthropology.

While the central concern of the encoding/decoding studies remains the account of the text, and while the diversity of the research focus is centred around a particular television programme, rather than around a critique of audience-text bonding, we will continue to produce writing about such programmes which situates the research more as apologue than as critique. It is time to look again at anthropology, and at ethnographic research techniques, to re-evaluate their use in cultural studies audience research both as a heritage and as a future direction. It is time to learn our lessons from the pioneering work which has been done and to develop strategies for cultural critique which provoke critical appraisal while retaining respect for and appreciation of the popular texts which accompany and orchestrate our lives.

NOTE

This chapter first appeared in *Australian Journal of Communication*, 16 (1989).

REFERENCES

Ang, I. (1985), *Watching Dallas: Soap Opera and the Melodramatic Imagination*, Methuen, London and New York.
Brunsdon, C. and Morley, D. (1978), *Everyday Television: 'Nationwide'*. BFI, London.
Buckingham, D. (1987), *Public Secrets: EastEnders and its Audience*, BFI, London.
Clifford, J. (1986), 'Introduction: partial truths', in J. Clifford and G. Marcus (eds) (1986), *Writing Culture: The Poetics and Politics of Ethnography*, University of California Press, Berkeley and Los Angeles.
Clifford, J. and Marcus, G. (eds) (1986), *Writing Culture: The Poetics and Politics of Ethnography*, University of California Press, Berkeley and Los Angeles.
Craik, J. (1987), 'Soft soap', *Australian Left Review*, 102, (November/December 1987), 34–7.
Fiske, J. (1987), *Television Culture*, Methuen, London and New York.

Gitlin, T. (1978), 'Media sociology: the dominant paradigm', *Theory and Society*, 6, 205–53.

Gorden, R. L. (1987), *Interviewing: Strategy, Techniques and Tactics*, 4th edn, The Dorsey Press, Chicago.

Grimshaw, R., Hobson, D. and Willis, P. (1980), 'Introduction to ethnography at the Centre', in S. Hall *et al.* (1980), *Culture, Media, Language*, Hutchinson, London.

Hall, S. (1980a), 'Encoding/decoding', in S. Hall, *et al.*, *Culture, Media, Language*, Hutchinson, London.

—— (1980b), 'Cultural studies: two paradigms', *Media, Culture and Society*, 2, (1980), 57–72.

Hebdige, D. (1979), *Subculture: The Meaning of Style*, Methuen, London and New York.

Hobson, D. (1982), *Crossroads: The Drama of a Soap Opera*, Methuen, London.

Hodder, I. (1986), *Reading the Past: Current Approaches to Interpretation in Archaeology*, Cambridge University Press, Cambridge.

Marcus, G. E. (1986), 'Contemporary problems of ethnography in the modern world system', in J. Clifford and G. E. Marcus (eds), *Writing Culture: The Poetics and Politics of Ethnography*, University of California Press, Berkeley and Los Angeles.

Marcus, G. E. and Fischer, M. M. J. (1986), *Anthropology as Cultural Critique: An Experimental Moment in the Human Sciences*, University of Chicago Press, Chicago and London.

Morley, D. (1980), *The 'Nationwide' Audience: Structure and Decoding*, BFI, London.

Morley, D. and Silverstone, R. (1988), 'Domestic communication – technologies and meanings', paper presented to the 1988 International Television Studies Conference, London, July 1988.

Nightingale, V. (1989), *Researching People as Audiences: The Cultural Studies Experiment*, PhD thesis, Macquarie University.

Pearson, G. and Twohig, J. (1975) 'Ethnography through the looking glass: the case of Howard Becker', in S. Hall and T. Jefferson, (eds), *Resistance through Rituals*, Hutchinson and C.C.C.S., University of Birmingham, London and Birmingham.

Pratt, M. L. (1986), 'Fieldwork in common places', in J. Clifford and G. E. Marcus, (eds), *Writing Culture: The Poetics and Politics of Ethnography*, University of California Press, Berkeley and Los Angeles.

Roberts, B. (1976), 'Naturalistic research into subcultures and deviance', in S. Hall and T. Jefferson, (eds), *Resistance through Rituals*, Hutchinson and C.C.C.S., University of Birmingham, London and Birmingham.

Rosaldo, R. (1986), 'From the door of his tent: the fieldworker and the inquisitor', in J. Clifford and G. E. Marcus (eds), *Writing Culture: The Poetics and Politics of Ethnography*, University of California Press, Berkeley and Los Angeles.

Said, E. (1982), 'Opponents, audiences, constituencies and community', in H. Foster, (ed.) *The Anti-aesthetic: Essays on Post-modern Culture*, Bay Press, Port Townsend, Washington.

Traudt, P. and Lont, C. (1987), 'Media-logic-in-use: the family as locus of study', in T. R. Lindlof (ed.), *Natural Audiences: Qualitative Research of Media Uses and Effects*, Ablex, Norwood, New Jersey.

Tulloch, J. and Moran, A. (1986), *A Country Practice: 'Quality Soap'*, Currency Press, Sydney.

Turner, V. (1977), 'Frame, flow and reflection: ritual and drama as public liminality', in M. Benamou and C. Caramello (eds), *Performance in Postmodern Culture*, Coda Press, Madison, Wisconsin.

Wartella, E. (1987), 'Commentary on qualitative research and children's mediated communication', in T. R. Lindlof (ed.), *Natural Audiences: Qualitative Research of Media Uses and Effects*, Ablex, Norwood, New Jersey.

Willis, P. (1977), *Learning to Labour: How Working Class Kids Get Working Class Jobs*, Gower Publishing, Aldershot.

—— (1980/76), 'Notes on method', in S. Hall, *et al.*, *Culture, Media, Language*, Hutchinson, London.

Part IV

Popular Culture and the Media

In this final section, the essays are concerned in various ways with the articulation of the media and popular culture. Their concerns take various forms – from broad discursive analyses of cultural and media texts to empirical audience research. Noel Sanders and Helen Grace both develop their analyses in response to high profile events or series of events within popular culture while John Tulloch and Marian Tulloch and Pam Gilbert and Sandra Taylor test theoretical accounts through the interpretative and empirical treatments of texts and audiences. In this section, the cultural specificity of the pieces is quite pronounced and so this introduction will primarily concern itself with providing some cultural background.

One of the longest-running scandals in contemporary Australian popular culture has been the so-called 'dingo baby' case – the disappearance of baby Azaria Chamberlain, taken from a tent in a camp ground at the foot of Ayers Rock in October 1980. The parents, Michael and Lindy Chamberlain, discovered the disappearance; Lindy claimed to have seen a dingo (a wild dog, known to scavenge for its food) leaving the tent with something in its mouth. While this explanation was initially believed, subsequently 'strange' behaviour from the Chamberlains fuelled a rumour mill that ultimately led to the couple being charged with the child's murder. The Chamberlain's defense – 'the dingo did it' – has become a popular culture slogan over the last decade. The couple's background, religion, sexuality and personal attributes have been the subject of continuous press and television commentary as well as of a Hollywood film starring Meryl Streep and Sam Neill (called *A Cry in the Dark* outside Australia, *Evil Angels* within it). And despite the eventual quashing of Lindy's conviction and a large compensation payout from the government which pursued her, many Australians continue to believe that Lindy did it. It is not surprising that Australian cultural studies has interested itself in the way in which the case was represented – the media's role in the formation of the popular notoriety of the Chamberlains – and in the way in which liminally popular discourses arose in order to provide alternative explanations to those suggested by the law, the press or other institutions: an oral commerce in 'dingo-baby' jokes, inside information from friends in the police, gossip about Seventh Day Adventist ritual practices and so on. Noel Sanders' essay is written in 1982, relatively early in the saga (the final episode occurred in 1992 with the compensation payout and the Chamberlain's divorce) and at a stage when the jury was still out, literally, on what the official explanation of Azaria's disappearance was to be. What Sanders provides is not a complete history but a rich contemporary account of the 'incontinent, excessive discourse[s] that subverted the official attempts at closure' and that actively refused the official 'sense' currently being made of the case. It is worth noting that this is not an exercise within the genre of tracing 'resistance' through 'the popular'; the voices of 'the popular' compete with the dingo for the role of villain in this media melodrama.

Helen Grace's essay also requires some contextualisation. During the 1980s, and as in most Western countries, the headlines in Australian newspapers were dominated by the economy – in particular by a new breed of risk-taking speculative businessmen. While by no means unique, these 'larrikin' capitalists were hailed in the Australian press as genuine local heroes, taking on the international corporations and outdoing them at their own game. Alan Bond, Rupert Murdoch, John Elliott and Christopher Skase – some of whom we encountered in the context of Tom O'Regan's history of Australian television – became media 'stars', celebrated as the saviours of Australian capitalism. Within such a context, Helen Grace's ironic application of structuralist narratology to the media representation of these characters seems especially appropriate. Her piece has a wider relevance, too, in its neat demonstration of the crucial relationship between myth and money in popular culture.

Grace's starting point is the changes in style and content visible in the business sections in our newspapers as 'business' acquired its centrality to diagnoses of our social condition. Despite the invisibility of the 'real action' of business and its frequent failure to actually produce anything material, the media have – improbably – turned business into a realm of performance, a spectacle. Grace suggests this spectacle itself takes place within a fictionalised world (the world of futures, junk bonds, debt itself). Indeed, the everyday economic life of the nation is 'a daily soap opera, full of the most extreme occurrences'. Hence the deployment of Proppian narrative structures, cutting through the level of discourse and operating at the level of structure in order to 'deconstruct the seriousness and self-importance of the world of business and to bring to bear a certain scepticism about its claim to so much attention'. Grace concludes with the caustic observation that the only real problem in applying Proppian categories to such a world lies in differentiating between the heroes and villains.

The topic of television and violence has been one of the hardiest perennials of mass-communication research, although most of it has taken place in America. Over the last few years in Australia, however, there have been a number of fresh attempts to deal with this issue; Stuart Cunningham raises it in *Framing Culture* and the chapter from John and Marian Tulloch takes a new look at it in this section. The provocation for the current interest is the Australian Broadcasting Tribunal's (ABT) inquiry into TV violence and the report from this inquiry which was published in 1990. The ABT inquiry virtually dismissed the whole 'effects' tradition and indeed the proposition of any simple relationship between representations of violence on television and changes in social behaviour. What it did accept was that there was genuine community concern about the depiction of violence on television – in news, as well as in drama – and it went on to ask for further work to be done: in educating the audience about television production and about existing regulatory and classificatory mechanisms in order to assure a more informed and thus well-protected audience; and in attempting to understand in more qualitative ways exactly what audiences did with such representations – in particular, 'at-risk' groups such as children. While it disappointed many who wanted more draconian measures, the ABT report was intelligent and balanced, delivered (it should be said) amidst quite strong community pressure to legislate for narrow restrictions on what could and could not be shown and equally vigorous pressure from the television networks in defense of their right to present 'the real world', warts and all, to their viewers. What was clear from the report, however, was the failure of *all* traditions of research into television violence to deliver any substantial understandings of audience responses.

John Tulloch and Marian Tulloch have responded to this challenge by bringing to bear an unusual combination of disciplinary perspectives onto the topic of television violence. Normally the disciplinary frameworks of developmental psychology and cultural theory would be seen as opposed; in this study John and Marian Tulloch explore the benefits of using both sets of methodological assumptions in complementary ways. The range of strategies used is subsequently far greater than is usual in cultural studies audience research. Sociocultural discourse analysis occurs alongside more traditional quantitative techniques, ethnographic audience interviews and textual analysis. The interplay between theoretical approaches is rich, with interpretative moves deriving support and conviction as they set agendas for, or respond to, the more quantitative information. Work this ambitious is unlikely to prove its points quickly or categorically and as one reads the piece one certainly comes to recognise the complexity and scale of the problems approached. But even in this summary of what is clearly a large and continuing study there are detailed and specific insights into how children's dealing with TV violence is related to 'complex class, gender and age-influenced agendas of their own'.

The complexity of the problem of understanding children's responses to the popular media concerns Pam Gilbert and Sandra Taylor too. In the book from which their chapter is drawn, *Fashioning the Feminine*, Gilbert and Taylor consider how the appropriation of popular culture texts into school curricula participates in the construction of femininity. Their interests are multiple in that they are addressing an audience of educators who need to consider 'how readily can the dominant discourses of the classroom work with issues as complex as the role of the popular cultural text in the lives of teenage girls', as well as a feminist cultural studies and audience interested in the way in which 'cultural texts are "made", in patriarchal consumer culture, in the sub-cultures of young women, and in the dominant culture of the classroom'.

Fashioning the Feminine looks at a range of texts and classroom practices; in the excerpt chosen, it enters the familiar territory of the reader of romance fiction to discuss the implications of its use within the classroom. While Gilbert and Taylor accept the importance of the relatively optimistic work of researchers such as Janice Radway, they want to complicate the conclusions customarily drawn from this work. First of all, they make use of Canadian and Australian research to emphasise how age- and culture-specific Radway's conclusions are. The use made of the romance was very different in a Canadian study of early teenage girls, where the novels assumed enormous power over the girl's view of reality – operating as 'manuals for ensuing femininity'. In Australian studies of slightly older girls, differences in class seem to be implicated in the nature of girls' responses to romance fiction. Gilbert and Taylor then ask what makes the difference:

> Why girls continue to read romance, and to claim an 'emotional involvement' with such generically ritualistic novels, is, of course, the key question. And to add a rather different perspective to this question, it can be considered from another angle. Given that reading practices are learned and reading positions are adopted, why is it that some girls have learned reading practices and adopted reading positions which reject the stereotypes offered through romance fiction?

In a small ethnographic study of girls reading a new group of novels, *Dolly Fiction* (produced by a popular teen-girl magazine called *Dolly*), they try to shed light on these differentials.

Given the now conventional position on romance fiction – crudely, the textually worrying but experientially empowering line – Gilbert and Taylor take an unpopular and possibly even old-fashioned position (I am thinking of their aesthetic objections to the form) in their conclusions. They are particularly brave, it seems to me, in their categoric insistence that for all their pleasures and for all the possibility of multiple readings, romance fictions do not 'serve women well'. Notwithstanding the kinds of pleasures Radway's Smithton women reported, Gilbert and Taylor maintain that romance novels 'grow out of consumer-oriented discourses which have vested interests in constructing groups of women as identifiable and therefore commercially marketable; and they grow out of patriarchal discourses which depend upon the continuation of unequal heterosexual couplings and domestic labour'. Given that their interest in the classroom focuses their critique on practices that actually might help to make a difference, one can see the usefulness of Gilbert and Taylor's attempt to stop the cultural studies pendulum swinging too far away from questions about the ideological effects of popular cultural forms.

Chapter 9

Azaria Chamberlain and popular culture

Noel Sanders

Two prints from Goya's *Los Caprichos* alternately show an innocent, cherubic child torn apart by clerics or lawyers, and a raging semi-domestic beast which someone (who? – the people?) is trying to bring under control. But these scenes are enigmatic; forms are violently juxtaposed against an undefinable, desert background. Rules of perspective fail to apply, and, as both Gombrich and Foucault have observed, while Goya's work appears to represent a stage in a continuous narrative, the narrative itself is obscure. The images are neither of a 'genre', nor do they 'represent' anything.[1] They are not illustrations 'of any known subject, either biblical, historical or genre'.[2] The forms themselves appear cast without meaning onto a scene which itself does not exist; they are 'born out of nothing'.[3] At best, we are linked with 'an old world of enchantments and fantastic rides, of witches perched on the branches of dead trees'.[4] The timeless world of oral narrative is invoked, but the figures themselves seem to have become as silent as the landscape without contours on which they have been thrown. In the absence of a readable topology, a logic of forms and spaces cannot arise. The only way the forms connect is in unspeakable acts of violence – infanticide, parricide, massacres of innocents. The participants themselves become monsters, and lack of a visual causation allows human motives and 'animal instincts' free interchange. In Goya's scenes, 'nothing can assign them their origin, nature or limits'.[5]

The silent theatre of the Azaria disappearance has taken place in Australia against just such backgrounds, with the narrative emerging only in dislocated episodes, as new evidence was brought to light and was reported in newspapers and on TV. The scene and images may be there, but as in Goya, there is no return to the 'natal scene' or terrain. Yet for the television and print media public that watched the Azaria Chamberlain matter unfold, both the natal terrain and the theatre of death, the silent and contourless centre of the continent, were transformed and known via a series of metaphors that filled the unspoken areas with new signs and meanings, filling the silence of the 'unconscious' landscape with an unauthorised speech (gossip, jokes, laughter) and with speculation that exceeded the official discourses of forensic experts and the coroner's findings on Azaria's disappearance – an incontinent, excessive discourse that subverted the official attempts at closure. Similarly, the emptiness of the interior, hitherto only known to many from the discourses of tourism which emphasised lack of habitation (by whites), primalness and 'rugged beauty' (which Michael Chamberlain's camera relentlessly captured, in the fashion known to other Australian tourist shutter bugs), became populated by a dramatis personae with a range of speaking parts that were not merely those of the Chamberlains or the coroner, Denis Barritt.

DEATH AND SPECTACLE

'Serialised news' and Azaria Chamberlain were made for each other. From the opening of the inquiry into Azaria's death in October 1980 to the televised findings of the coroner's inquest on 21 February 1981, Eyewitness News on Channel 10, in Sydney, presented daily revelations alongside serialised snippets on how to make the home safe for children and how to control home finances. Against the dramatic unfolding of crisis within the Chamberlain family, and the daily revelation of new evidence were set the minutiae of the perils of suburban living and the instability of family life, the threats being both *technical* and *social* (accident insurance problems or marital breakdown).

At the same time, we got the dramatic televisual revelation of the centre of the continent, its dangers, the dangers of tourism, the failure of conservation and the ungratefulness of the centre's trustee inhabitants (dingoes, Aborigines). As an unfolding TV spectacle, the Azaria case provided daily dramatisation and documentarisation of the Dead Centre. Only the conquest of another 'feminine' upsidedown world – the moon landing of the late 1960s – had attracted as large an audience (2 million) as watched Denis Barritt engaged in perhaps the most boring forty-five minutes of anticlimax in Australian TV history. The closure of his discourse 'I am satisfied . . . I am satisfied . . . I am satisfied' seemed, however, to contain the 'sense of discovery' and the adventurousness of the TV audience only for a while: Barritt relied on the backdrop of the Rock and its remoteness, together with the picturesque cast of dingoes and Aborigines, to provide a decent acceptable narrative of the eyewitness sort, but perhaps these elements in combination had set in motion wider narratives – epic, mythical – so much the stock-in-trade of an emergent film industry, rather than the cosy soap opera in exotic surroundings (an outback *Holiday Island*) that showed up on TV.

On television in Australia, non-urban settings are sought in which to place anything from margarine ads to long-running serial dramas – and for a predominantly urban TV audience. Rolling highlands provided the backdrop for one of the most successful ads of the late 1970s, Mojo's Amoco ad, and 'pastoral' scenes continue to construct an ideology of mobility (for the young adult audience), and (for women buying food) family stability in the down-home mode, with a healthy family fed (paradoxically) on fresh, unprocessed fodder. On the other hand, these displaced urban scenarios are also deathly and threatening – as, for instance in the 1981 Project Australia ads, in which a voice over aerial shots of endless arcadian beaches tells both of the beach as representative of Australian values such as egalitarianism, and as the place of threat in a country without land borders over which an enemy might invade. The outback itself is variously known. The Leyland Brothers go there as mates, conquering the land by turning it into TV; Bill Peach goes there, and, via TV, tells you how you can go there; Harry Butler, on the other hand, was there already and alternately horrifies you by rising above its violence and desolation, and engages your sympathies with his respect for the 'little fellas' he finds there.

Ayers Rock – the 'Rock', as it is consistently known in the media coverage, is known not only through tourist advertising and travel docos, but also through art. Its monumentality appears both as valuable sculpture (a good risk) and as something uplifted, altar-like, a navel that is all that remains after the umbilical cord with the rest of the world has been severed. (It appears with Phar Lap, as the only nonhuman 'redhead' that appears on Australian 'Redhead' match covers, along with other famous redheads like Elizabeth I, Churchill and Van Gogh). The fact of the Rock already having become aestheticised and symbolised in this way is certainly taken up in Barritt's findings where he exploits the Rock's existence as a 'found object', a principal 'subject' for amateur art/tourist photographers:

> Pastor Chamberlain, a keen photographer, photographed the effect of sunrise on Ayers Rock, took other photographs and returned at 8 a.m. Thereafter the family breakfasted and went sightseeing around the northern side of the Rock . . . they then went to Maggie Springs in that area, including the fertility caves, where *they* observed a dingo watching *them*.[6]

(My emphases: the camera angles high up in the rocks in Peter Weir's *Picnic at Hanging Rock* also suggests that visitors to remote, picturesque spots not only see, but are seen, sometimes by malevolent eyes.) Similarly, dingoes themselves are rendered painterly and photogenic in Lindy Chamberlain's account: 'I dropped the beans. I could see the dingo quite clearly. It was a beautiful gold colour with sharp pointed ears and it was having trouble getting through the gap because of a bundle in its teeth' (*Woman's Day*, October 1 1980).

Ayers Rock in particular signifies the immemorial and also the immortal – the permanence and security that transcend the social and historical (as in the insurance ads). For instance, an article in the *National Times* 10 May 1981) notes: 'Tourism's blue rinse brigade makes way for adventure seekers . . . besides the lure of spaciousness, this country offers two other "s's" – safety and political stability.' A photo of Ayers Rock accompanies the article, which is captioned: 'They like Australia's safety and stability.' But further than this, the role of 'rock' – of 'the Rock', here – is to signify immortality and permanence in distinctive opposition to other elements – as quite the opposite of what Azaria herself signifies (having the distinctive features of human, vulnerable, soft and small against the Rock's masculine, hard, impenetrable magnitudinousness). Plants, such as the ones that left traces on Azaria's clothing, also appear in this system of signs; in a treeless landscape, they, apart from the Aborigines and dingoes, are the only animate terms, but like both Aborigines and dingoes, they appear as witnesses, accomplices and perpetrators of the crime, mediating between the other two signs, and ultimately subject to scientific scrutiny, bound to forensic biological, botanical and anthropo-logical discourses in a way that the Rock and Azaria are to aesthetic discourses (say, Barritt's contention on ABC TV, February 20 1981, that 'whoever removed Azaria Chamberlain's body must have had some knowledge of botany, but again it is speculation', versus Lindy Chamber-lain's 'Azaria was a beautiful dream', her reminiscence that Michael Chamberlain had been 'quite passionate about dingoes (on a former holiday to Cape York) and said what good looking dogs they were' (*Woman's Day* 1 October, 1980), or Michael's assertion after the inquest findings that, as God's creations 'dingoes are beautiful creatures'.

The Rock, then, although it is 'known' previously in other ways (its redness, its role as a symbol of Australian fortitude and strength in isolation), signifies somewhat differently as part of the triad Rock-plant-Azaria. For instance, Lévi-Strauss notes in *The Raw and the Cooked* that in myth sign systems, 'stone or rock appears, then, as the symmetrical opposite of human flesh'. Elsewhere, he elaborates: 'Myth enlists three calls to which the hero (TV viewer?) must reply or keep still . . . these are the calls of rock (immortality/human flesh), hard wood (animal flesh), and rotten wood (cultivated plants).' Although it is not intended that this distinction be wholly carried through to the present discussion, Lévi-Strauss's conclusion is useful in providing evidence for an 'appeal' to a media audience based on a knowledge, or perceived knowledge, of the scenario the media-reading public might be able to decode. Each of the elements in the scenario issue, out of their muteness, a call which is both visual (scopic) and aural ('invocatory', in Lacan's term[7]) which asks the reading/viewing subject to recognise something, whether it is the 'self-evidence' of the family setup and the role that a young baby plays in it, or the grandeur and permanence of the Rock. Yet, while the visual evidences are there, the voices (Azaria's cries, Lindy's shouts on the one hand, the voice of a confessor – dingoes are, after all, voiceless dogs – on the other) are absent. Lévi-Strauss has this to say about the arrangement of mythic elements in the myth he studies:

> These things that emit sounds (calls, silent appeals, here) . . . must be chosen in such a way that they also possess other sensory connotations. They are operators which make it possible to convey the isomorphic character of all binary systems of contrasts connected with the senses, and therefore to express as a totality, a set of equivalences connecting life and death . . . silence and noise.[8]

It was to these absent voices that viewers answered. Sometimes it was in the terms indicated by Lindy Chamberlain and Denis Barritt, filling in the absent voices with their own affirmations. More often, however, it was in a negative way, replacing the words in the cartoon bubbles with subversive calls and answers, challenging the closure of the Chamberlains' and Denis Barritt's narratives through jokes and gossip and conjecture, releasing the libido of media texts (infanticide, as well as otherwise unspeakable forms of family violence) and allowing an approach to the death drives to be made, in the direction of *jouissance*, but at the expense of a 'pleasurable' reading.[9] The myths of the '*continent*', its stability, safety, but, paradoxically also, violence, had become rather '*incontinent*', excessive (through jokes especially), and messy. Perhaps the 'overflow' that popular cultural forms such as jokes and rumour enact on the contained nature of the official narratives is summarised by a dingo joke of the time which goes: 'How do you bring up a baby?' 'You stick your finger down a dingo's throat.'

AZARIA AND THE AUSTRALIAN FILM INDUSTRY

Big media events like the Azaria Chamberlain affair set into operation reading and decoding practices that are both synchronic and diachronic. From a synchronic point of vantage, they are set alongside other media events which require the same type of reading practices, rhetorics and media literacies to understand them. They also require the recognition and operation of the same sorts of 'self-evidence', such as common mythology, common recognition of the necessity for a political status quo, the integralness of the family to social life and an appeal to the avoidance of violence (except one's own) at all costs. In its synchronous aspect, the Azaria Chamberlain inquest and its coverage occurred at the same time as the hunger strike in Northern Ireland by Bobby Sands, and his subsequent death. During this, the media turned their attention from highlighting the militancy of the IRA to Sands's non-violent, self-sacrificial act, whilst converting prevailing ideologies about self-sacrifice (good if it's within the guidelines of Project Australia) into negative images of aggression. At the same time, however, against Thatcher's intransigence, Sands's approach could be seen as adding to the possibility of British victory. And, into the bargain, the inherently violent nature of confrontation in Northern Ireland could be temporarily circumvented: news reports switched from reporting the day-to-day struggle to medical reports on the increasing deterioration of Sands's body. (At the same time, the arrest of the Yorkshire Ripper also focused attention on the how rather than the why of Sutcliffe's murders.) For one reader of the *Sydney Morning Herald* (Letters, 8 May 1981),

> when people, such as Sands, are willing to give their life in protest against what they regard as a serious social injustice *in place of* [my emphasis] violence against their enemies, they do something very profound for the whole of humanity. They show that even in the face of the most appalling injustices in the world, one does not have to do violence to others.

Only to oneself, then: violence is precluded by images of self-sacrifice, which is certainly as Project Australia would also have it.

It was perhaps in the context of this sort of hypocrisy (and also in the failure to recognise Sutcliffe's female victims also as, at some level, sacrifices to the preservation of heterosexual responses to monogamous marital self-sufficiency) that the media's representation of the Azaria affair fell short. It was not able to pull off, on home territory, a reportage of the Azaria affair that did not in some ways also include the possibility of a sacrifice. The idea that both sacrifice and self-sacrifice are appropriate concepts in the decoding repertoire has been built up in many forms in Australia in the last century or so, bridging the sacrifice made by soldiers in wartime, to the sacrifices made by women in all forms of work, to the sacrifices we all must make to keep the country from anarchy. Metaphorical sacrifice and self-sacrifice and actual sacrifice resulting in death become interchangeable. And this is especially so when a set of reading and decoding practices must be used on diverse material which should be given individual treatment: it all comes to look as if it's a multi-media event – different responses, but somehow all supposedly attainable with everyone using the same tools for getting at it. (Lindy Chamberlain herself, in an interview for TV, said to have been given five days after Azaria's disappearance is reported (in the *Sunday Telegraph*, February 7 1982) to have said that 'We have agreed to the media coverage because we felt that there was a reason for her death, and that somebody needed this to bring them back to God. But God must allow this to happen for people to realize that his way is the best way and that he has the last say.')

The reading practices involved in understanding the Azaria affair in relation to other 'hot' news items involves the media in the business of crossing thematic elements and intertwining levels of discourse at some points, and keeping them separate at others (as it has in more recent times, keeping up its Australian union-bashing activities on the one hand, while pulling out the stops for Solidarity pluck). However, there is a diachronic dimension in which it is not so much immediately contemporaneous 'stories' that are relevant for understanding how things are read (or how further meanings, not necessarily legitimised, are made available) but rather texts/issues/events that have gone before that are important. For instance, in a paradigm of 'disappearance stories' in Australia, the Azaria affair takes its place alongside others (also involving females or juveniles or both) from 'the lady of the swamp', through the Beaumont children, to Juanita Nielson.

In some writings, this addition to the repertoire has been called 'intertextuality' and it roughly covers the instance of reading in which more than one text is actually being 'read' where only one appears to be on the screen or page that a person is actually looking at a particular time.[10] Within the category of such 'inter-texts' overlaid on the Azaria texts, and which at least partially determine the way in which the latter are read are some of the key Australian movies of the last decade. Some of these movies, for instance, use a similar backdrop of outback emptiness, filled with threatening quasi-animistic 'presences', as for instance in *Picnic at Hanging Rock*. Here a group of young women goes on an expedition in a remote colonial time to a rocky uplifted place, split with passes through which the visitors go. One of the party dies – but neither the death nor the body is seen. The responsibility for the murder/disappearance is on the one hand animist: causation for the death of the young woman is located outside of society, and outside history – in (super)natural forces or extra-human animacies. At the same time, a contradictory reading presents itself: throughout the movie, the camera has tracked the girls and put them under surveillance, looking down at them from particular watchful points of vantages in the rocks above, so that the intervention of a murderous human agency must also be read into the film's 'meaning'. The same sort of contradictory readings of the Azaria texts seem in part to result from an overlay with *Picnic*: for instance, while Barritt 'found' that a dingo has abducted Azaria, and that she had, by an appeal to the 'unknown life' of Aborigines, been disposed of by 'persons unknown' (read: Aborigines), contradictory readings were produced through the implication of white intervention at some level: 'On the probabilities, I find that at Ayers Rock a scissors would be a tool used by a white person rather than an Aborigine.'

Another intertext that overlays and intertwines with the Azaria text is another Peter Weir movie, *The Last Wave*. Here also, there are unidentified causations which propel and enigmatise the film's narrative, and here also these are aligned with Aborigines – driven underground and, apparently, living in the sewers of Sydney. The disasters in the film involve catastrophes to skyscrapers and rains of mud. The elaboration of the myth of Aborigines as both the possessors of the power to upend white social life and at the same time to 'preserve' and resymbolise it in the form of white capitalist society is at much at work here as it is in the text of Barritt's findings that imply that Aborigines may fit the bill for the 'person or persons unknown' who disposed of Azaria's body (*Daily Telegraph*, 23 February 1981).

Ideologies of how city folk are alienated socially have often been constructed in Australian films in terms of a displacement to non-urban spaces – an inversion of ideologies of colonial isolation, where instead of a new innocent speech there comes the recognition of solidarity that follows on the confession of a crime (whether as convicts, women or Aborigines). In the bush, the alienation of/from urban white, male society takes its voice from, and in, a discourse of confession, and following on that, the declaration of war fought for (two common) goals. This goes as much for films such as *Eliza Frazer* and *Journey Among Women* as for *Mad Max* (*1* and *2*). The possibility of the Bush or the outback as a setting for voicing the alienation of city life was fully realised in both the official discourses on Azaria's disappearance and the excessive gossip/ rumour/joke discourses that 'exceeded' the former. But here the alien-ation that might have resulted in confession and declaration were pre-cluded by another discourse – equally one of alienation and exclusion – namely, that of tourism.

SYMPATHY FOR THE DINGO

Tourism in Australia constitutes a range of practices, not least of which are reading and viewing practices. The TV ads mentioned above that use rural and outback settings to sell goods, as well as the 'nationalist' army and Project Australia ads, all depend on the assumption that Australians are as much tourists in their own country as are overseas visitors and are equally attuned to 'stability' and to the potential aggressors who/which might threaten this. In identifying a dingo as the culprit in the Azaria affair, Denis Barritt was as much identifying a tourist hazard (and a barrier to the continuing 'innocence' of nature and the land) as a potential killer. But further, this identification itself functioned as a displacement of *threat* inasmuch as the placing of the Chamberlain affair functioned as a displacement of urban family stability and its problems into the outback.

Animals as threatening of the social fabric have long been imaged as both individual in their cunning and collective in their overwhelming, plague-like force. To take only two examples, from the 1920s: a rat scare in 1920 had occasioned an item in the *Sydney Morning Herald* that read:

(if the Minister of Health and Motherhood) wishes to find an all-pervading evil waiting to be eradicated, let him tackle the rats which have grown in numbers to a most alarming extent of late. Perhaps the overcrowding of houses by human residents in pushing out the rats which cannot now find house-room in their former haunts, or perhaps a strike is on amongst the rodents, who have stopped work, and can find time to stroll about the city streets.[11]

Again, in the 1920s, the rat scare provided D. H. Lawrence with a resolution for the discussion between Calcott and Somers on the threats to Australian 'integrity':

It was a period when Sydney was again suffering from a bubonic plague scare: a very mild scare. . . . But the town was placarded with notices 'Keep your town clean', and there was a stall in Martin Place where you could write your name down and become a member of the cleanliness league, or something to that effect. . . . The battle was against rats and fleas, and dirt. The plague affects rats first, said the notices, then fleas, and then man. All citizens were urged to wage war with the vermin mentioned.[12]

Between this and Denis Barritt's findings on dingoes have come the rabbit menace and fruit fly campaigns of the early 1950s (all couched in Movietone newsreels in similar vein) and the mid-1970s – rats-eating-Australia campaigns that characterised the Packer-inspired anti-inflation campaigns. Barritt's findings in the Azaria case take these displacements a stage further, but in the same direction. Here the enemy is the dingo, and those – such as conservationists – who would protect it:

In a territory whose economy is based, in part, on tourism, it is strange that [there are not representations from] the body that is responsible, if not liable, for the overall conservation policy of the Uhuru National Park. In an area where advanced planning is in hand to meet the accommodation requirements of upwards of 6,000 people a night, a policy of conservation seems to have been activated that has as its primary aim the intermingling of tourists with an ever-increasing number of dingoes, desert death adders, desert brown and king brown snakes. The dingo is dangerous and known to be dangerous. Prior to 17 August, 1980 the conservation authorities had received several instances of dingoes attacking children. The significance of the dingoes' range and territory was known to rangers . . . and known to be in areas where children might be exploring in the many areas of interest around the Rock. The conduct of dingoes around the campsites together with their propensity to enter tents was known, or ought to have been known. The propensity of a dingo, reared by *homo sapiens*, and treated in a domestic environment to violently attack children was known, yet in the face of this knowledge dingoes have been retained and allowed virtually to infest the area as a tourist attraction. I would hope that the moral responsibility to protect children visiting the National Park appears to have been avoided in the past, [and that] the legal consequences of any such action in the future should lead to *the elimination of any species dangerous to man* from such parks, or at least any such areas frequented by tourists. Every person in our community is under an obligation to conserve human life, and those charged with the added task of conserving life in the National Parks ought to remember and apply *the primary tenet of our land*. If those charged with the protection of wild life in the National Parks would rely on laws forbidding the destruction of such creatures, then they ought to be made to publicize the dangers that exist and are permitted to exist within such parks. . . . Such publicity should be included in any tourist promotion to fulfil the requirements of fair advertising. The case clearly shows that *a choice has to be made between dingoes and deadly snakes on the one hand, and tourism on the other*. The two should not be allowed to co-exist, *providing traps for decent people where our forebears set traps for deadly creatures*.

Dingoes are not and never have been an endangered species: despite efforts by man they have retained their position as the most dangerous carnivore of the canine species on this continent. Tourists in National Parks should be allowed to examine fauna in its natural state, *but I maintain only at a safe distance*. . . . *All animals dangerous to man [should be] safely enclosed or eliminated*.

(All emphases are my own; this portion of the text of Denis Barritt's findings were excluded from the most comprehensive transcript, *Sydney Morning Herald*, 21 February 1981, but can be found in TV recordings of the inquest findings.)

To offset the popular notion that Azaria was somehow herself a sacrifice (acknowledged by Barritt himself in his assertion that 'the name Azaria does not mean, and has never meant, "sacrifice in the wilderness"'), a scapegoat, a more visual sacrifice, was enacted. Twenty-seven dingoes died in an act of scientific self-appeasement. Azaria's death was a 'mystery' and could not be *seen*, but the death of the dingoes could; so could the sacrificed goat in the Adelaide Zoo experiment. This televisual sacrifice in the name of forensic science seems, at first sight, to be an externalisation of the sacrifice that is made by scapegoats in general, but also perhaps of the sacrifice that oneself is supposed to be making – in other words, the visual realisation of sacrifice and self-sacrifice promoted by such outfits as Project Australia.

Georges Bataille has interesting comments to make about the relationship between sacrifice and the spectacle of sacrifice that may illuminate the huge public support for the underdog (the dingo) that was perhaps the real focus of discourses on sacrifice in the period leading up to the handing down of Barritt's findings. Of sacrifice in general, he notes that: 'For people to be finally revealed to themselves, they would have to die, but they would have to do so while living – while watching themselves cease to be.' This however is impossible – the sacrifice of self is unimaginable because the act itself cannot be made visual. So, argues Bataille, the sacrifice or scapegoating of an animal arises as a solution, even though sympathy with (through identification with) the animal will also be a strong dynamic of this sacrifice.

> In principle, death reveals to people their own natural, animal being, but the revelation never takes place. For once the animal being that has supported them has ceased to exist. . . . In sacrifice the sacrificer identifies with the animal struck by death

A circle is in motion: on the one hand, the human sacrifice is an unspeakable proposition, a narrative that turns back on, and destroys itself, identifying with Lindy Chamberlain's assertion (*Woman's Day*, 1 October 1981) that:

> They're making up all sorts of dreadful stories because of Michael's religious connection. That Azaria was a sacrifice. That her name meant Bearer of Sin. That we dressed her in black. Can you imagine that? Always dressed her in black?

However, the identification with the other sacrifice, the animal one, is also untenable in that the 'identification with the animal struck by death' is also precluded on the grounds that this is not just any animal, but the dingo, represented on no coat of arms, and with strong ties with other underdogs in popular mythology.

Like the coyote of California, the dingo stands in a mediating category, between the wild and domestic. In a taxonomy of Australian animals, dingoes occupy the same space as, say, the fox in English folk narratives or the coyote in American tales. Dingoes, foxes and coyotes in these stories have in common that they try on big things, hatch big plans, but always muck them up. They get the blame, but it is for a crime that they themselves never actually benefit from, despite the devastating punishments they incur in the process. All of them perhaps occupy the 'neighbour' category prescribed for 'fox' in Edmund Leach's structural analysis of animals in English folktales:[13] trustworthy up to a point, but forgiveable in breach of that trust. Furthermore, as the rats in the foregoing quotes may have acted as metaphor for 'reds' in the red scares of the early 1920s, so also the dingo stands as a metaphor for thieves, criminals and the poor in Australia, as metaphor for aggressors against property, in fact, rather than as murderer.

Hence, the widespread 'sympathy for the dingo' movement is as much a refusal to accept the scapegoat as it is a protest against injustice. Even in Lindy Chamberlain's words, 'the dingo has *taken* my baby', the dingo is a thief rather than a murderer, and its representation as murderer is itself contradicted by such popular 'definitions' as that of 'a dingo's breakfast' ('a drink of water and a good look around', as cited in the *National Times*, March 1981), a situation that applies to an increasing number of Australians living below the poverty line.

Inasmuch as the dingo maps in with images of other folklore characters such as the coyote (or Roadrunner, or Tom of *Tom and Jerry*), there is also a lot of sympathy for the dingo. In Roadrunner cartoons, for instance, the coyote's fate is usually to be torn to pieces, but then to turn up in one piece again. If indeed the dingo is a displacement for the unspeakable, but nevertheless much spoken of, rumoured sacrificial fate of Azaria, then the dingo's own fate (confirmed by the Adelaide Zoo experiments in the eyes of the TV audience) mirrors that of Azaria as narrated by her mother: 'I wanted someday to find a shred of her clothing to know what happened so the world would know . . . but not my beautiful Azaria torn to shreds by dingoes'. Or later: 'At that stage, Michael was full of hate for all dogs, especially dingoes and, minister of religion though he is, he could have torn them limb from limb' (Woman's Day, 1 October 1981).

In part also, the sacrificial displacement of baby into dingo was produced by the 'appearance' of Azaria as in fact whole and well in the large photograph of the child held up by both the Chamberlains at the end of the Barritt inquest 'to show what a beautiful baby she was' (*Daily Mirror*, 23 February 1981). The photo, perhaps a metre across, was certainly big enough for the TV cameras there present, and presented, or rather re-presented, Azaria as 'a beautiful dream', the 'princess', 'such a little lady', or 'quite the most beautiful baby I have ever seen' that Lindy Chamberlain spoke of in her *Woman's Day* interview. The appearance of a 'whole' Azaria via this image and its visibility to the cameras might also have given impetus to rumours that another being, the dingo, was the dead underdog.

POPULAR CULTURE: A LAUGH AT LIFE

The most bourgeois of all phenomena, gossip, comes only because people do not want to be misunderstood. The destructive character

tolerates misunderstanding, but not gossip. . . . The destructive character obliterates even the traces of destruction.

(Walter Benjamin, *The Destructive Character*)[14]

Ayers Rock and the Olgas comprise the visible ends of a huge sedimen-
tary conglomerate of great geological and scenic importance.

(Denis Barritt, *ABC*, 20 February 1981)

In drawing attention to the function of gossip, jokes and speculation as
an extension and partial subversion of dominant/dominating decoding
practices in reading and viewing, and then discussing these in terms of
something called 'popular culture', I have perhaps been perpetuating a
notion of 'popular culture' that has recently come under scrutiny and
criticism (for instance, by Tony Bennett in his 'Popular culture: a teaching
object', *Screen Education*, 34 (1980). Specifically, one of the points that
are taken up in such recent discussion concerns the dangers in taking up
the idea of 'popular culture' as only an oppositional category – the study,
say, of working people's or unemployed people's culture defined in terms
of what it is set against (elite culture, hegemonic bourgeois culture). And
in Australia, the idea of a confrontation between, as Bennett put it,
'forms that are opposed from "above" and those that emerge from
"below" ', certainly coincides with the Australian soft spot for the 'ocker
knocker' as the local form of apolitical anti-authoritarianism. Gossip,
rumour and jibes certainly may have been bourgeois forms in the world
that Benjamin knew (see first quote above), but in Australia, they constitute the productive remains of working-class oral virtuosities that have
been increasingly converted to literate ones by schooling and the media.
Denis Barritt's comments (second quote above) might almost be a metaphor for the relation between rich hegemonic signifiers such as Ayers
Rock and the 'invisible' but still active 'conglomerate' from which it
obtrudes.

However, an important aspect which a discussion of 'popular culture'
in Australia might start with is this: the way in which oral practices such
as joke and rumour articulate silences in 'official' discourses, such as
those of the media, in such a way, as to destroy their legitimacy and the
'self-evidential'[15] regimes of sense that they perpetuate. In the dingo-baby
jokes that proliferated in early 1981, the function of the rumoured sacrifice is taken over by the dumb animal (dingo), the silent continent,
the silent race[16] (women, Aborigines), socially and sexually persecuted
minorities, voicing the subject who is 'subjected', but not yet subjectified,
socialised or sexualised. For example:

1 *What did one dingo say to another outside the maternity hospital?
Shall we eat here or take away?*

2 *What could have changed the course of history? A dingo at Bethlehem.*

Baby jokes, and dingo-baby jokes, traverse the space of socially constructible meaning, articulating what has been evacuated from 'official' language and laughing at the vulnerability of that language. As popular culture, baby jokes in general deal usually with the torture, mutilation and death of humans before they have themselves become capable of language, when, as babies, they have yet to enter the Symbolic of language, when they are still 'speechless' – in this sense, baby jokes are not about babies so much as about being the oppressed of a situation in which one likewise 'has no voice' – e.g. being poor. Baby jokes 'make sense' by laughing at 'made' sense.

In the gossip and speculation that surrounded the reportage of the Azaria case then, media and magisterial discourses were elaborated and made to exceed themselves, making a non-sense of officially articulated closure of sense ('Dingo did it', for example). The recent discussions on 'popular culture' that appeared in *Screen Education* have tended to reduce the anti-authoritarian and anti-hegemonic force of popular cultural practices by reducing a theory of resistant cultural forms to an algebra with dominant discourses and practices on one side of the equation and subdominant discourses and practices on the other. Rather than reducing the force of popular cultural practices in this way, in order to produce an account of how hegemony is attained and maintained (which is also necessary, but perhaps not at the expense of a 'popular' notion of 'popular culture') and to produce a reasonable 'teaching object' out of what is, after all, not only a set of cultural practices, but also the subject of a range of discourses on those practices by the people who engage in them, perhaps an 'engaged' study of popular cultural practices in Australia might consist in identifying, elaborating and perpetuating ruptures that dominant discourses and practices either exclude or incorporate or reinterpret or reanalyse or resymbolise.

Gossip, rumour and joking are subdominant forms in which the 'play' of meaning is, anyway, produced, is acknowledged and exceeded. 'Making sense' of the various practices that constitute 'the social whole', as Francis Mulhern[17] has proposed for a study of culture ('the unity of those practices that produce sense'), may be only one part of such a study. But equally, 'making sense' also means doing so *at the expense of sense*, by indicating its limits, and in the 'making' of this 'sense', identifying whose 'sense' it is and how it has been constructed; and also, by carrying it to an extreme, showing how tenuous is its legitimacy and capacity to enact and perpetuate hegemony. The algebra of an 'above' and 'below' must perhaps still be taken into an account, for it is not only an algebra with 'a' and 'b' terms, but also excess and whys.

NOTES

This chapter first appeared in *Interventions*, 16 (1982).

1 E. H. Gombrich, *The Story of Art*, 13th edn, Phaidon, London, 1977; M. Foucault, *Madness and Civilization*, Vintage, New York, 1973.
2 E. H. Gombrich, *Story of Art*, p. 385.
3 M. Foucault, *Madness*, p. 280.
4 ibid.
5 ibid.
6 *Sydney Morning Herald*, 21 February 1981.
7 Cf. J. Lacan, *The Four Fundamental Concepts of Psychoanalysis*, *passim*, Penguin, Harmondsworth, 1977.
8 C. Lévi-Strauss, *The Raw and the Cooked*, Harper & Row, New York, 1970, pp. 153–4.
9 This distinction is a reference to one made by R. Barthes (e.g. in *The Pleasure of the Text*, Hill & Wang, New York, 1976) between a text, such as the realist novel, which produces in the reader a sense of pleasure and the fulfilment that comes with consumption, as against the text of *jouissance* – bliss, orgasm, rupture, loss, unrest. This latter category is supposed to describe the effects of reading, say, avant-garde novels or seeing avant-garde films.
10 'Intertextuality' seems like a very useful term for indicating the way in which the way one reads a sign in one text is also supported by the way one has read the same sign (e.g. 'dingo' or 'Ayers Rock') in another text. The introduction by Leon S. Roudiez to J. Kristeva's *Desire in Language*, Blackwell, Oxford, 1980, p. 17, warns, however, that 'the term has . . . been much used and abused on both sides of the Atlantic'. So here's one for Australia.
11 *Sydney Morning Herald*, 10 May, 1920, and quoted by H. McQueen in his *Social Sketches of Australia*, Penguin, Harmondsworth, 1978.
12 D. H. Lawrence, *Kangaroo*, Penguin, Harmondsworth, 1978, p. 56.
13 E. Leach, *Lévi-Strauss*, London, 1974, p. 56.
14 W. Benjamin, *One Way Street*, London, 1979.
15 Cf. An interview with M. Foucault, 'Questions of method', in *Ideology and Consciousness*, 8 (Spring 1981), 6.
16 Cf. J. Kristeva, 'Signifying practice and mode of production', *Edinburgh Magazine '76*, 1, 66 on women as 'the silent race, silent support of the symbolic function, permanent appeal to a forbidden incest, object of anguished male identification'.
17 F. Mulhern, 'Notes on culture and cultural struggle', *Screen Education*, 34 (Spring 1980), 32.

Chapter 10

Business, pleasure, narrative
The folktale in our times

Helen Grace

> Money demands constant vigilance. To become poor, one only has to
> let oneself go. But to enrich oneself requires greed. Our relationship
> to money demands a tension which is not reducible to any other. It is
> through money that the Order confronts us. The monetary act is always
> aggressive.
>
> (André Amar in *The Psychoanalysis of Money*)[1]

Within the last few years, a noticeable shift has taken place in the layout
of the business pages of daily newspapers in Australia. Some of the
changes which are observable have affected the whole of the newspaper,
such as the increased tendency towards a kind of television-style 'programming' layout in which we are dealing not so much with time slots
but rather with 'space slots'. For example, in the *Sydney Morning Herald*
each day there is a special supplement, a kind of spatial filling of the
paper with material directed at specific readerships (television viewers,
computer buffs, gourmets, potential tourists, investors, home renovators,
followers of fashion, seekers of pleasure and weekend entertainment).
Each of these consuming readerships is addressed directly, the special
interest which the newspaper takes in these readerships revolving largely
around the fact that they have disposable incomes, which can be delivered
to advertisers. Other social groupings – potential readerships such as
street kids, single parents, junkies – are not directly addressed, because
they do not have large disposable incomes; they are not spoken *to* but
only spoken *about*. And in another magazine section of the paper concerned with social problems they are constituted as objects of spectacle.
(This section of the paper takes over from what used to be the women's
pages, until feminism challenged this compartmentalisation. My interest
in this chapter, however, is with the men's pages, since these have certainly remained and have in fact been extended.)

The greater the disposable income of the consuming readerships, the
greater the social problems will be to which they are called upon to
respond. Street kids are the current favourite and so great is the fasci-

nation with them that a local advertising industry body has recently begun a campaign to set up an inner-city refuge for them, amidst a blaze of publicity for the advertising industry.

Meanwhile, the 'social problems', (debt, current account deficits, balance of payments imbalances), which are caused in part by the level of consumption encouraged in the other 'space slots', are analysed on the editorial pages and, of course, in the business pages. They are not, however, regarded as 'social problems', a category which always implies a particular social group, the 'disadvantaged'. Instead, the effects of economic, as opposed to personal, recklessness are regarded as universal problems, responsibility for them being placed with the population at large. Such consumption-induced problems becomes everyone's responsibility, rather than the responsibility of the sector of the population for whom 'welfare' is the solution, 'welfare' in this case, of course, being provided at the level of industry assistance, subsidy and tax concessions.

On the business pages, the visual content has recently increased and we are now confronted with dramatic graphs and charts, the drama being emphasised by the widespread use of non-zero baselines, which greatly exaggerate rises and falls. Large portraits of businessmen are also a feature of the new business pages. While it is their business dealings which have made them prominent in business circles, the use of a particular style of photography constitutes them as important to the person in the street. The newspaper photograph – which must compete with television news for impact – is part of the process of putting into circulation a set of images of power. Such images become individualised in the portrait of the businessman. In this way the man becomes important, is recognised in the street – becomes a recognisable figure beyond the narrow confines of the business world. But representation must play another important part before this world can be seen as a place of action and excitement equivalent to a football stadium on Grand Final day.

On the surface, there is nothing to see in the business world. Deals are done in secret. The telephone is used a lot, and people talking on the telephone do not present an exciting spectacle. Columns of stock prices are less interesting to read than the telephone book and the intricacy of deals remains hidden behind dense legalistic language. On the whole, then, no spectacle is immediately observable. So it has to be produced by emphasising, as a site of action, one particular aspect of its operation. The site chosen for this emphasis is the floor of the stock exchange. Here the constraints manifest at every other level of the business world are suspended in a frenzy of activity giving the appearance of complete chaos. The spectacle is such that visitors' galleries, where spectators as well as speculators can observe the action, are provided as part of the architecture of these sites of the arbitrariness of capital's value creation. At the time of the October 1987 stock market 'correction', photographs of the figures of hysterical floor traders represented the events to a mass audience more powerfully than did the numerical figures of falling prices, since for those who had no interest in the workings of business, it was hard to see that the paper losses being referred to were in any way real. The presence of the market and the focus on its site suggests that a freedom in the determination of value is at play – everything is out in the open, so that the value which is acquired in this process is seen as a real and natural one. Given, then, that the existence of the market is a crucial rhetorical device in maintaining the belief that freedom exists, it is hardly surprising that its site should become the centre which represents the spirits of energy, activity, virility.

We are constrained at every turn by Western philosophy's divisions – logic, ethics, aesthetics, all knowledge belonging in one or other of these categories. In this structure, there can only be a consideration of the true, the beautiful, the good. Each realm is autonomous, with its own set of concerns, its own rules. Rather than casting aside this structure altogether, I choose to work around it. Along the edges, those who scavenge for the cast-off scraps resulting from attempts to fit recalcitrant bits of information into these realms will find some rich pickings in the border skirmishes, the incursions into foreign territories which take place in these regions.

Aesthetics proper has nothing to do with logic and ethics, notwithstanding the assumption of a high-minded truth and goodness expressed by art, which is manifest amongst high cultural followers of aesthetic experience. It certainly has nothing to do with money, a distasteful substance, which does not fit into any of philosophy's knowledge categories. Money appears only as an abstraction, which does not oblige philosophy actually to handle it. (To do so would verge on usary – which itself is caught up in a long history of ambivalence and persecution.[2]) There do exist a number of key works which could be said to belong to a philosophy of money.[3] Monetary theorists, however, have no trouble with the idea of appropriating an aesthetic dimension in order to give concrete form to their own concerns:

> Monetary theory is like a Japanese garden. It has esthetic unity born of variety; an apparent simplicity that conceals a sophisticated reality; a surface view that dissolves in ever deeper perspectives. Both can be fully appreciated only if examined from many different angles, only if studied leisurely but in depth. Both have elements that can be enjoyed independently of their whole, yet attain their full realization only as part of the whole.[4]

The particular success of the Japanese economic effort renders the use of the Japanese garden metaphor all the more appropriate. My reason for quoting Friedman is to point to the ready use of language's poetic function which is made by theorists whose disciplines will have nothing to do with poetics or aesthetics on the whole. For emphasis, however, it is left to a function of *language* to produce the desired effect and to carry the power of arguments which are presented initially in forms which belong to the realm of logic rather than aesthetics.

In the title essay of the book to which I've referred here, an elaborate argument is developed to produce a formula representing the optimum quantity of money within a community. It takes into account the distinction between the nominal and the real quantity of money and the distinction between the alternatives open to the individual and those that are open to the whole community. (So here we also enter the realm of ethics, which is disallowed by aesthetics and logic.) The optimum quantity of money is expressed in the following way:

$$MRY = IRD(O) = r_E = \left(\frac{I\ dR^*}{P\ bt}\right),$$
$$MPM = MNPS_M = MNPS_B = r_B = 0$$

Clearly, this form does not belong to a consideration of aesthetics, unless one concerns oneself with issues of typography or layout, issues which are quite extrinsic to this abstraction. What we are presented with in formulations like this is an attempt to quantify a social experience. One may approve of such an attempt, admiring its elegance, or one may regard it as somehow missing the point of the social experience as being beyond representation. Either way, the dominance of quantitative research is well established, for reasons which are accounted for in simple, seemingly innocent assertions such as: 'modern man likes to measure',[5] itself a displacement of another more subjective explanation, which always remains hidden from these speculations – that is, modern man *is* the measure of all things.

But it is also too simplistic to dismiss a formulation like this as being concerned entirely with the quantification of social experience. Another function is at play here which is of more importance to us – the desire to produce a model which represents what is described. A displacement, a representation. Whenever a model is built and applied, there is a sense in which we enter a structure of similarities and contrasts, or in other words, language and metaphor. This structure, in a certain way, is accounted for by the category which Foucault calls the classical episteme, in which a reflective model of reality applies:

> Up to the end of the sixteenth century, resemblance played a constructive role in the knowledge of Western culture. It was resemblance that largely guided exegesis and the interpretation of texts; it was resemblance that organised the play of symbols, made possible knowledge of things visible and invisible and controlled the art of represent-

ing them. . . . Painting imitated space. And representation – whether in the service of pleasure or of knowledge – was posited as a form of repetition; the theatre of life or the mirror of nature, that was the claim made by all language, its manner of declaring its existence and of formulating its right of speech.[6]

In those fields called the hard sciences and in the area of proper knowledge, it seems that this classical mode is still current, at a certain level, and repetition, notwithstanding its bad press in the debate with difference, returns endlessly.

Money is like desire and, these days, probably more interesting. Money is desired, not for its own sake solely, but because of its abstract value – that for which it can be exchanged. Increasingly what it is exchanged for is not a positive value, an object, a commodity, but, more likely, its own negation – debt. Money is used to buy debt. Its very absence renders it desirable for its own sake. It is the classic fetish in many ways because it stands for something else, it replaces the object which it ostensibly represents. It displaces its own referent. It becomes pure signifier, replacing its signified. In the process, money ceases to exist. Most money economies are today run on debt.

Here I am conflating Freud's and Marx's ideas on fetishism, although, on the whole, I think Marx is probably more useful to my analysis. More recently, however, a new dimension of anxiety has been added to the problem of money and debt, which perhaps adds to the value of a psychoanalysis of the economy. This is the problem of 'contagion'. Contagion occurs when investors, in assessing credit risk, group together corporations by nationality, management style or financial structure. If one such corporation fails, then all others like it may be affected, having a harder time on the financial markets.[7]

In Freud's absurdist story, we understand that fetishism is the end-result of a process of disavowal, in which a discomforting reality is displaced and condensed onto another object. The originary, primal instance of disavowal is the encounter with the reality of the absence of the maternal phallus, itself a displacement of the (boy) child's fundamental fear of castration. The fetish object takes many forms, one of the most interesting and problematic being the phallic woman, a figure in which an absence is replaced by the very form of the absent object, so that the body of woman becomes phallus. As women have entered certain sectors of the workforce, a certain anxiety seems to have emerged and a displacement of woman as representation of desire and pleasure has begun to take place. Increasingly, the sex objects are men, partly in terms of their bodily attributes but partly also because of what might be called their mind attributes; the bright young executive or bond dealer, who outsmarts the competition.

Man, as we know, is a rational creature, whereas woman is not, strictly speaking. She always stands outside reason. As the oft-quoted Archbishop Whately once put it: 'Woman is an irrational animal which pokes the fire from the top.'[8] Women become hysterical. Hysteria, after all, is named after the body of woman. Its symptoms include amnesia; *attitudes passionelles*; feelings of cold; *cephalalagia adolescentum*; deafness; *délire ecmnésique*; neck cramps; *idées fixes*; palpitations; disturbances of smell and speech; stammer, stupor; tears; throat constriction; tremor; disturbance of vision – to mention only those of particular relevance on the floor of the stock exchange.

Although woman is associated with hysteria, it is man whom we most see in states of morbid excitement; all of the symptoms mentioned are now most often to be found on sporting fields or amongst floor traders. (It is worth noting that even in Charcot's time, the most dramatic of the hysterics were men.) Notwithstanding all the knowledge we now have of woman, all the work which women have done themselves to solve the problem which was never theirs to begin with, it is man who remains the great mystery, and it is his world which is filled with the most bizarre rituals, posing as reality. One enters as a fascinated anthropologist (literally).

Let us then consider that realm of absolute reality – the world of economic reality. But we find that, in reality – if there is such a place – we are dealing with fictional entities: futures trading (commodities which do not yet exist); junk bonds (which symbolise the only logic which operates in this field of danger – the greater the risk, the greater the return, *if* there is a return at all); something which is called credit, but which is in fact, debt; and the problem of what the banks refer to as LDCs (less developed countries) – the terrifying reality of Third World debt, in which, in a movement of the most profound poetic justice, the entire economic system of the Western world is threatened because of its enthusiasm for creating debt in order to extend credit.

Clearly then, a world of high fiction is observable, a daily soap opera, full of the most extreme occurrences. Everyday economic life has become a fiction of terrifying realism, a horror scenario with such convincing special effects that, at times, you really feel you too are there, in the middle of it.

One of the tools for analysing economic reality might be through the insights of structural analysis of narrative, in which a common language can be identified. To apply a descriptive or analytic system in this way appeals as a means of breaking out of the entirely personalised description of occurrences which the business pages produce. These pages give a sense of uniqueness to every individual occurrence within the world of business, regardless of the repetitive monotony with which operations are carried out from one corporation to another, or from one businessman to another. Such an analysis will make it possible to deconstruct the seriousness and self-importance of the world of business and to bring to bear a certain skepticism about its claim to so much attention. Propp's *Morphology of the Folk Tale*[9] contains a useful method of analysis to apply to what might be identified as the narrative structure of the business pages, because in this context we are dealing with folktales (although not precisely in the sense in which Propp understood them) – urban myths in which villains abound and heroes and princesses may also appear in the unfolding stories which are serialised daily.

My application of Propp's structure is only partial, since his analysis is complex, and I have only attempted to apply the spheres of action of the dramatis personae rather than the full list of thirty-one functions of the characters, although this could certainly be attempted. To this extent, my application of Propp could be said to be concerned more with the anatomy rather than the physiology of the narrative, since I merely identify certain major players, without describing their functions in relation to each other in great depth. As might be expected, the narrative we are dealing with is not hermetic, so that it is not a perfect one; in particular, it is never resolved because, of course, it remains unfinished. This means that certain spheres of action predominate, especially that of villainy, and the identity of the real hero remains unclear. This is a distortion which ultimately limits the applicability of Propp's structure.

My application of the structure is also limited to – or, rather, governed by – the photographs appearing on the business pages, which, in my view, suggest the possibility of describing a classical narrative, one which is cinematic or televisual, rather than literary. It is this cinematic or televisual aspect of the narrative, based on a heightened realism, which allows for a dissolution of boundaries between fiction and reality, so that a continuity between representation and 'real life' is made possible. To illustrate this, in November 1985, businessman Alan Bond's daughter was married in an excessive public spectacle in Perth. A church was redecorated for the event; a floating dance floor was installed on the Swan River. The event was *produced* like a Hollywood movie, with sets built and prepublicity arranged. The event was not actually televised live, as a royal wedding would be, although national news programs picked up the story. Two days later, on the local Channel 9 (owned by Bond) an episode of *Dynasty* was televised, which featured the remarriage of Crystal to Blake, in a televisual spectacle equalled only by the Bond wedding. One event was displaced onto the other in a basic metonymic structure.

In Propp's classic narrative analysis, seven spheres of action of the main dramatis personae are identified: the spheres of action of the *villain, the donor* or *provider*, the *helper*, a *princess* (or sought-after person) and of her father, the *dispatcher*, the *hero* and the *false hero*. If we now briefly consider some of the functions of the dramatis personae it becomes clear that we are concerned only with the early part of the folktale.

Here, functions numbered 2 to 6 by Propp have some applicability within the narrative of the business pages:

2 *An interdiction is addressed to the hero*. Don't borrow beyond your capacity to repay, or don't pay too much for assets.

3 *The interdiction is violated*. Expansion in the present market requires extensive capital, which, for companies which are not blue-chip, may only be raised through considerable risk-taking – the selling of, for example, junk bonds, which, of course, are imaginary scenarios.

4 *The villain makes an attempt at reconnaissance*. A meeting is sought to discuss matters of mutual interest and the possibility of a merger.

5 *The villain receives information about his victim*. Insider trading is engaged in, which weakens the position of the hero.

6 *The villain attempts to deceive his victim in order to take possession of him or of his belongings*. The leveraged buyout or hostile take-over; the hero's companies provide cash flow and are asset-stripped.

End of the first part of the story. Break for advertisements. Or, if it's a mini-series, end of the first two hours, followed by a preview of tomorrow night's episode.

The second part of the story is, of course, only a partial narrative: the hero and the villain join in direct combat (Function 16); the hero reappears after great vicissitudes, having been discredited or branded (17), and the villain is defeated (18). The initial misfortune or lack is liquidated (19) – legal challenges may have proved successful, for example. The law can sometimes function as a magical agent in this story. The hero returns (21) but is still pursued by the past (22). Before being fully restored to heroic status, he must prove himself, in, for example, another country (23), undertaking a particularly difficult task – for example, the restructure of a group of companies or strike-breaking, in which the unions are defeated in court (25). As a result, the hero acquires a new appearance; builds a marvellous palace; puts on new garments; is shown to have a sense of humour, and to be a man of the people; all is forgiven (29). The villain is punished – placed in receivership (30), and the hero is married and ascends the throne (31). This final stage of the story is much more fanciful, and aspects of it never appear on the business pages, although some parts may be dealt with in the social pages, or in gossip columns. (There is also a gossip column in the business pages, in which rumours can be put into circulation, resulting in bigger stories being developed – and more circulation for the newspaper.)

While this narrative is taking place, photography plays a role in defining the characters. Always a popular character, the *villain* and his sphere of action are not too difficult to establish, and he is the most readily identifiable of the characters in the story. He may be recognised according to his political persuasion. Paul Keating and Simon Crean might be regarded as villains for one side, John Elliott, Rupert Murdoch and Alan Bond for the other. On the business pages of a daily newspaper like the *Herald*, however, the Elliott-Murdoch-Bond group is more likely to be presented as villain, Elliott, because photographically he *looks* like a villain, a thug – or an especially rough and tough rugby league player (there is always an ambivalence at play between villainy and heroism), Murdoch since he represents the competition for the Fairfax press, and Bond, who, at the time that this photography was being studied (1988), was in a fierce legal battle with the Fairfax proprietors over financial advice (given to Warwick Fairfax, in his attempt to finance the takeover of the *Herald* from the rest of the Fairfax family).

The images of Bond have undergone a noticeable change and the process of transformation into villainy is observable over a period of years. From images of the affable businessman, national hero and winner of the America's Cup in 1983, Bond begins to be represented as the belligerent manipulator of the media, in his disputes with for example the Broadcasting Tribunal. Political conspiracy is suggested photographically by association. In a photograph taken at the funeral of Larrie Adler (a prominent businessman who died suddenly of a heart attack in early 1989) a passing moment becomes a decisive one. Two important men, Alan Bond and former Premier Neville Wran, are shown together. It is almost a forensic picture, taken from a considerable distance with a telephoto lens. This is suggested not only by the grain of the image, but also by the fact that a smaller section of the frame has been greatly enlarged for emphasis. The photograph was carried on the front page of the business section, reproduced on a large scale. It is a suggestive photograph, indicating perhaps that Bond has friends in high places who will look after him, friends in the Labor Party, no less. The link, an accidental one, an arbitrary one, is made by pure association, but once made, implies a great deal, suggesting that something sinister is at play in the relations between Bond and his business associates and social contacts. This is a reading based on *photographic* details: grain size, image cropping, image size, lighting, depth of field and so on. Bond has also been represented as the archetypal fat capitalist, an image reminiscent of 1930s political art (Heartfield and Eisenstein). Taken from a vocabulary which is no longer considered to have currency in left cultural discourse, such an image can be used with no difficulty and without self-consciousness by the conservative press in the late 1980s. Finally, the caricature is completed when the figure becomes illustrated as a cartoon.

The sphere of action of the *donor* or provider is also represented by association. In the narrative indicated above, the state becomes the donor, providing the hero with a magical agent (money, a deal, a joint venture). But material assistance at this level is not enough – misfortune or lack has to be liquidated. The hero has to be transfigured, and in this narrative this happens through the operation of influence: social accept-ance and the company of politicians who hold power. For example, a photograph has appeared on the business pages of a daily newspaper with a caption reading 'Labor's WA business friends' showing the Prime Minister and the Western Australian Labor Premier surrounded by prominent businessmen. This represents the sphere of action of the *helper* and also operates through association.

Some interest is added to the narrative by the sphere of action of a *princess*, or sought-after person, and of *her father*. Photographs of women are rare on the business pages and when they do appear, that presence is marked. In this example (a photograph of Patricia Cross, from the *Herald*), the subject of the photograph is a merchant banker, but this is of less interest to us than the style of photography deployed, since it clearly marks out *difference* from the representations of powerful men. Femininity becomes a kind of ambivalent strength in this context. A photograph like this is so different on the business pages that it alerts us to something else at play. One might take a simplistic view and conclude that this 'something else' is merely sex. But such a reading is problematic because it assumes that women are only permitted to enter these spheres because of their physical rather than their intellectual attributes, which is simply not the case. The economic commentator, Max Walsh, has derived some of the authority of his discourse, at least in his television shows, from the presence of powerful women, who are smart, confident and knowledgeable.[10] However, the photograph undercuts the possibility of such power: a certain aloofness (achieved photographically), soft waves, a gesture of the hand, all speak desire rather than authority – the sought-after person. It was in trying to understand what this photograph is doing on the business pages that I first began to consider the possibilities of constructing a narrative analysis of the images, since it was the style of photography rather than the expertise of the subject which stood out so startlingly.

In Propp's structure, the sphere of action of the princess is continuous with that of her father: 'The princess and her father cannot be exactly delineated from each other according to functions. Most often it is the father who assigns difficult tasks due to hostile feeling toward the suitor.'[11] However, in our narrative, there is no father. This is a world of younger men, smart young men like the Charlie Sheen character in *Wall Street* – lean, hungry and prepared to do anything. Older men are displaced by the young; patricide is implicit. The father figure is either a caricature, like the representations of Reagan as Mickey Mouse, or a paternal func-tion is taken on at the level of the sign, so that glasses, perched on the nose, or prematurely grey hair may sometimes signify mature authority.

The sphere of action of the *dispatcher* may be arbitrarily attributed to a figure like Sir Peter Abeles, owner of an airline and dispatcher of the pilots' union.

The most problematic sphere of action is that of the *hero*. Notwithstanding the fact that our narrative is dependent on a hero, in fact there are no really clear candidates for this position. This is perhaps the paradox of our story. As noted earlier, it is not difficult to find a villain for the story, but at any point any possible hero can be turned into a villain. The hero does not exist (or cannot be clearly delineated from the villain, who in turn cannot be delineated from the *false hero*) because of a crisis which belongs to ethics rather than aesthetics. This crisis was expressed locally with the appointment of a new head at the Australian Graduate School of Management in 1988 and the admission that the AGSM was engaged in what has been described as 'a low-key search for someone to teach ethics' rather than leveraged buyouts.[12] 'The entrepreneur's day of leveraged growth has passed . . . because the big banks were the only ones with enough money to fund it, and they're no longer willing to lend. "You can't play the game without any chips." '[13] The business community and business students don't want to know about innovative balance sheets anymore, it seems. Harvard has been given $20 million to fund a school of ethics and now everyone wants one. Opportunities for philosophy graduates have, as a consequence, never looked better (or worse).

NOTES

This chapter first appeared in Rosalyn Diprose and Robyn Ferrell (eds), *Cartographies: Poststructuralism and the Mapping of Bodies and Spaces*, Allen & Unwin, Sydney, 1991.

1 André Amar 'A Psychoanalytic study of money', in Ernest Borneman (ed.), *The Psychoanalysis of Money*, Urizen Books, New York, 1976, p. 283.

2 For an instance of the contemporary return of anxieties relating to the handling of money, and in particular the anti-Semitism attached to it, see Connie Bruck, *The Predators' Ball: The Junk Bond Raiders and the Man who Staked Them*, Simon & Schuster, New York, 1988. This book deals with the rise of the US merchant bank, Drexel, Burnham Lambert and in particular its junk bond specialist, Michael Milken.

3 The best known of these is of course Marx's *Capital*. Less well known, but of considerable use to us because of its aesthetic emphasis is George Simmel's *The Philosophy of Money*, trans. Tom Bottomore and David Frisby, Routledge & Kegan Paul, London, 1978.

4 Milton Friedman in the preface to *The Optimum Quantity of Money and Other Essays*, Aldine Publishing, Chicago, 1969.

5 Martin Shubik, *Games for Society, Business and War: Towards a Theory of Gaming*, Elsevier Scientific Publishing, Amsterdam, 1976, p. 60. For a much more interesting and more rigorous account of claims like this see Ian Hacking, *The Emergence of Probability: A Philosophical Study of Early Ideas about*

Probability, Induction, and Statistical Inference, Cambridge University Press, Cambridge, 1975.

6 Michel Foucault, 'The prose of the world', in *The Order of Things: An Archaeology of the Human Sciences*, Vintage Books, New York, 1973, p. 17.

7 'The "threat" of corporate debt'; editorial, *Sydney Morning Herald*, 1 February 1990.

8 Quoted by I. A. Richards in *The Philosophy of Rhetoric*, Oxford University Press, Oxford, 1936, p. 6.

9 V. Propp, *Morphology of the Folk Tale*, University of Texas, Austin, 1975.

10 For example, Carol Austin, on the 'Carleton-Walsh Report' on the ABC, and Glenda Korporaal, on the Sunday morning business programme on Channel 10, which Walsh hosted. Curiously, Sunday morning business programmes have begun to disappear, so perhaps the moment of fascination with money has passed, along with the entrepreneurs, whose lives have been relegated to the status of last year's top rating soapies.

11 Propp, *Morphology*, p. 79.

12 *Sydney Morning Herald*, 19 February 1990, p. 29.

13 ibid.

Chapter 11

Understanding TV violence
A multifaceted cultural analysis

John Tulloch and Marian Tulloch

In Australia policy debates about 'the culture of violence', about the gun laws and about television and video violence have intensified over the last three years. In Melbourne in 1988 sixteen people were killed by gunmen with semi-automatic weapons in two different incidents. At the time of writing in 1991, another 'massacre' has left eight people dead in a Sydney shopping mall, leading to renewed speculation in *The Bulletin* cover story about the link between the visual media and violence. As *The Bulletin* notes, the 1988 incidents led to a National Committee on Violence Report in 1990 which found that 'Australian society's tolerance of violence . . . extends to the way in which we deal with disputes in the home, the way we accept it in the sporting arena and our preference for it in entertainment such as films and television' (Warneminde, 1991: 22). Also in 1990 came the Australian Broadcasting Tribunal (ABT) report, *TV Violence in Australia*. This report, commenting on the inconclusive evidence from 'the vast body of research on the topic of television and violence' and the 'limitations inherent in the research techniques', argues that 'new approaches are necessary to make progress in violence research' (ABT, 1990: 90).

An important feature of both these Australian government-sponsored reports is the emphasis on sociocultural rather than psychologistic contexts of violence. The ABT report concludes:

> Many factors contribute towards the manifestation of violent action. Not least among these are the social pressures arising from poverty, unemployment, low self-image, family breakdown, stress, challenges to traditional values, attitudinal conditioning and prejudice. A part of this, and it is only one part, is the role of the media.
>
> (ABT, 1990: 90)

The ABT report is important for theories about TV violence in at least two ways. First, it insists, as above, in tying the 'problem' of TV violence into societal violence. It encourages us, in theory if not in its own analysis (which is influenced by Barrie Gunter's 1985 social-psychological research), to examine television violence in the context of institutional violence – the class violence of unemployment, the gender violence of bashings within the family, the prejudiced violence of racism. Second, it emphasises the responsibility of television professionals and of consumers, as well as of governments, to address the issue of television violence.

To take this view is to adopt a position which emphasises the agency of people – of TV producers and audiences – at least as an equal with that of censorious governments. Television is not, in our view, a structure functioning (for good or bad) independently of people's choices; and nor are members of its audience passive dupes or simple 'effects' of its structure.

Our current research represents an attempt at a new, critical approach to an old debate. It is interdisciplinary in so far as it combines developmental psychology with cultural theory: age difference (not to mention gender and class difference) having been notably absent from the analysis of 'children and television violence'.

Our own theoretical assumptions led us to take each of the points we have traced in the ABT report seriously. That is:

1 we assumed that a crucial nexus point for current research is precisely where television *represents* the relationship of violence to the structural and institutional 'factors' which the report itemises as significant causes (unemployment, family breakdown, challenges to traditional values, etc.); and in doing so, makes choices for or against violent responses or solutions;

2 we looked for those 'violent' television texts where producers do indeed seem to be taking their responsibility seriously by actually questioning institutional violence and offering 'alternatives to its expression';

3 we examined audiences' active response to the texts (not individualistically but according to factors of age, class and gender) in cognitive and attitudinal terms, as well as in terms of behavioural options designed to assess social tolerance of violent solutions. We were, in the words of the ABT report, positioning violence 'in conjunction with more positive, prosocial motivations and attitudes'.

TV TEXTS AND INSTITUTIONAL VIOLENCE

Each of the television texts chosen in our research programme *questioned* institutional violence: a British documentary by Ken Loach discussed police violence towards picketers during the 1984 British miners' strike over pit closures; an episode of the Australian soap opera, *A Country Practice* examined domestic violence; *Tour of Duty* challenged (via a major character) the claim that the US military was in Vietnam in the interests of the indigenous people; an episode of *21 Jump Street* questioned the violence of basic training in the army; a *Doctor Who* episode examined the issue of 'video nasties' in the context of economic and political power; and an Australian studio talk-back programme debated violence in sport.

MULTIFACETED AUDIENCE STUDY

Our audience study, which drew on about a thousand school students, consisted of a number of different measures: (1) narrative summaries of 'what it was about' drawing on students' everyday explanatory discourses; (2) small group interviews which encouraged students to reactivate and elaborate the texts' discourses about violence in ongoing debate; (3) cognitive option questionnaires investigating students' understanding of acts of violence in their narrative context; (4) behavioural option questionnaires examining students' tolerance of violent solutions in a range of television genres; (5) semantic differentials to assess students' feelings, attitudes and emotions toward heroes, villains and victims of violence.

Because of limited space, we will discuss findings according to these different measures in relation to one text only – but one which exercised the ABT report significantly as a programme 'featuring fictional violence and entertainment violence' – *Tour of Duty*.

THE TEXT

There is not the space here to undertake a detailed textual analysis of the *Tour of Duty* episode chosen. Suffice to say that, as with all our texts chosen for the project, we showed students in school time an extract of about twenty minutes' duration. A fairly substantial section of the narrative was needed to avoid the 'stimulus/cue' approach to television texts which has been one of the limitations of traditional 'effects' research (Livingstone, 1990). At the same time, we could not show the whole episode and complete the audience measures in a standard school period.

The edited sequence was long enough to contain the central debate between, on the one hand, the major running characters (Lt Goldman and Lt Anderson) who were following orders to 'bring the Katu villagers into the war against the Viet-Cong' by arming them with modern weapons, and, on the other hand, Katim, a former American soldier, now living in the Katu village, who argues that the Bravo unit is there not to help the villagers, but for its own selfish ends. Arming the natives will, he argues, destroy Katu culture and 'make them a target' in the war. This is, indeed, what happens. The local South Vietnamese commander, Major Tung, has only harassed the villagers in a minor way until this period. However, he attacks the village with mortars after the armed

Katu help the US soldiers attack what they suppose to be a V-C trail, but in fact turns out to be Tung's illegal opium supply route. Tung uses his influence in Saigon to have the Americans ordered out, and then enters the village to take the guns and kill the few remaining Katu who have survived the earlier attack. The Bravo troupe hear gunshots, return to the village and wipe out Tung's men. Tung escapes. Anderson goes after him and is about to be shot in the back by the hiding Tung when Katim shoots Tung. The final sequence of our extract has Katim looking down quizzically at the gun which, despite rejecting modern weapons earlier, he has just used to kill a man.

Our textual analysis focused on the central discursive conflict between Goldman/Anderson and Katim, examining the way that the agents of this violence/anti-violence debate are positioned by conceptual and presentational images of setting (the native village), generic schemata, narrative structuration, change of topic and camera angle. In particular, we examined camera and audio support for the 'expressive' Katim against the 'bureaucratic' ('I have my orders') Goldman; but how the subsequent verbal confrontation between Goldman and Tung (as well as gestural and verbal differences between Goldman and Anderson) reposition this 'human'/'bureaucratic' dialogue in favour of the American soldiers. This revaluation of the American position, despite the earlier textual support for Katim, is then confirmed narratively as the soldiers (cued by Katim's angry plea 'teach them to live; don't teach them to kill') help the Katu farm, fish and build. Goldman's 'Give them weapons – bring them into the twentieth century' discourse is thus *temporarily* converted via Katim's 'local culture' one into action which, as the soldiers say, gives them the satisfaction of 'building up, instead of tearing down'; temporarily, that is, until Tung's mortars and guns go off. At the conclusion of the narrative Katim has been proved right; the native culture has been destroyed. But the Americans have been shown to be far from selfish: they are victims as much as agents of bureaucratic 'orders' from above.

AUDIENCE SUMMARIES

Immediately after seeing the *Tour of Duty* text, students ($N = 241$) were asked to write an account of 'what it was about'. Summaries of this kind are 'topics of discourse' (Van Dijk, 1984), semantic reductions of the macro-structural and lower-level propositions in the text according to some notion of heirarchical meaning and salience. As Van Dijk says, 'a summary is a type of discourse providing (a personal variant of) the macro-structure of the discourse it summarizes' (Van Dijk, 1977: 157).

Like Van Dijk, we assume that summaries are both cognitive and social phenomena in so far as they are *shared forms* of social representation. Summaries represent both what respondents understand cognitively and their attitudinal position to the extent that 'what that was about' reflects the *salience* of aspects of the narrative to the respondent, e.g. Grade 4, working-class female (Gr 4 WCF) – *Tour of Duty*

> It was about – The war, vilence [violence] but it wasn't as bad as other vilence movies. I think that it should be shown on T.V. at a late time so that people at a little age won't be able to watch it. It is good that they don't swere [swear] alot. In most of the other movies they show close ups of the shootings and the loud swereing.

Here the respondent is summarising consciously in the context of *a 'TV Violence' research project*; while the 'swearing and violence' notion of salience is probably attributable to her parents. In this sense, her parents' discourse about 'the problem of television' established a pre-text for her summary, which the research process made discursive. Compare this with the following more 'macho', male peer-group oriented responses to *Tour of Duty* from a Grade 7, middle-class male (Gr 7 MCM) and a Grade 10 working-class male (Gr 10 WCM).

> Should have shown more action, less talking. Not very violent.'
>
> (Gr 7 MCM)

> I liked the movie *Tour of Duty*. It had a lot of violents [violence] in it. The end was really action because I thought he had shot him in the back. It is a good movie to watch.
>
> (Gr 10 WCM)

Systemically, both in the summaries and interviews, it was boys (usually senior working-class boys) who criticised our research texts for 'not enough action', 'not enough violence', 'no blood and guts'. In these cases it is likely that the students were articulating their pleasure in 'TV violence', *in contrast to* the 'parental' discourse quoted above, or as 'claims to masculinity' (Connell, 1983). Physical aggression, swearing, drinking and driving are among 'the very limited claims that can be made by people who, because of the age and class structure, have very few resources' (Connell, 1983: 29).

Given that violence is so clearly a matter of cultural constraint and social construction (by age, gender, class, ethnicity, etc.), the way that the causes of violence are represented in the media is of crucial importance. As Van Dijk notes, 'The problem of media influence is complex . . . but it should be stressed that this influence may be substantial for those topics that (a) are found relevant and salient, and (b) about which people do not have direct information from other sources' (Van Dijk, 1984: 9).

Unlike sports violence and possibly domestic aggression, issues such as police, military or racial violence may well be areas of interest (and often class, ethnic or gender-based relevance) that students have little or no direct knowledge about. As two Grade 7 working-class boys said to us in interview about the Loach documentary,

> I'd say it was pretty interesting because you hear about it on the news and all that about the police have gone and done this and done that, but you never actually see what they do.

> And they just show the police walking around and holding back all the people. They don't show like this does all the other blood and guts and that sort of stuff.

Dominant media associations of violence with out-groups (blacks, miners, etc.), while at the same time representing police as defenders of the community *against* violence (Potter and Reicher, 1987), establish 'frames of tolerance' for violent solutions. It matters, for instance, that blacks are more readily associated, among whites, with violence, that minority racial groups are commonly associated in the media with social problems, rather than being seen as partly determined by them, because of the cognitive implications that can easily follow; for instance, the search for cognitive coherence by tying the causes of the social problems to the inherent characteristics of the minority groups (Tajfel, 1981; Van Dijk, 1984). Similarly, the conventional script for the police as 'helper' or 'traffic cop' ('walking around and holding back all the people') is – as these two boys are beginning to perceive – at the expense of other schemata which associate them with institutional violence.

This emphasis on sociocognitive aspects of 'violence and television' shifts our attention away from the ABT report's focus on 'public perceptions of violence' to understanding violence as between this and that group, between this man and that woman, between white man and black man, etc. We assume (with Van Dijk most recently; but before him a long tradition of 'European' critical theorists, e.g. Goldmann, 1968) that discourse is functional and strategic. Consequently, we also believe that group-based scripts and schemata 'are a specific form of attitude structure', that these 'attitudes are represented as propositional structures' ('blacks cause problems, take our jobs', 'police help the public, hold back demonstrators, catch criminals'), and that these propositional structures are 'not arbitrary but effective for their relevant uses and functions' (Van Dijk, 1984: 33). Fundamentally, this assumption understands the notion of discourse (in so far as discourse is the self- and other-representation of in-groups and out-groups) as socially and economically *interested*. In particular, we agree with Van Dijk that 'group schemata, the situation models (and hence the stories), and the strategies of their use are not arbitrary but rather related to the relevant social dimension (interests, aim) of the dominant group' (Van Dijk, 1984: 39) – whether we, for the purpose of analysis, see this group as composed of age, gender, class, ethnicity or national affiliation.

Take, for example, this interview response to *Tour of Duty*:

> About people in the army that were trying to help the villagers. . . . Help them – 'cause they're way behind and we've got all the stuff and that: like television and all those things, and they're just trying to help them by giving them a few things.

This summary by a working-class Grade 10 boy indicates clearly the sociocognitive nature of explaining 'what it was about'. The culturally advanced group is nominated both exclusively – 'They', the violent US soldiers – and inclusively – 'we', who have got 'television and all these things'. This exclusive/inclusive assimilation positions this member of the *Tour of Duty* audience as part of a dominant in-group (the consumption-rich West) represented in the text by the US soldiers who are in Vietnam to bring the out-group (the villagers) 'into the twentieth century'. Alternatively, audiences could be positioned so that the US forces were seen as an out-group, as in the following summary from a Grade 10 middle-class girl:

> The American soldiers were stationed in the village to disable the route of arms to the Viet Kong. They were stationed to help – or so they liked to think, bring the Katu natives into the 20th Century. They were assigned to protect the Katu, yet did a brilliant job at upsetting their culture (- western influences) and turning their previously peaceful lifestyles into something out of a horror movie.

The essence of this sociocognitive approach is that responses to violence on television are not simply individualistic, behaviouristic or psychologistic, but are part of 'the whole causal or rational "background" for the understanding of actions and events in the social world' (Van Dijk, 1984: 22). It is this causal and rational 'background' which generates the 'gist' of the boy's summary of *Tour of Duty*. It is here that the 'audience perceptions of TV violence' assumptions of the Australian Broadcasting Tribunal (influenced strongly by Gunter's 1985 'perceptual analysis' work in the UK) need to be given a more systematic grounding in concepts of cultural and societal (in-group and out-group) functions.

We were interested to see just how many and how wide-ranging these summarising discourse topics were, how they differed for different age, gender and class groups, and also how these group-based sociocognitive factors would influence perceptions of behavioural options in violent situations.

Table 11.1 Discourse topics expressed as a percentage of total number of summaries

	Grade 4	*Grade 7*	*Grade 10*
Pro-US	43	45	69
Pro-villager	10	14	20
Non-specific description of events	21	15	6
Historically specific summaries	13	8	9
Historically 'other'	10	5	3
Research-focused summaries	9	17	8
'Meta'-textual summaries	0	5	6

For *Tour of Duty* the most favoured discourse topics were (as expressed in Table 11.1.):

1 pro-US (e.g. US soldiers were the good guys helping the villagers against the enemy; were arming the villagers to bring them into the twentieth century; were helping the peace-loving villagers attacked by the villainous Tung, etc.);
2 pro-villager (e.g. they wanted peace and were made a war target by the US soldiers; they had their culture destroyed by the US intervention; it was terrible that the villagers were killed when it was unnecessary to bring them into the war, etc.);
3 non-specific description of events ('about soldiers and fighting', 'about some people fighting other people/helping other people', 'about guns and shooting', etc.);
4 historically specific summaries ('about the Vietnam War');
5 historically 'other' (= Asian), war-genre influenced summaries (US soldiers fighting against the Japanese, the Koreans, etc.);
6 research-focused summaries ('about violence'); and
7 'meta'-textual summaries ('sick show', 'cliché-ridden', 'not realistic', 'through American eyes', etc.).

As Table 11.1 indicates, pro-US and pro-villager discourses are the most frequent, and increase systematically with age; with non-specific and historically inaccurate discourses appearing less frequently in older groups.

These figures hide, however, substantial class differences. The pro-US discourse topics contained four distinct variants, of which 'arming the natives to help them defend themselves and bring them into the twentieth century' was the most significant. In *all* grades this was the most favoured response among the middle-class students:

Gr 4 (MC) = 30%, GR 7 (MC) = 29%, Gr 10 (MC) = 42%

Among working-class students, the far less precise category (non-specific description of events) was the most favoured of all in grades 4 and 7:

Gr 4 (WC) = 39%, Gr 7 (WC) = 30%, Gr 10 (WC) = 9%
(cf. Gr 4 (MC) = 13%, Gr 7 (MC) = 0%, Gr 10 (MC) = 0%)

However, in Grade 10, working-class students, like middle-class students, most favoured the pro-US 'bringing them into the twentieth century' discourse topic: Gr 10 (WC) = 43%.

As regards pro-villager responses, though sympathy with the villagers is roughly the same for working-class and middle-class students in Grades 4 and 7, there is a marked shift to middle-class support in Grade 10: Gr 10 (MC) = 36%, Gr 10 (WC) = 3%.

Whereas precision in recognising the storyline as set in the Vietnam War is a middle-class phenomenon at Grade 4: Gr 4 (MC) = 20%, Gr 4 (WC) = 0%, incorrect, 'war-genre' influenced responses (US versus Japan, Korea) are primarily a working-class phenomenon at Grade 4: Gr 4 (WC) = 27%, Gr 4 (MC) = 2%

There is also a gender factor here, with 14 per cent of males to 5 per cent girls responding in this way at Grade 4. The only other substantial gender difference in *Tour of Duty* summaries was for girls to respond with the 'about violence' discourse topic more often than boys:

Gr 4 (F) = 13%, Gr 4 (M) = 5%
Gr 7 (F) = 19%, GR 7 (M) = 15%
Gr 10 (F) = 14%, Gr 10 (M) = 3%

The anti-macho, anti-US summaries, when they appeared, were always female: 'It seemed to be about a bunch of American soldiers with a lot more brawn than brains on location in Vietnam during the war shooting a lot of people and apparently protecting the locals' (Gr 10 MCF).

A marked difference between summaries of *Tour of Duty* and those of all the other texts we used in the research is the very low number of 'don't know' responses when asked to summarise 'what it was about': only one student offered this response out of 241 students' summaries for *Tour of Duty*. This should be compared with the 36 'don't know' responses out of 179 students' summaries for *Doctor Who*, a science fiction programme which is made for children as well as adults. The very low 'don't know' frequency for *Tour of Duty* indicates very considerable familiarity (even at Grade 4) with fictionalised 'solder' scripts. However, the recognition of *specific* war scenarios (Vietnam, Korea, etc.) varies according to age and class.

Summaries as narrative

As well as semantically reducing the text as topics of discourse, many of the students' summaries are also mini-narratives having complete or partial structures consisting of Summary, Setting, Complication, Resolution, Evaluation and Coda.

> *Tour of Duty* was about US military soldiers and Tungs soldiers fighting [Summary] the US soldiers were told on the radio that they had the wrong place so they left [Setting/Orientation]. When they were a couple of metres a way from the village they heard a gun shot [Complication] so they went back to the village and helped the South Veightnam people. Then a lot of shooting and a killing of a couple of people [Resolution]. I liked it [Evaluation] but I thought there was to much violence but thats what it would be like in the war so its okay [Coda].
>
> (Gr 4 MCF)

As this example illustrates, these summary narratives can oversimplify or often misunderstand the textual narrative without this subverting the structural coherence of the students' tale. The US soldiers, for instance, are not told on the radio that they are in the wrong place, but rather that somebody (whom they and the narrative assume to be Tung) has intervened in high places to pull them out, thus enabling his further massacre of the natives. Yet this misunderstanding does not prevent the Grade 4 student from offering a complete (Summary, Setting, Orientation, Complication, Resolution, Coda) and coherent narrative.

We were interested to examine these mini-narratives in terms of age, gender and class variation. Because of limited space, we will discuss only the Grade 4 summary narratives here.

The students' summary narratives could focus on the discursive position and subjectively viewed action of each of three major protagonists.

1 Major Tung – the villain:

> About Vietnam War – district chief wasn't telling the truth and didn't want anyone to know about it – jealous that villagers had good fighters so he fought to get them out.
>
> (Gr 4 MCM)

2 US soldiers – the heroes:

> about Americans teaching tribe how to protect themselves from the enemy.
>
> (Gr 4 MCM)

3 Katim and the villagers – the victims:

> about war, violence and death – I thought it was upsetting for these village people.
>
> (Gr 4 MCM)

> about how different groups work together. . . . The Indians teach them to have some peace.
>
> (Gr 4 MCM)

The fact that different members of the audience can focus on different actants and their different discursive positions is due, first of all, to a quality of narrative itself: i.e. that 'a tale, even a very simple one, always relates simultaneously the various intertwined fortunes of several actors' (Bremond, 1977: 52). Bremond rightly criticises the classic narrative theory of Propp for its simplistic linearity. For instance, Propp's crucial function 'Villainy' (Complication) is in fact two functions, not one. The villainy represents an *action* for the villain, but also a *state* for the victim. This state (of deterioration) of the victim is then normally redressed by a further action by the hero – punishing the villain, who himself is thus reduced to a state of deterioration.

In part, the narrative of *Tour of Duty* does follow this simple narrative pattern, and this structures the summary narrative of our Grade 4 student quoted above.

Deterioration of villagers → Improvement

    because of unworthy villain (Tung)

Improvement of villain (Tung) → Deterioration

                    because of worthy
                    helper (US Army)

The metaphorical 'marriage' (Propp's concluding function) would be the alliance between the US army and the Katu villagers against, not the corrupt South Vietnamese ally, Tung (who is a textual alibi for the failure of the US war in Vietnam), but the 'real' enemy, the Viet-Cong. This alliance is mooted both at the beginning of the episode's narrative as the cause of all further action (going to the village, arming the natives 'to get them into the war') *and* also is the conventional final equilibrium of the *series*-text (the *generic* narrative). However, the actual episode ends differently, since nearly all the villagers are killed and so cannot be allies for the US (Katim, in fact, leads the remnants off to another country).

This play, or tension, between the episodic and generic narratives (killing the villagers/killing the Viet-Cong) means that an audience may either identify with one narrative or another: i.e. with the 'Indians teach them some peace' discourse, or with the 'Americans teaching the tribe how to protect themselves against the enemy' discourse, which in many students' summaries (including some even at Grade 10) collapsed Tung and the V-C together.

Given the totally negative representation of Tung (brutal, evil, arrogant, dishonest, slyly powerful, hints of pederasty) there was little likelihood that audience members would identify with his position. A further point of interest, however, is how far Tung's position is even *understood* in the sense of students having a causal chain of explanation (Philo *et al.*, 1977) like the other two positions, i.e.:

1 the Indians are at peace, and so can teach the US soldiers to have some peace;
2 the US soldiers are empowered by twentieth-century technology and weaponry, and so can teach the natives to fight the Viet-Cong enemy by giving them modern weapons;
3 Tung is profiting from the local opium trade, and so doesn't want villagers with modern weapons threatening his supply trails which pass close to the village.

The textual predicament with this *Tour of Duty* episode is that its particular narrative *problematises* violence itself (that of the US military as well as that of the enemy) – which is obviously a difficulty for a war genre. In an important sense (in so far as the US soldiers are sufficiently influenced by Katim's discourse to talk of it being a happy change 'building things up instead of tearing them down') the episodic narrative *reverses* the classic narrative tale where the initial state of equilibrium is destroyed by the villain.

Initial equilibrium → Lack (Villainy) → New equilibrium (destruction
of villain; marriage of hero
and victim)

In this *Tour of Duty* episode, the initial situation (the villagers at peace) is, according to one major (sympathetic) American agent, destroyed by the *heroes*. Theirs is the 'villainy' (complication) – the arming of the natives; and this complication brings the predicted results: the villagers 'become targets', the chief and many of the tribe die, their safety and their culture is destroyed, and they must leave not only their region but even their country with Katim. The primary objective of the Americans' narrative – alliance to win the war – in this case fails.

To examine the degree of identification and recognition of these separate narrative positions, we coded the sequences according to their three discursive and causal perspectives.

A Tung runs opium trade and steals from villagers (1a)→Tung angry
at arming of villagers and orders disarming (1b)→Tung, angry at

attack on his men and insults of US colonel, orders return of his opium (1c)→Tung attacks village (1d)→Tung enters village (1e)→Tung (heard not seen) kills chief, villagers (1f)→Tung escapes, is shot (1g).

B US army wants villagers as allies versus V-C (2a)→They arm natives to 'bring them into the twentieth century' (2b)→They attack 'V-C' trail and find it is Tung's men carrying opium (2x)→US army help natives farm, fish, build (2c)→Mutual happiness marked by a party (2d)→US soldiers withdraw (2e)→US soldiers return to village→US soldiers fight Tung and kill his men (2g).

C Village culture, happy the way they are (Katim) (3a)→Katim predicts arming natives will make them victims, says 'help them to live' (3b)→Katim watches villagers help army attack 'V-C' trail (3c)→Villagers (including children) die in Tung's mortar attack (3d)→Katim says proved right, Americans are big children who destroy things (3e)→After Tung enters village, more villagers dead, Katim tortured (3f)→Katim shoots Tung (3g).

By mapping the students' summary narratives, differentiated first by class, then by gender, we were able to establish a narrative matrix which gave a sense of the narrative *field* of any one group. We immediately see that the middle-class group's summaries establish a larger narrative field (25 per cent more narrative moves than the working-class students).

Working-class

			1e		
2b		2d		2f	2g
3b	3c	3d		3f	3g

Middle-class

1a	1b	1c		1d	1e	1f	1g
2a	2b	2c	2x		2e	2f	2g
	3b					3g	

The *Tour of Duty* matrix reveals that inclusion of the 'Tung' narrative in summaries is a middle-class rather than working-class phenomenon at Grade 4 (accounted for, if we break these maps down further, primarily by middle-class boys); and inclusion of the 'villagers' narrative is a working-class rather than middle-class phenomenon (accounted for primarily by working-class girls).

Working-class males

a	b	c	x	d	e	f	g
	2b				1e		
				3d		2f	2g

Working-class females

a	b	c	x	d	e	f	g
	2b	2c		2d		2f	2g
	3b	3c		3d		3f	3g

Middle-class males

a	b	c	x	d	e	f	g
1a	1b	1c		1d	1e	1f	1g
	2b	2c	2x		2e	2f	2g
	3b						3g

Middle-class females

a	b	c	x	d	e	f	g
	1b			1d	1e	1f	
2a	2b	2c			2e	2f	2g
	3b						3g

In the case of the soap opera, *A Country Practice* summaries, it was the Grade 4 middle-class girls who mainly accounted for the largest narrative field; in the case of the war genre, *Tour of Duty* summaries, the middle-class boys provided a significantly larger narrative field. In both cases middle-class students provided a larger narrative field in their summaries.

Their kind of analysis, of course, ignores numbers of responses to any one narrative move – it only indicates the degree of narrative spread of the summaries in any one group. When we examined the responses quantitatively, we noticed that for both the *A Country Practice* and *Tour of Duty* texts, the working-class group had proportionately a greater number of responses in significant 'violence' narrative moves (i.e. in *A Country Practice* the 'husband bashes wife' narrative move, in *Tour of Duty* 'US soldiers arm the Katu', 'US soldiers return to fight' 'US soldiers kill the enemy'). To put this another way, in the case of *A Country Practice*, 59 per cent of working-class compared with only 26 per cent middle-class total narrative moves were 'husband bashes wife'. In the case of *Tour of Duty*, 65 per cent of working-class and 37 per cent of middle-class total narrative moves were in the 'arming the Katu', 'returning to fight' and 'killing Tung's men' categories. There was no difference between girls and boys on this 'violence' measure, each group providing 42 per cent of their total narrative moves in these three categories.

Rather than assuming on the basis of this evidence that working-class Grade 4 children respond 'more violently' to *Tour of Duty*, however, we should first of all remember that middle-class children provide a greater proportion of 'complete' narratives in their summaries than working-class children, which may partly be a class-based function of language use.

Our behavioural options would give more information about different class tolerances of violent solutions.

Behavioural options

This research was not designed to examine 'behavioural effects' of television violence. In the first place, we do not accept that television violence 'stimulates' or cues violent acts in this way. Rather, violence in society is a matter of institutional values and structural control. Second, we believe that people's behaviours are significantly governed by their values: for example, in the soap opera we used in the research, the husband would not have been violent to his wife (when her career seemed more successful than his) if his actions had not been dominated by the patriarchal notion of the man as 'good provider' that underpins the traditional family structure. In this sense violence has an institutional context in 'the traditional family', and an underlying ideological 'cause' in patriarchal values.

Consequent to this assumption about institutional, structural and ideological determinants of violent behaviour, we wanted to examine students' *values vis-à-vis* such behaviour in institutional settings – including their tolerance of violent solutions. Students were given a series of behavioural options in relation to physically or verbally violent incidents in the texts they watched. The four behavioural options were determined according to two behavioural axes: a violent/non-violent axis; and an active/passive axis. Thus, for instance, for the soldiers to go out and shoot the enemy rather than farm is active violence (AV); whereas to call out a warning to Anderson so that he can shoot Tung is passive violence (PV) in so far as Katim himself commits no violence, but still conforms with institutionalised violence. In contrast, to escape from the scene of violence (whether in the case of Katim or the battered wife in the domestic violence episode) is passive non-violence (PN-V); while appealing to the 'law' (the police, high command, etc.) is active (AN-V) and 'pro-social' in the sense of using existing (or creating new) institutional structures as alternatives to violence.

1 When the US soldiers are working in the village fields:

   a they are wasting their time; they should be out killing the enemy (AV);
   b they should be defending the village, they are soldiers not farmers (PV);
   c they are doing something more worthwhile than teaching villagers how to shoot (AN-V);
   d it is wrong, because they should have left the village as Katim asked (PN-V).

2 After the battle, Katim should have:

    a not become involved in the killing but afterwards worked with the villagers to remake a peaceful community (AN-V);

    b called a warning to Anderson so that the American soldier could shoot Tung (PV);

    c escaped with the villagers and found another peaceful place to live (PN-V);

    d followed Tung and shot him (AV).

In each case, one of the options was textually prescribed and narratively legitimated (i.e. Katim did shoot Tung to save Anderson, because the latter had just helped save the remnants of the villagers). But not all the textually legitimated options are violent (e.g. the soldiers did farm rather than defend the village).

Students were asked to tick the best answer, and put a cross next to the worst answer. A log linear analysis of the relation of age, class and gender to positive and negative choices was conducted for both sets of options.

1 The US soldiers working in the fields

Responses to the US soldiers working in the fields varied significantly with gender (partial $\chi^2(3) = 21.26$, $p<0.001$). More girls (84 per cent) than boys (61 per cent) felt that in farming the soldiers were doing something more worthwhile than shooting; while more boys (33 per cent) than girls (12 per cent) believed that they should be defending the village rather than farming. The text, in this case, legitimises both responses; since it legitimises the farming via the discourses of both Katim and the soldiers, but it visually illustrates the failure of the Americans to defend the village in the death of so many villagers during Tung's first and second attacks.

The choice of worst option interacted significantly with age and class (partial $\chi^2(6) = 18.2$, $p<0.01$) with more middle-class than working-class (Gr 4 MC = 77%, WC = 39%; Gr 10 MC = 85%, WC = 59%) rejecting the 'active violent' response. While Grade 7 students do not differ in choice of this option (MC = 72%, WC = 74%), when violent options are combined a higher proportion of middle-class students in each grade nominate a violent solution as their worst option.

2 Katim shooting Tung

Students' evaluation of options open to Katim were significantly related to their grade (partial $\chi^2(6) = 23.65$, $p <0.001$) and class (partial $\chi^2(3) = 11.1$, $p<0.01$). Younger students (Gr 4 = 53%) more frequently chose non-violent solutions than older students (Gr 10 = 33%). Whereas 40 per cent of Grade 4 and 44 per cent of Grade 7 believed that Katim should not have become involved in the violence of the ending, but should have waited to rebuild the village afterwards, only 29 per cent of Grade 10 chose this option. On the other hand, there was a sharp increase in Grade 10 in the PV option of calling out a warning to Anderson (Gr 4 = 11%, Gr 7 = 2%, Gr 10 = 26%); a solution which maintained Katim as a pacifist yet saved Anderson's life. However, the most favoured option at year 10 (and the second most favoured at Grades 4 and 7) was the textually legitimated one of Katim shooting Tung (Gr 4 = 35%, Gr 7 = 34%, Gr 10 = 41%).

Middle-class students were significantly more likely to choose the active 'alternative to violence' option than working-class students (MC = 47%, WC = 28%), whereas working-class students opted for Katim shooting Tung significantly more often (MC = 25%, WC = 49%). As we have seen, at Grade 10 the 'alternative culture' of the villagers was noted in summaries significantly more often by middle-class than by working-class students; whereas the violent action was understood as 'about US army fighting to protect villagers from district chief' significantly more often by working-class (26 per cent) than by middle-class (8 per cent) students.

Overall, in relation to the physical violence questions, working-class students favoured violent solutions significantly more than middle-class students. Perhaps surprisingly, only in relation to the 'farming vs defending the village' option was there a significant gender response in relation to violent behaviour. In fact, there were markedly few gender effects (compared with class and age effects) in relation to *Tour of Duty*.

The behavioural option responses confirmed the initial impression given by the students' narrative summaries: a greater tolerance for violent solutions among working-class students.

What is noticeable from our analysis of student summaries is that our three significant 'violence' moves establish a narrative structure in line with the *generic* narrative rather than with the narrative tension we have described in this particular episode:

US soldiers arm villagers to defend themselves→(They cannot defend themselves)→US soldiers return→They kill Tung's men.

For most students (but with a significant working-class weighting), the narrative tension between the two American discourses (Lt. Goldman's and Katim's) simply fails to impact. What accounts for this? Later in the article, we will examine discursive logics which *working-class* students use to diminish this contradiction.

But first we argue that quite specific features of the text make it easier for students to accept the conventional 'American goodies kill Asian baddies' script:

1 The primacy of the visual (MacCabe, 1974). Katim uses a gun to kill Tung and thus save the American soldier, Anderson. No words are exchanged; the significance is in the action (Katim uses a gun) and in the visual interaction between the two men (guns *are* needed, despite Katim's earlier view). It is particularly noticeable that the only time grade 4 students mention Katim by name or function ('the chief's adviser') it is when he is shooting Tung.

2 The discourse of contemporaneity. The natives are represented as primitives, and the developing narrative defines the task of the US soldiers as 'bringing them into the twentieth century' by both violent means (giving them guns) *and* peaceful means (farming/fishing/ building). We should note the use of contemporary American music over the farming/fishing/building scenes – 'bringing them into the twentieth century' audibly as well as visually, culturally as well as militarily. This motif is then developed as a complete narrative unit in the 'Party' (or 'Celebration' as one Grade 4 student called it).

3 The use of narrative sub-units. We should note that the 'bringing them into the twentieth century' theme establishes its own 'initial situation' of peace and fulfilment, which overtakes the earlier one of the 'authentic' village culture. The natives are taught modern methods, and at the party their 'alliance' seems complete as each group enjoys the cultural display of the other, and American men dance to contemporary rock music with Katu women. Even Katim (perenially a stern observer of violence in the narrative) smiles as he watches. *This* initial situation is disturbed by the villain when Tung attacks the village with mortar shells. Thus we have a mini-narrative (embedded in the larger one):

Initial equilibrium ('Twentieth-century alliance')→Lack (Tung's villainy)→New equilibrium (US soldiers kill Tung's men, Katim kills Tung).

4 The embedding in Katim's discourse of information which potentially disturbs his own position. 'Bringing them into the twentieth century' turns out to be saving the villagers from poverty and feudalism. Thus, in describing Tung to the US soldiers, Katim says:

He comes around a couple of times a year, bullies the young men, tells the village how much their taxes are going to be, steals a few chickens, then he goes. . . . So long as they're poor and no threat to him, they have an uneasy peace. You've probably changed all that. . . . I'd rather you hadn't come at all. These people mean absolutely nothing to you or your superiors. You just want to use them.

This becomes, in one Grade 4 summary: 'about villagers and enemy who stole chickens and mucked the place up – the US soldiers were on a mission to help the villagers and train them to fight for themselves.' In this student's summary narrative the 'peace' of the village at the beginning is far from ideal; a 'lack' rather than an initial plenitude, which it is the Americans' function to repair.

Nevertheless, the presentation of the villager's perspective is not insignificant in these summaries (nearly 25 per cent of the total narrative moves). And as students got older, fewer (though still a majority at Grades 7 and 10) accepted the conservative resolution of the generic narrative. How then did different age groups evaluate the character (Katim) who carried the anti-violence (anti-generic) narrative message?

Semantic Differentials

In making its anti-violence character use a gun, the *Tour of Duty* text certainly compromised its message. But to what extent did Katim now become a violent character? How did this perception vary according to age, gender and class? Just how positively did these different groups feel about Anderson (given that he was violent too, initiating the final shoot-out)? If he was viewed more positively than Katim, on what measures of his personality and his actions?

Students in all groups completed semantic differential questions on Katim and Anderson according to ten binarily-opposed concepts (good/bad; intelligent/stupid; strong/weak; reasonable/emotional; pleasant/unpleasant; non-violent/violent; normal/unusual; victim/aggressor; fair/unfair; efficient/inefficient) on a five-point scale. For both characters patterns of response indicated underlying dimensions of evaluation (a maximum-likelihood factor analysis with varimax rotation was performed on the semantic differentials of each character).

In Anderson's case a positive/negative dimension (positive = good, intelligent, pleasant, fair, normal) was distinct from assessment of aggression (aggressor, violent, strong). The extent to which he was positively evaluated in the student group as a whole was not related to whether he was seen as aggressive. In contrast, the positive/negative evaluation of Katim included non-violence and victim categories as part of the positive dimension. There was a significant class difference in the evaluation of Katim, $F(1,219) = 8.48$, $p<0.05$, with middle-class students viewing him more positively than working-class students. No significant group differences occurred in the overall very positive evaluation of Anderson.

On the aggressive dimension, however, the main effect of class, $F(1,219) = 20.0$, $p<0.001$, was modified by a significant class × gender × age interaction, $F(2,219) = 6.75$, $p<0.001$. While overall, middle-class students saw Anderson as more aggressive, this view was shared by Grade 10 working-class boys but not by Grade 4 middle-class girls. In contrast to Grade 10 working-class boys, Grade 10 working-class girls typified – and even exaggerated – the general working-class perception of Anderson as not aggressive.

As class appears the most important variable in the evaluation of both Katim and Anderson, the interrelationships in the perception of the two characters can be fruitfully examined by contrasting the responses of working-class and middle-class Grade 10 girls (see Figures 11.1 and 11.2). These figures show the mean ratings for both Katim and Anderson by these two groups.

For the working-class girls Anderson is more 'positive' than Katim on every factor except reasonable/emotional (and arguably, even the emotional is read here as a positive category, since, compared with the cooler and more 'bureaucratic' Goldman, it is, as interviews revealed, Anderson's more impetuous 'backchat' to Tung which appeals to the students as 'funny'). These working-class girls rate Anderson markedly more pleasant than Katim, more intelligent, more fair and, despite the fact that Katim fires only one shot in the episode (to save Anderson's life) *considerably less violent* than Katim! In contrast, the middle-class girls rate Katim markedly less violent than Anderson, more normal, more fair, more reasonable, and no less good or intelligent. If, as we will see later, working-class Grade 10 girls found *Tour of Duty* 'serious' but not particularly 'involving', this was *not* because they identified with Katim's 'serious' ideas. On the contrary, it seems that they were not especially involved in the discursive debate between Katim and Anderson. For them, there was really no debate – Anderson won hands down. Notably, both working-class and middle-class girls and boys at Grade 10 saw Anderson as markedly more efficient than Katim, a sign of his 'twentieth-century' superiority.

Three explanations may account for the class differences in recognising and evaluating violence in *Tour of Duty*, exemplified most forcefully in the contrast between Grade 10 working-class and middle-class girls. These explanations are to do with (1) different *perceptions* of what constituted violence, (2) different *ideological* positions *vis-à-vis* Katim and the villagers, (3) different *tolerances* of violent solutions.

1 The working-class girls uniformly saw Katim as a 'half-way' character between positive and negative. In other words, all but one of the evaluations of Katim by this group fell within the neutral '3' category or within 0.5 of it (while their most positive mean rating for Katim was the 'good' classification at 2.46). In contrast, the middle-class girls ranked Katim well to the positive side of neutral on all but three categories (reasonable, pleasant and efficient) and these three

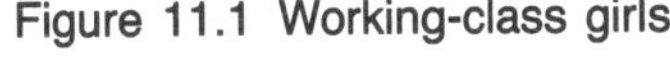

Figure 11.1 Working-class girls

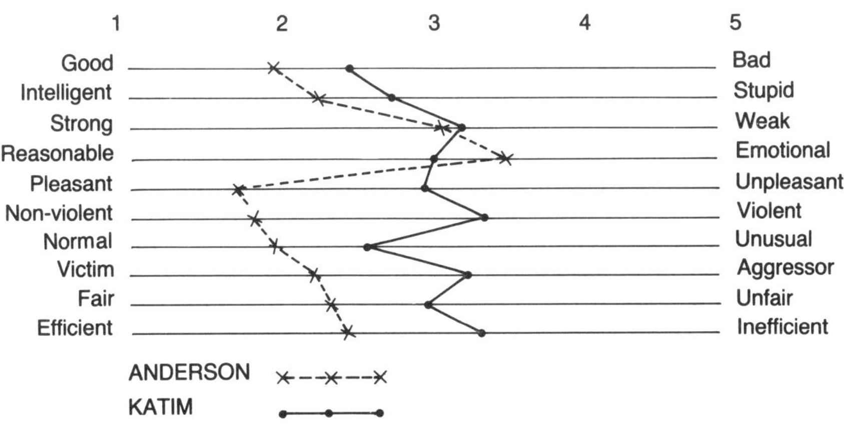

Figure 11.2 Middle-class girls

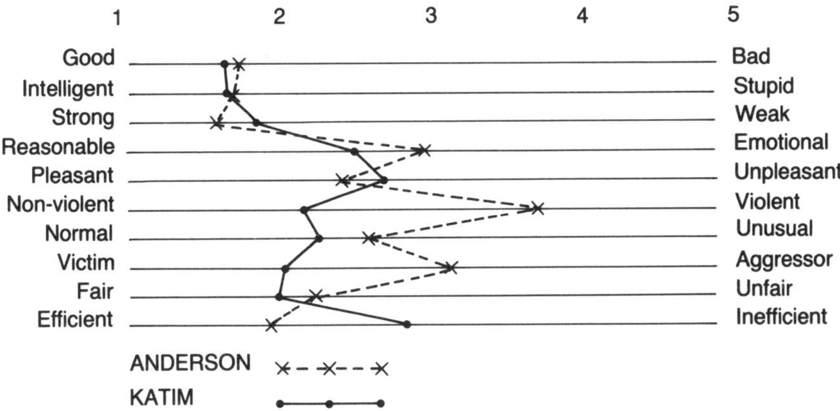

were still on the positive side of neutral. In other words, for middle-class Grade 10 girls Katim was a 'goodie' (particularly in the good, intelligent, non-violent, fair, victim cluster) whose violent action at the end was vindicated by his status as 'good victim'. Consequently his shooting of Tung was not *perceived* as violent – just as Anderson's violence was legitimated among working-class Grade 10 girls by *his* equivalent cluster of 'goodie' values (particularly good, intelligent, pleasant, normal and fair) and so also was not perceived as violent.

2 These differences of perception of Katim as 'goodie' are themselves underpinned by differing ideological attitudes towards the villagers'

culture. Students' narrative summaries showed that there was a marked divergence at Grade 10 as between working-class and middle-class focusing on the villagers and on Katim's wish to retain their traditional culture. Whereas 36 per cent of middle-class summaries at least partially sympathised with Katim's position on village culture, only 3 per cent of working-class ones did. Symptomatically, it was a Grade 10 middle-class girl who wrote: 'It seemed to me about a bunch of American soldiers with a lot more brawn than brains on location in Vietnam during the war shooting a lot of people and apparently protecting the locals.'

3 Working-class students, as we saw from the behavioural option responses, are significantly more *tolerant* of violent solutions. This greater tolerance *vis-à-vis* the 'normality' of violent solutions may help account for the very marked difference of perception of Anderson, with Grade 10 working-class girls perceiving him as non-violent with a mean of 1.83 and middle-class girls perceiving him as violent with a mean of 3.75!

However, this explanation cannot work for Grade 10 working-class boys, since their Katim/Anderson semantic differential graph is much closer to the middle-class ones than to the working-class girls. Anderson *is* rated as violent and aggressive by Grade 10 working-class boys (with a 'violent' and 'aggressor' mean close to that of the middle-class girls), while Katim is seen as a non-violent victim. Yet, for these boys, Katim and Anderson rate almost identically as good, strong, pleasant, fair and efficient. If they are equally 'goodies', but Anderson is much more aggressive and violent, how do these boys maintain the greater ideological identification with Anderson and the other American soldiers that we have noted? Or, to put it another way, given that their sympathy for *both* Anderson and Katim could lead to apparent contradiction, as in the following student's summary: 'The peace side looked after the village and cared for them and taught them to use guns', how do students discursively work through this paradox of the 'peace side' being defined as those that 'taught them to use guns'? We examined this discursive strategy by talking with Grade 10 working-class boys. It helped reveal some of the students' logics in use. We turn here from quantitative to qualitative analysis.

INTERVIEWS

We chose television texts which *debated* violence for our research project. The taped discussion our researcher had with school students about these programmes subsequently allowed them to debate what the texts debated. Unlike the summaries which asked the students for the gist of the show, or the questionnaires which examined cognitive understanding and behavioural attitudes, this was the place where the text's discourses about violence could be reactivated in on-going debate. Discussion is a process by way of which students may come to a more developed understanding than they brought individually to the text; but, in doing so, they expose the process by which they negotiate what may be contradictory propositional structures.

We took small groups out of the larger class for these discussions while the latter were completing the summaries and questionnaires. How would the discourses they used in discussing *Tour of Duty* compare with those used by the classmates in their summaries? To what extent would the discussion and questionnaire responses throw light on each other? To what extent would focused questions from the researcher lead them to discursive aspects of the text which they had not clarified for themselves?

To speak about a topic like television violence is an interactional as well as a cognitive accomplishment, requiring conversational strategies from the speakers. 'Topics are not just "there", but may be suggested, introduced, negotiated by the parties of a conversation. They may be challenged and changed after specific conditions, or changes may be interactionally "refused" by the other participants' (Van Dijk, 1984: 57). In interview situations, the interviewer tends to assign the discussion's relevance and coherence, monitoring the interview, changing the topic and so on. To begin with, our interviewer simply asked interviewees what happened and what they thought of the show, explaining that 'there are no right or wrong answers'. Later she asked more focused questions. Our question-answer format would encourage students to expand on their thoughts about causes and consequences in the text as they were asked to explain and evaluate what happened.

In the interview discussed here, we took four Grade 10 working-class boys, Simon, Shannon, Acheleus and Johnnie outside the school immediately after the screening of *Tour of Duty*. Our interviewer, Hannah, began by asking the same question which the students who were completing summaries were asked: 'What do you think the video was about?'

> Simon: 'About people in the army that were trying to help the villagers and that.'

This 'gist' response was the one we found strongly in summaries at Grades 4, 7 and 10. Hannah's follow-up question, however, enabled her to get behind Simon's topic of discourse to his 'worldview'. This clearly influenced his understanding and reading of the text and established a high-level propositional schema working out of his own situational experience (within consumer culture) as a member of the 'developed' world.

> Hannah: 'Can you be a bit more specific?'

Simon:	'Trying to help them get up to date and all that stuff. Help them – 'cause they're way behind and we've got all the stuff and all that; like television and all those things, and they're just trying to help them by giving them a few things.
Hannah:	'Who were the ones that were helping and who were the . . . ?'
Simon:	'Oh, the blokes in *Tour of Duty* or whatever. The blokes on *Tour of Duty* and like, I don't know, the army or something.'
Hannah:	'How about you Shannon?'
Shannon:	'They're just trying to teach them how to defend themselves, and know which is right and which is wrong.'

Again, Shannon's response of 'trying to teach them to defend themselves' was a dominant one in the narrative summaries. Simon seems vague ('the army or something'), even confused about the strategic reason the text offers (three times) for the army unit's presence in the village. But he is clear, as is Shannon, on the superiority in culture, civilisation and knowledge of 'us'/the Americans over the villagers. In fact the text offers no examples of the soldiers 'giving them a few things' remotely comparable with the advantages of television (other than the pleasure of hammed-up rock and roll music; and fishing with a hand-grenade!). Moreover, the villagers themselves have, via Katim, quite complex and nuanced notions already of what 'is wrong' (including in that category imperialistic Americans who 'like big children, come in and break things, and leave for others to clear up the mess'). Despite these textual positions, the Grade 10 boys are starting from the assumption that the villagers will gain from 'contact'. So, though they will sympathise with Katim and his anti-violence discourse, it will be difficult for these boys to identify with it. It will be hard for them to believe Katim that the villagers are best left with their culture unchanged. Our cognitive option questions revealed that working-class Grade 10 boys were very low in understanding that the 'US soldiers arm the Katu natives so that they can help the US fight the enemy'. Only 11 per cent chose this option, compared to 68 per cent who chose 'to bring them into the twentieth century and help them defend themselves better' (though we should note that middle-class Grade 10 boys scored even higher on this response at 81 per cent). At one level, *Tour of Duty* was about the soulless machinations of war as *real-politik*, where 'orders' from above might vary in degree of corruption, but at best paid little heed to the cultural interests of the war-zone inhabitants. But, apparently lacking a structural understanding of war politics (the US *using* rather than helping the villagers), Simon and Shannon, cued by Lt Goldman's 'to bring them into the twentieth century' discourse, import to the text the superior 'helping' civilisation of television and moral probity (know which is right and which is wrong').

The next speaker, Acheleus, begins with a *generic* response which in fact draws on this assumption of American cultural 'normality'.

Hannah:	'OK. What did you think about the video? Was there anything you liked about it?'
Acheleus:	'It's the same as other videos on violence.'
Hannah:	'What do you mean?'
Acheleus:	'Oh, have guns; somebody dies, somebody lives . . .'
Hannah:	'So, what did you think about that?'
Acheleus:	'It's normal; that's what I think.'
Simon:	'Yeah, it's normal.'
Hannah:	'Sorry?'
Shannon:	'It's just normal.'
Hannah:	'What do you mean? Can you explain what you mean by that little bit?'
Shannon:	'You're used to it; used to seeing that sort of stuff. It's nothing new.'
Hannah:	'So what – do you – did you like that or dislike that?'
Shannon:	'Yeah, it was good.'
Hannah:	'Can you say a bit more?'
Shannon:	'I got nothing else to say.'
Hannah:	'Why did you think it was good?'
Shannon:	'I don't know; because I liked it.'
(laughter)	

Analysis of the semantic differential evaluation of the story of *Tour of Duty* isolated two separate factors: one of 'entertaining' (including 'interesting' and 'exciting'), and one of 'serious' ('not funny', 'realistic', 'violent', and 'disturbing'). Boys (particularly working-class Grade 10 boys and middle-class Grade 7 boys) tended to fall into the 'entertaining' but not into the 'serious' category, whereas older girls tended to find the show 'serious' rather than 'entertaining'. The Grade 10 working-class boys (together with younger middle-class boys) were the group that found it the *most* 'entertaining'. Consequently, Acheleus's and Shannon's generic response ('same as other videos of violence', 'you're used to it') is not surprising. This group of working-class boys don't find the programme especially 'serious'; they 'just like it' and find Hannah's insistence on probing further rather pointless and amusing. For Simon, Shannon and Acheleus this is just another 'US good guys help the weak and under-developed against the bad guys' scenario, which is 'just normal' in war movies – as well as in 'factual' discourses like news coverage of US soldiers fighting Iraq on behalf of the Kuwaitis. At this point in the discussion, the *difference* of this *Tour of Duty* episode *vis-à-vis* Katim's

anti-violence discourse seems not to have been noticed amidst general
pleasure in the 'normal' narrative of 'have guns; somebody dies, somebody lives'.

However, Hannah persists, and on further questioning about the video,
Simon creates a topic change which reveals somewhat more ambivalence
that originally appeared.

> Hannah: 'How about you Simon? What did you think about
>   the video?'
> Simon: 'Oh, they might have been trying to help them in the
>   wrong way by giving them guns, because they lost a
>   few lives in the village and that. Some people got
>   killed. Oh, they could have helped them in other ways:
>   with food and all that, instead of guns.'
> Hannah: 'So that was something that you didn't like about it,
>   was it?'
> Simon: 'Yeah like; yes, something like that.'
> Hannah: 'Was there any particular parts that you didn't like?'
> Simon: 'Oh, the only bit was when they started shooting
>   everyone at the end; that was the only bit. They prob-
>   ably – I don't know – probably needed it in the story
>   anyway.'

If linked to Katim's explanation of why it is wrong to give the villagers
guns (which Simon's topic change draws on here) – that it will make
them targets – the killing of most of the villagers at the end justifies
Katim's anti-violence discourse and is a colossal textual critique of the
American presence. Simon has, however, already justified the American
presence in the village, and to avoid contradiction he *justifies* the killing
in terms of his pleasure in the entertaining ('exciting') qualities of the
text: 'they probably needed it in the story anyway.' This is a strategic
dialogic move by Simon. Rather than following textual causality via
Katim's prediction ('give the villagers guns→they become a target→they
will be killed'), he resorts to a 'meta-textual' explanation (that the narrative 'needed' these killings for its enjoyment) to establish functional
coherence between his own speech acts, his own propositions about the
text. Here the *pleasure* response of 'entertaining' but not 'serious' among
Grade 10 working-class boys seems a more powerful determinant of
reading and interpretation than textual logic.

Acheleus, who as we will see values Katim as 'best' character, uses a
different strategy to make the text cohere despite his acceptance of the
contradictory 'helping'/'making them a target' textual discourses.

> Hannah: 'What about you? Did you – any bits that you didn't
>   like?'

Shannon: 'No, only when they killed the villagers.'
Hannah: 'Who was that?'
Acheleus: 'Major Tung.'
Shannon: 'Yeah, Tung.'
Hannah: 'You didn't like that part? Any parts that you didn't like in it Johnnie?'
Johnnie: 'Probably about what he said too.'
Hannah: 'What part was that?'
Johnnie: 'The villagers got shot.'
Hannah: 'Acheleus, what about you?'
Acheleus: 'Nothing, I liked it – but it was sad the villagers getting shot. Because they were defenceless, which is no good – shooting people defenceless. It's not good.'
Hannah: 'Can you say a bit more about the defenceless . . . ?'
Acheleus: 'Well, they took their guns. They – the villagers, they didn't want to fight, and then that major, Major Tung, just ordered to shoot them.'

Whereas Simon uses a meta-textual proposition to make his interpretation of the text cohere, Acheleus (faced with the self-presentational problem of explaining why he so much enjoyed a text that was 'sad' because the defenceless were killed at the end) draws on a textual displacement: Katim's pacifism is related narratively, not to the Americans who put the villagers at mortal risk, but to the gun-toting villain, Tung. Via the temporal 'causality' established by 'and then' (in the sentence 'the villagers didn't want to fight and then Major Tung just ordered to shoot'), Acheleus constructs a 'passive villagers proved to be wrong in the face of the strong villain' scenario; whereas in fact the villagers are skilled warriors, *are* armed and are therefore not defenceless. Indeed, the violent finale is begun by a villager shooting one of Tung's men with a gun. It was initially the *Americans*, not Tung, who put the villagers in the firing line by giving them guns. This displacement of textual cause/ consequence relations of violence from the American soldiers to Tung enables Acheleus to both value the episode as a 'normal' shoot-em-up ('have guns; somebody dies, somebody lives') and also value the quite contrary, pacifist and cultural position of Katim – as the continuing discussion illustrates.

Hannah: 'Was there anyone that – was there anyone that you thought was – I mean, was there a best character, like a good character?'
Acheleus: 'That Indian guy that speaks English.'
Hannah: 'Uh-huh. Why did you think – why was he the best character?'
Acheleus: 'Because he disagrees with the guns, and he sort of

doesn't like the Americans like getting . . . he wants
the Indians to stay as they are. Like, they didn't know
any of those guns didn't know how to work them out,
but defend themselves with spears.'

Despite saying earlier that this was enjoyable as a typical 'video on
violence', Acheleus is actually valuing Katim for the cultural association
Katim makes between preserving the villagers lives ('no guns') and preserving their traditional culture ('staying as they are'). This is also in
contradiction with Simon's opening proposition that the Americans are
helping the natives out of backwardness, with which nobody disagrees at
any stage. However, the semantic and semiotic richness of the 'American'
discourse compared to the relative poverty of Katim's single voice and
'serious' words comes to Acheleus' rescue. With the others, he names
alternative 'best' characters – and they all choose Americans.

Hannah:	'What about anyone else? Did you have a best character? Someone that you thought was the best character?'
Simon:	'That one – the black one that was singing the song. Everything that he said he put a humorous side to it . . .'
Hannah:	'So, why was that?'
Simon:	'Because he was pretty funny.'
Hannah:	'Shannon, what about you?'
Shannon:	'The black guy that he was talking about, because he made it more enjoyable – the movie – instead of it just being violence all the time.'
Hannah:	'Uh-huh. So why was it more enjoyable with him?'
Shannon:	'Because like he made it funny, instead of sad and killing and that.'
Acheleus:	'There's another guy, the one with the peace sign on his head.'
Shannon:	'Yeah, 'cause he felt sorry for that girl that died.'
Hannah:	'Oh yeah. Who was . . .'
Johnnie:	'I don't know his name.'
Acheleus:	'The one that – the guy with the laugh on his face.'
Shannon:	'Yeah, with all the stuff on it.'
Hannah:	'So what was about him that was . . .'
Shannon:	'He got attached to the villagers; especially the little ones.'
Johnnie:	'The little ones, yeah.'
Shannon:	'And when he was leaving you saw the guy, and then these little kids turn around and look at him. And he looked at everyone sad because he had to leave.'

Hannah: 'Johnnie, was that – was he your favourite? The one with the peace sign?'
Johnnie: 'Oh no, this other guy. The guy that was counting down; then he count from three to twenty-seven.'
Hannah: 'Oh yeah, why. Why was he your . . . ?'
Johnnie: 'Oh because, he want to get those VCs because – like he want – oh, I don't know how to say it.'
Hannah: 'Because he . . . ?'
Acheleus: 'He wanted to defend the villagers.'
Johnnie: 'Yeah, that's it. I'd say that.'
Hannah: 'What was it about the VCs – the VC trails that . . . ?'
Shannon: 'Tung. He's talking about Tung.'

Tung's crime, for these boys, was not simply that he kills 'defenceless' people; but also that he terminates the 'humorous' and 'funny' bits: i.e. the party where the 'black guy' and others are doing a pastiche rock song for the villagers until Tung's mortars put an end to it. In that sense it is *Tung* who makes 'it just being violence all the time'. Given that for Grade 10 working-class boys being 'funny' was a major factor in their enjoyment of the text, this made Tung both a killjoy and a killer of children. Two of the boys' 'best characters' were involved in these two activities that Tung killed: he killed off the black soldier's humour, and he killed 'the little ones' that the soldier with the peace sign cared for. Consequently, this one violent scene embedded American actions in humour and pathos (over the dead little girl in the arms of the soldier wearing a peace sign). Indeed, it is through those two qualities (humour and pathos) that Katim is displaced by the American soldiers textually, just as surely as he is displaced in the boys' conversation by the other American 'best characters'. Katim seems humourless, the Americans have humour (*and* rock music – the closest the text gets to Simon's television culture). Further, the soldier with the peace sign also represents the Americans' pleasure, in farming the village, that they are at last 'building things up instead of tearing them down' – thus appropriating Katim's pacifism for the Americans. It is they who are now 'helping' the villagers.

The boys' responses to the 'best character' conversation reminds us how rich a TV serial like this one is in continuing characters. A 'family' of different soldiers is filled out in terms of personality, motivation and social issues week by week, offering much stronger points for pleasure and identification; while the solitary Katim, however sympathetically portrayed, is expelled from the series' narrative at the end of one week. Our data indicated that 84 per cent of working-class Grade 10 boys in our sample (together with 88 per cent of middle-class boys, 66 per cent of working-class girls, and 50 per cent of middle-class girls) are 'sometimes' or 'often' viewers of the series, so most of them will have seen this family develop over time. In our *Tour of Duty* episode, the soldier family is simply widened to include (via the soldiers' relationship with the children) the villagers – another appropriation of Katim's role. The 'family' reading is further inflected according to the age, class and gender of the students, Grade 7 working-class girls, for instance, quickly and enthusiastically chiming in that what they liked best about the episode was 'the boys' (the American soldiers), but also that they found their relationship with the Katu children 'cute'. This 'liking the boys' may well have also been a major factor explaining the differences between Grade 10 working-class male and female semantic differentials for Anderson, given that he was consistently nominated as the favourite among the American soldiers.

We should be reminded by the boys' discussion, too, of the semiotic richness of the audio-visual text that they are interpreting. In the case of the 'party' sequence that the Grade 10 boys are talking about, audio signs (the music), gestural style (the 'funny' miming to the music) and visual icons (the peace sign) together make up the powerfully 'entertaining' text that these boys enjoy. In this sequence, the soldiers are dressed as 'funny Indians', in contrast to Katim whose 'Indian' vestimentary coding is permanently and seriously as 'other', not modern American, thus excluding him from the entertaining 'family'.

Also humorous (with his order to Tung, 'You get on out of here in thirty seconds. . . . One, two, three . . . oh to hell with it 27, 28, 29') is Anderson – Johnnie's favourite character. Yet Johnnie finds himself unable to fully comprehend or verbalise what it is Anderson is opposing in Tung. He links him with the Viet-Cong that the US army is officially fighting. Our cognitive option questions indicated, in fact, that a high 29 per cent of working-class Grade 10s (compared with 5 per cent middle-class) thought that Tung was working with the V-C. This higher percentage of Grade 10 working-class than even Grade 4 working class (22 per cent) possibly indicates the effect of 'generic knowledge' of the Vietnam War among the older students. It is in the light of this cognitive data that we also need to interpret the behavioural option responses which indicated a significant difference between middle-class Grade 10s (65 per cent) and working-class Grade 10s (39 per cent) who thought that the best response to Tung's aggression was for the Americans to lodge an official complaint about Tung's drug-running with the South Vietnamese high command. If it was not clear to working-class Grade 10s that Tung *was* South Vietnamese, a complaint to that high command would not have been a logical step.

Tung was, perhaps, for our Grade 10 conversation group, less an actual historical representation of South Vietnamese corruption and exploitation, than (returning to their generic discourse) 'the bad guy in the movies'.

Hannah:	'Was there anyone that was your worst character?'
Shannon:	'Tung.'
Simon:	'Tung.'
Hannah:	'Why was that?'
Shannon:	'Because he was the bad guy.'
(laughter)	
Hannah:	'Sorry?'
Shannon:	'Because he was bad! He was mean to the villagers. He's just a mean character.'
Acheleus:	'He's the bad guy in the movies.'
Hannah:	'But can you sort of say a bit more? Why did you think . . . ?'
Shannon:	'You know, because he was mean, and he was the leader of the meanies . . .'
Hannah:	'What do you mean by mean?'
Shannon:	'Like, he was mean to the villagers. Like, he came back and he tried to kill them all. And he was just mean.'
Acheleus:	'He's the bad guy.'
Shannon:	'Yeah – he's mean.'
Acheleus:	'Everybody hates the bad guy in the movies.'
Shannon:	'Because they're mean.'
(laughter)	

The boys quite deliberately and humorously resisted Hannah's attempts to get deeper into the actual history of South Vietnamese corruption (Tung's opium trade) and the culpability of their American allies. So, finally, Hannah focused the discussion with her own topic changes. She wanted to probe deeper into the boys' responses to the argument between Katim and the soldiers.

Hannah:	'Who is Kaytum?' [Mispronounced 'Katim']
(silence)	
Hannah:	'Who is Kaytum?'
Simon:	'I don't know.'
Hannah:	'We've talked about him a little bit already.'
General:	'Oh, the Indian.'
Hannah:	'What did you think of him.'
Shannon:	'That he was good for trying to defend the villagers' rights – you know, how they wanted to stay as what they were. Because bringing guns there is making them a target as well, because if they left there without the guns they wouldn't be. He was just standing up for that.'
Hannah:	'What did you think of him Simon?'

Simon:	'Well, he was the one that – he didn't really want to take the guns and that. He wanted them just to live how they were – wanted to get food, that's all. Because he knew it would've been like a death threat and that, 'cause that would have made them a target; and I don't know what else.'
Hannah:	'Johnnie.'
Johnnie:	'I don't know.'
Hannah:	'You didn't think anything about him?'
Johnnie:	'They all said it.'
Hannah:	'How about you?'
Acheleus:	'Same thing as I said. He's good – tried to defend the tribe.'
Hannah:	'Why do you think the Americans were in the village?'
Acheleus:	'Because they had the orders to teach them how to shoot. They had the orders to protect them as well. That's why they were there.'
Hannah:	'Why do you think the Americans were in the village?'
Shannon:	'Basically the same as him.'
Hannah:	'Simon?'
Simon:	'Oh, to help them defend themselves and have a better life.'
Hannah:	'And what did you think about that?'
Simon:	'Oh, it was alright, but the guns – they didn't really need the guns. They could've just helped them growing crops and stuff like that; and make them get their own food.'
Hannah:	'What did you think about that?'
Shannon:	'What?'
Hannah:	'Why – the reason that you said the Americans were in the village.'
Shannon:	'Because they were there to help them defend themselves, and they needed to use weapons; and also better methods of farming and that.'
Hannah:	'What did you think?'
Johnnie:	'The same as those two.'
Acheleus:	'He don't say much, eh?' (laughs)
Hannah:	'How about you? Anything to add?'
Acheleus:	'No.'

By the end of the discussion the boys had clearly said all they wanted to. They had not fully worked through the contradiction in both supporting Katim's desire to preserve native culture and believing in the American mission to provide the villagers with 'a few things' like television and rock music. They had not pinned down the economic source of Tung as 'bad guy' (the opium trade) – thus supporting the evidence of our Grade 10 narrative matrix which indicated that it was middle-class rather than working-class boys who identified the 'cause' of the Tung narrative. Nor had they noted the relevance of this kind of activity to the American presence in Vietnam. They recognised that the American soldiers were under orders, but did not articulate the proposed use of the villagers to fight the Viet-Cong (and thus make them a target whether or not there was a corrupt Major Tung around). Some of them at least did not even make the distinction between South Vietnamese allies and Viet-Cong.

We have here analysed just one interview. Other interviews contained different conversational strategies; but overall there was a tendency to inflect initial macro-propositions in terms of psychological or emotional processes. The interviews about *Tour of Duty* used the *same* discourse topics that we found in the students' narrative summaries: pro-US, pro-villager, historically specific, Asian-'other', research-focused, meta-textual. In our quantification of discourse topics we were able to get a sense of how widespread in different age, class and gender groups specific macro-propositions were. Only via the interviews, however, can we examine the discursive logics which situate these macro-propositions in interactional situations. Further, by understanding these discursive logics, we can begin to understand the sociocognitive positions which must be engaged with before more advanced theories of social processes will be understood by teenagers.

CONCLUSION

We have tried to show in this article how traditional quantitative techniques may be combined with critical qualitative approaches to throw more light on the hoary research question of 'children and TV violence'. Rather than assume that television itself is, monolithically, a 'social problem' in this regard, we have treated it as an agentive institution as regards both producers and audiences. One of our findings is that, according to a number of different measures, working-class students are more tolerant of violent solutions in relation to this particular genre than middle-class students (perhaps an appropriate response from a social group itself more subject to societal violence than others); and we have tried to show how working-class boys negotiate an 'entertainment' text which offers both violent and 'pro-social' solutions. In this way we have used semantic differential measures to quantify the notoriously subjective concept of 'pleasure' that critical theorists have been drawn to recently.

Of particular value, we believe, is the treating of both television material and students' responses to it as serious and complex texts, valuable for study in their own right – rather than the familiar behaviourist assumption of active (usually bad) television 'stimuli' and passive children – the 'children as a vulnerable group' syndrome which the Australian Broadcasting Tribunal Report reproduced yet again. We strongly agree with the report's call for 'a move to better equip children to understand the processes of television through media education classes' (ABT, 1990: 98). But part of that move must be the recognition that children, like television itself, are *agents* in the field of TV violence, with complex class, gender and age-influenced agendas of their own. It is these sociocognitive agendas which engage both with violence *and* with 'alternatives to its expression'. Unless these are first understood, and their relationship to television violence further researched, we will be no further forward in understanding the 'influence of television violence on children'.

NOTE

This chapter has not previously been published.

REFERENCES

Australian Broadcasting Tribunal (1990), *TV Violence in Australia* vol. 1, ABT, Sydney.

Bremond, Claude (1977), 'The morphology of the French fairy tale: the ethical model', in H. Jason and D. Segal (eds), *Patterns in Oral Literature*, Mouton, Hague, pp. 49–76.

Connell, Robert (1983), *'Which Way Is Up?' Essays on Sex, Class and Culture*, Allen & Unwin, Sydney.

Van Dijk, Teun A. (1977), *Text and Context*, Longman, London.

—— (1984), *Prejudice in Discourse: An Analysis of Ethnic Prejudice in Cognition and Conversation*, John Benjamin's Publishing Company, Amsterdam.

Goldmann, Lucien (1968), 'The sociology of literature: status and problems of method', *International Social Science Journal*, 19(4), 493–516.

Gunter, Barry (1985), *Dimensions of Television Violence*, Gower, Aldershot.

Livingstone, Sonia (1990), *Making Sense of Television: The Psychology of Audience Interpretation*, Pergamon, Oxford.

MacCabe, Colin (1974), 'Realism and the cinema: notes on some Brechtian theses', *Screen*, 7(27).

Philo, Greg, Peter Beharrell and John Hewitt (1977), 'One-dimensional news – television and the control of explanation', in P. Beharrell and G. Philo (eds), *Trade Unions and the Media*, Macmillan, London, pp. 1–22.

Potter, J. and Reicher, S. (1987), 'Discourses of community and conflict: the organization of social categories in accounts of a riot', *British Journal of Social Psychology*, 26, 25–40.

Tajfel, Henri (1981), *Human Groups and Social Categories*, Cambridge University Press, London.

Warneminde, Martin (1991), 'Massacre in the mall: the culture of violence', *The Bulletin*, August 27, 22–4.

ACKNOWLEDGEMENTS

Our thanks to our research assistants on this project, Julie Crittle and Hannah Sharp.

Chapter 12

Reading the romance

Pam Gilbert and Sandra Taylor

While it is relatively straightforward to consider the textual construction of romantic ideology in a series like *Dolly Fiction*, the possible effect of romance reading upon young women has always been contentious, and the argument has rightly been put that studies which recognise the 'complex relationships between social context, reader and text' (Taylor, 1989) are urgently needed. Two such studies – one by John Willinsky and Mark Hunniford in Canada (1986), and another by Maylyn Lam in Australia (1986) – go some of the way towards exploring these 'complex relationships'. Both of these studies investigated pre-teen and teen romance readers who were identified by school reading surveys, and both offer examples of the ways in which these readers – all of them young women – make sense of their romance reading.

A major problem with studies of this nature is that young women have learned a great deal about what counts as a 'response' to a book, and what counts as fiction, and studies which attempt to unpack statements about response must take this discursive positioning into account. There are recognisable ways of talking about books; there are recognisable sets of assumptions about what constitutes a story; and, currently, there is a recognisable emphasis in language and literature teaching which claims to value the 'personal' response of a reader to a text.

As we have argued earlier, reading is not an idiosyncratic activity: reading is learned. Romance fiction is therefore 'readable', because its generic conventions are recognisable and familiar. Series novels, in particular, rely upon instant recognition of the genre. They hold out the promise of more of the same, the series title acting as a brand name guaranteeing the quality. Readers are thus actively discouraged from making idiosyncratic meaning from the texts. These are not 'open' texts which offer space to textual play. Formula novels must appeal quickly and easily to thousands of readers, and, like franchised fast food, must not disappoint. Consequently the possibility of a multiplicity of responses is undesirable because it makes the success of the series less predictable. Interesting evidence of this was described in Radway's account of how the romance bookseller/guide in her study had to show her romance readers how to read particular texts which threatened to break out of the conventions of the typical romance genre (Radway, 1984: 63–4). Once readers are positioned to accept – and to desire – romance ideology, particular textual conventions are usually quickly recognised.

Studies that have been made of young romance readers do offer interesting material about the ways in which young women talk about their readings of romance fiction. The Canadian study by Willinsky and Hunniford, for instance, largely replicated – with forty-two grade 7 girls from a lower middle-class neighbourhood – Janice Radway's work with adult romance readers (1984). But Willinsky and Hunniford found significant differences between the ways in which the young women and the older women claimed to make use of the romances and talked about their romance reading. Willinsky and Hunniford claimed that the young readers were 'on the verge of a total surrender on a number of counts'; they were 'taking more from the books than the adults, more than many of us in education would want to ask' (1986: 21). When the girls completed a questionnaire listing reasons for reading romances, the statements 'because I wish I had a romance like the heroine's', and 'because I like to read about the strong, virile heroes' were scored as the two most important reasons for reading. This was quite different from the older women's responses, where 'for simple relaxation' and 'because reading is just for me; it is my time' were key reasons. Interviews with the girls supported this emphasis. The books had, according to Willinsky and Hunniford, become a 'beginner's manual for ensuing adolescence' (28). One might add that they serve more as manuals for ensuing femininity than for adolescence.

Maylyn Lam's work with forty-two older working-class and middle-class girls in an Australian high school (1986) indicates, however, a less complete acceptance by these girls of the world presented by romance fiction. While many of these older girls were still firm romance readers, they could feel the disjuncture between romance novels and the 'everyday reality' of their lives more keenly. One of the groups of girls Lam interviewed had stopped reading romance, and this group of ex-romance readers suggested in interview that this was largely because they no longer wanted to subject themselves to the pain of the disjuncture. However, other young women in Lam's study continued to enjoy the romance formula. The books still seemed 'real' and 'compelling' to many of them, largely because, Lam suggests, they were offering 'a view of the world in which feelings are of paramount importance' (1986: 44), a view of the world which Lam suggests is a crucial perspective for young women.

Like the younger readers, these 14 and 15 year-olds observed the lessons in love and relationships offered through the novels – and enjoyed this focus in the texts – while becoming increasingly aware that the world of the romance was not their own world. Lam's comments at the end of her study indicate something of this dilemma for the older readers.

> The Banyule readers' reflections on how and why romance fiction appeals to them defies the attempt to pigeonhole their responses into a theoretical framework. The girls do not articulate an awareness of 'the ideology of romance', but are quite capable of advancing a critique of the literary, social and sexual content of the novels. They are aware of differences between the boys they know and the fictional heroes who inhabit the *Sweet Valley* world. They are able to define ways in which the novels make them feel envious and inadequate, and are quite conscious of the low social status that is attached to their reading preferences. Yet they continue to read romances, reporting a degree of emotional involvement which is no less intense for the ambivalent nature of the pleasures that the books offer.
>
> (1986: 56)

Why girls continue to read romance, and to claim an 'emotional involvement' with such generically ritualistic novels, is, of course, the key question. And to add a rather different perspective to this question, it can be considered from another angle. Given that reading practices are learned and reading positions are adopted, why is it that some girls have learned reading practices and adopted reading positions which reject the stereotypes offered through romance fiction? How differently positioned are these girls who are *not* romance readers from those who are, and how might alternative positioning facilitate such learning? Are there other subject positions available to non-romance readers which make it easier to resist romance ideology as it is developed through formula fiction? And what might a study of such readers tell us about romance reading?

Social class membership has not been a key factor in the studies by Willinsky and Hunniford, Lam or Christian-Smith, but it could be argued that the lived social and cultural experiences of girls as members of oppressed and disadvantaged groups may be significant in positioning some girls more readily to adopt romance ideology – and to accept romance fiction – as the most promising method of resolving the contradictions of becoming feminine. For instance Taylor's work with an inner-city group of Australian girls found that those who came from non-English speaking backgrounds were more attracted by romance fiction than were other girls in the class (Taylor, 1989).

Given this interest in the possible influence of social and cultural experiences on the construction of romance readers, we did undertake a small-scale study of a group of girls who are not normally romance readers, but who saw themselves as 'readers', and were keen to read a new attractively packaged series of romance fiction. A neighbourhood group of three girls aged 11 to 13 was well-known to one of us. The girls all come from middle-class family backgrounds, their parents have university educations and professional occupations, and the girls are all seen to be successful at school. The lived experiences of these girls were experiences of privilege – all of them had professional career aspirations and expectations of economic security.

With this background for the girls, we wondered what would be their interest in reading a new romance series like *Dolly Fiction*, and what their reaction to such a series might be. The girls were asked if they would like to read books from a new romance series. While all of the girls had read some formula romance novels before, and had clear textual expectations of such books, the girls did not call themselves 'romance readers'. They liked a wide variety of material – adventure, mystery, science-fiction, historical romance, fantasy. However, when they were shown the first eighteen of the brand new *Dolly Fiction* series, they were happy to read them. *Dolly* magazine is very popular with girls of this age, and the link from the fiction to the magazine was obviously attractive. While none of these girls actually bought *Dolly* magazine, some of their friends did, and they had also been able to borrow copies from the municipal library.

The girls were asked to read as many of the novels as they wanted, to keep a journal of anything they wished to note about the books, and then to talk to the researcher afterwards about their reading (the researcher was a well known and familiar adult to the girls). Initially the girls were asked as a group to select which of the eighteen they most wanted to read, and their discussions were taped.

Typically they used the back cover text, and the inside front cover extract to help them choose. One of the girls picked up the word play of several of the titles immediately, and all three seemed discerning in their selection. They seemed to know what they expected to like, and all rejected several titles immediately. They were after books that had a good 'storyline':

This looks like it might be OK. Not so soppy.

Perhaps this one might be a mystery.

This's got a different kind of twist.

They wanted books that were not what they considered to be 'typical romances', and one that they all seized upon as having potential was no. 11, *First Impressions*. *First Impressions* is not the usual romance, in that it is predominantly written from the viewpoint of the hero, Jack Darcy. However at the beginning of the book a page reads:

WARNING!
Before you start to read this book, I reckon you ought to know what

you're letting yourself in for. They say it's girls who are interested in reading about romance – but this story is written by a guy. And Jack Darcy's no ordinary guy, either. . . . Just so you don't get stuck with Jack all the time, I'm going to add my own comments at the end of every chapter, to make sure you get the girl's point of view as well. Happy Reading!
SIGNED
Liz Bennet

One other book in the first eighteen of this series was constructed like this. The rest were all ostensibly from the single viewpoint: the viewpoint of, as we noted earlier in this chapter, a girl who is usually not doing well at school, typically not able to organise her school, social and family life into any tolerable order, and often not confident in her own ability to be interesting or attractive to boys. For most of these girls the greatest crisis in their lives is likely to be what they'll wear to the disco, or whether they'll get a glimpse of their boyfriend at school before lunch. They are not, as Knodel suggested (1982), protagonists for some girls to admire. Consequently a romance book which purports to be from a male perspective seems to offer not only a novel narrative twist, but also a more valued, because more valuable, perspective. *First Impressions* suggests that it could be a male discourse about romance, a discourse which many women would see as potentially enlightening but also potentially unusual, interesting and more powerful. As one of the girls said, 'I know what girls think. I want to know what a guy thinks.' This has also been an emphasis in *Dolly* magazine, which runs a 'Boys on' feature every month, purporting to offer what boys have to say about a set issue, for example 'Casual sex' (July 1989), and 'Girlfriends' (August 1989).

The girls followed different patterns as they read the books. One of the three – the youngest – read thirteen of the possible eighteen in the two-week holiday period, but the other two lost interest fairly quickly. One read five of the books, and one four. The older girls seemed to complete as many as they did out of a sense of duty to the researcher. Their journal entries were short and not always complete. Both of the older girls apologetically explained that they had a number of other books that they wanted to read.

The youngest girl stopped on her thirteenth book, and didn't want any more. However, she said that she had quite liked the *Dolly Fiction*. One, in particular, had been very interesting to her, and she was quite surprised, and a little dismayed at her enjoyment of the book: 'I thought about this and thought – oh, how embarrassing – I actually got hooked into a romance book.' This devaluing of romance fiction had been a strong feature of all the girls' responses. None of them really wanted to like romance fiction. All of them assumed that the researcher and their parents thought such books were 'trash' or 'pathetic', and when asked why parents wouldn't like the books, the girls offered reasons like:

> Dad doesn't mind what I read, although he would think that reading stuff like this was a bit silly. He wouldn't understand why on earth I'd want to read books like that.

> The girls in the stories are just so pathetic.

> Mum says that whatever goes into your head has to come out in some way, so why fill it up with junk?

> The parents in the books are often stupid old bats yelling at each other and so on. . . . My family's not like that.

They also described how boys devalued romance novels:

> Boys wouldn't be interested, because of the reputation they've got. Because girls read them.

> Boys wouldn't like to read books like this. Think it's sissy to like books and romance and everything like that.

When asked what they thought about the possibility of working with romance fiction like *Dolly Fiction* in the mixed-sex classroom, all the girls were adamant that it would be a mistake. They argued that they wanted the opportunity to study other books at school, and they claimed that while some girls might appreciate the chance of working with books they knew and liked, this would be more than offset by the likely reaction of the boys. They were sure that boys would hate the novels, and laugh at their use. When pressured about what sort of girls preferred romance fiction, one of the girls suggested that such girls were probably a bit 'boy-crazy', but it was more than likely that they didn't really enjoy reading very much:

> these give them more satisfaction than other books. It's the girls that don't read much that read them. Because they don't want to go down into a long novel or anything but this is about something they might know something about. They think it's nice. I guess at school – maybe this isn't right – you're sort of considered a square if you're reading long novels but if you're reading these, people don't mind. This isn't like a proper fiction.

Romance reading may be seen, at least by some students, as a resistance to school authorised material – to institutionalised schooling – and research by Christian-Smith (1987) and Lam (1986), would seem to support this claim. But for these non-romance readers such reading was largely a waste of time:

It's a waste of reading.

You start talking about what's in these books. Speak like them. Act like them. Write like them and stuff like that. You start to think that everything's going to end up happily as soon as you meet the right person. Or who they think the right person is for them.

If you take this stuff seriously, if you think, 'Oh, this could be me', I think it could go a bit far and you could live in a world that isn't real. Some girls might think that – if they were stupid. . . . Guys just aren't like that. This is so unreal.

As with Taylor's work (1989), this 'unreality' of the books was a major, and quite unsolicited, focus of the girl's discussion. If the girls could not position themselves to accept and be seduced by the *fantasy* of the romance, then the other more obvious reading position to take up was that of the *reality* of the romance text.

They're supposed to be about real life but they're not like real life. It's about real life and they're making it *not* life.

Falling in love does happen but not like that.

No way are they realistic. Nothing ever happens like this. . . . All these spunky guys. Guys just aren't like that. They're just so unreal in appearance.

Yet the girls could see that in part it was the 'unreality' – the 'fantasy' – that was attractive to many of the readers who were romance fans.

Some girls . . . don't have boyfriends and they just like reading books instead of having the real thing.

The girls noticed how different the *Dolly Fiction* series was from other books that they had read, and how the series fared badly by comparison. One of the girls in particular was able to speculate about what generally made other books more interesting:

Other books are about adventure and mystery. These are all romance. They're pretty boring. You don't want romance to be the main part of your life. Of course it's got to be a big part because you've got to get married and everything, but there's all the school part and just having fun and lots of books just about school life aren't just about romance. I like other books better because with these you know what's going to happen. With the others you don't. . . . I like books that are about people my age. They don't really happen in real life. Fantasy books don't have any real life, but they make you feel as if it could be real life. With these, you suddenly meet the guy and you marry them – but it doesn't happen like that.

The girls were also critical of the way the romance books were written, and had much to say about the construction of the books. They commented upon their readability levels:

They're all about older people and yet it sounds like they're written for younger people.

Their narrative style:

These have all different people, but they're put together in the same way all the time. . . . They're very direct, like they always say, 'She felt this', or, 'She said this'. Other books tell you what they want to tell you, but they say it in an interesting way. They use more description. Much more interesting to sit down and read. These – you only keep reading to find out what happens at the end. With novels you also do that but you also enjoy reading them while you're reading them. They're much more artistically written if you know what I mean.

Their character framing:

The heroes usually know everything. They've just got to sort their girls out. The girls are all sort of mixed up. The man next to them helps them sort it out. They're all the same. The boys are really nice and intelligent and the girls are kissing their feet sort of.

Their stylistic artistry:

It's pathetic how they describe things, like, I wrote this one down: 'Tingling vibrations of electric currents racing through her body.' Pathetic. And there's all these exclamations. In one paragraph. Just listen . . .

The proofing and editing accuracy of the production:

There's so many terrible spelling and typing mistakes. It's awful. They've even got the guy's name wrong in this one.

These three girls are, we would suggest, differently positioned as readers than are many other girls. Their class and family backgrounds have encouraged the perception that romance is a devalued genre, both as a popular art form, and as a source of information about adolescent girls. And this matters to them. They are ready to link up with, at least at this stage of their lives, their parents and their teachers and to take up subject positions that seem to offer more authority. While versions of romance ideology may well be more attractive to them at different points in their lives, when they are differently positioned discursively, at this stage they perceive of infinitely more options than the world of *Dolly Fiction* offers. They will not easily take up the gendered subject positions that romance ideology constructs.

In addition, they want something else out of reading than romance fiction will give them. They like to read books, because they have varied and extensive intertextual experiences. They are able to be discerning about what they want in fiction, and for them, this romance series was, on the whole badly written, badly produced, boring and trite. They framed the series immediately – even before they had read any of the books – into a generic type which led them to anticipate particular textual and ideological conventions. And the conventions were drawn from discourses about success, schooling, marriage and adolescence which these three girls rejected. They did not connect with the lived experiences as privileged and successful middle-class girls. The texts could not appeal to them as a guide to teen relationships and adolescence, and yet once the fantasy of the texts was rejected, that was the only other dominant reading frame to adopt. As a guide to adolescent femininity, the series was unattractive. As young adult literature, it was also unattractive.

Girls and women know that romances are fiction: they are fantastic, unreal, impossible. But it is this unreality which many girls and women find seductive. While schools may not be able to alter significantly the discursive positioning of many young women, schools can offer approaches to working with texts which make it easier to recognise the constructed nature of texts, and which can begin the process of showing women ways in which they might reposition themselves discursively. It should not be surprising to us, for instance, that year 7 girls like those in Willinsky and Hunniford's study are still slightly confused about the textual construction of 'reality', but it should be a matter of some concern if older students were not able to examine ways in which texts construct different versions of reality, and to ask why this is possible. The question of what reality is constructed in literature is a key one, and in chapter 2 of *Fashioning the Feminine* we examined some of the concerns that feminist aesthetics has had with just this issue. As we argued there, we learn how to read texts, because we learn to take up various subject positions which allow the text to be framed in specific ways. The way in which some girls have already accepted romance fantasies as an apparent solution to the 'problem' of becoming a woman – a lover, a wife, a mother – positions them more readily to accept romance fiction as a discourse of relevance and interest.

If formula romance fiction does discursively belong to patriarchal systems of organising and defining reality, it should be a matter of concern to us that the genres are so attractive to certain groups of women. Why, for instance, do some women reject the subject positions formula romance fiction offers, and why are other women apparently seduced by them? Part of the answer to this must lie in the different discursive positions women can adopt in relation to romance texts. The lived experiences of some girls, as oppressed and marginalised groups, partially accounts for their willingness to accept romance ideology as an alternative solution to the patriarchal parameters of their present and future lives. But the representations of romance ideology in formula novels do offer the possibility of textually exploring these parameters in tangible form. Such an exploration will be more easily undertaken if girls' textual experiences are rich – if they have read of other ways to construct women's futures, and of other ways to speak of love. And if they have some understanding of the way in which language practices are social and cultural processes.

We accept that romance fiction, like many other popular cultural texts, connects strongly with some young women's lives, and we accept that there is a complex interplay between girls' conscious and unconscious desires which popular culture, through its powerful sets of interconnected images, links with. Fashioning the feminine in our society is big business, and it is unquestionably the dominant contemporary discourse influencing the construction of female subjectivity. But it is not the only discourse, and much of what *Fashioning the Feminine* argues for is that discourses 'not intended for her' (Rich, 1980: 243) – discourses not offering women speaking positions of authority – be replaced by others.

Romance ideology is not a discourse intended for 'her'. It is a discourse which locks women into passive and submissive response rather than active and independent action; a discourse which cannot construct a future for women without men; a discourse which necessitates the humiliating and crippling romantic inscription of the body. Romantic ideology operates through fairy tales and comics, through movies and television soaps, through magazines and commercial advertisements, to construct women's conscious and unconscious desires for love, for difference, for escape, for security, for sensuality in an apparently natural and inevitable way. The result is, as Ann Snitow (1984: 265) has argued so persuasively, that:

> When women try to picture excitement, the society offers them one vision, romance. When women try to imagine companionship, the society offer them one vision, male, sexual companionship. When women try to fantasize about success, mastery, the society offers them one vision, the power to attract a man. When women try to fantasize about sex, the society offers them taboos on most of its imaginable expressions except those that deal directly with arousing and satisfying men. When women try to project a unique self, the society offers them very few attractive images. True completion for women is nearly always presented as social, domestic, sexual.

Formula romance novels should not be protected from scrutiny because they are popular culture, nor because they are fiction, nor because they are specially written for women and give women pleasure. They do not grow out of discourses which serve women well. They grow out of consumer-oriented discourses which have vested interests in constructing groups of women as identifiable and therefore commercially marketable; and they grow out of patriarchal discourses which depend upon the continuation of unequal heterosexual couplings and domestic labour.

NOTE

This chapter first appeared in Pam Gilbert and Sandra Taylor, *Fashioning the Feminine: Girls, Popular Culture and Schooling*, Allen & Unwin, Sydney, 1991.

REFERENCES

Christian-Smith, L. (1987), 'Gender, popular culture, and curriculum: adolescent romance as gender text', *Curriculum Inquiry*, 17(4), 365–406.

Knodel, B. (1982), 'Still far from equal: young women in literature for adolescents', paper presented at the annual meeting of the National Council of Teachers of English Spring Conference, Minneapolis.

Lam, M. (1986), *Reading the Sweet Dream: Adolescent Girls and Romance Fiction*, unpublished M.Ed thesis, University of Melbourne.

Radway, J. (1984), *Reading the Romance: Women, Patriarchy and Popular Literature*, North Carolina University Press, Chapel Hill.

Rich, A. (1980), *On Lies, Secrets, Silences*, Virago, London.

Snitow, A. (1984), 'Mass market romance: pornography for women is different', in A. Snitow, C. Stansell and S. Thompson (eds), *Desire: The Politics of Sexuality*, Virago, London.

Taylor, S. (1989) 'Empowering young girls and young women: the challenge of the gender-inclusive curriculum', *Journal of Curriculum Studies*, 21(5), 441–56.

Willinsky, J. and Hunniford, R. M. (1986), 'Reading the romance younger: the mirrors and fears of a preparatory literature', *Reading-Canada-Lecture*, 4(1), 16–31.

Index